T0209928

The Art & Craft of Playwriting

Jeffrey Hatcher

WRITER'S DIGEST
BOOKS

About the Author

Jeffrey Hatcher is the author of numerous plays, including *Three Viewings, Scotland Road, The Turn of the Screw, SMASH, Sockdology, Compleat Female Stage Beauty, Mother Russia, Hanging Lord Haw-Haw* and *What Corbin Knew.* His plays have won many awards and have been produced throughout the United States, Canada, Mexico, Great Britain, Australia, Germany, Chile, Japan, and Malaysia. He taught for six years at the Playwrights' Center in Minneapolis, and has been a guest lecturer and playwright-in-residence at many colleges and theater centers, such as Carleton College, Macalester College, Denison University, and The Eugene O'Neill Theater Center. He has written TV movies for the Peter Falk series "Columbo" and is currently adapting his play *Three Viewings* for film.

WRITER'S DIGEST
BOOKS

An imprint of Penguin Random House LLC
penguinrandomhouse.com

ISBN 978-1-884910-46-3

Designed by Clare Finney

146122990

Permissions

Acknowledgments

This book began when Edward Stern, Artistic Director of Cincinnati Playhouse in the Park, selected my play *Scotland Road* to premiere there as the winner of the 1993 Lois and Richard Rosenthal New Play Prize. While we were rehearsing in Cincinnati I met Lois and Dick, and after the play opened, we kept in touch over the phone. A few months later Lois asked me if I would be interested in writing a playwriting text for Story Press. I'm grateful to Lois for this opportunity. Working on this book has proved to be a kind of refresher course in Playwriting 101. While I was reading plays, researching other texts, talking to writers and thinking about drama, I got a second education in the profession.

Many people deserve a lot of thanks. Lois and Dick Rosenthal, of course. Jack Heffron and Bob Beckstead at Story Press. John B. Santoianni, Charmaine Ferenczi and Jack Tantleff at the Tantleff Office in New York. And Ed Stern for bringing me to Cincinnati.

I'd like to thank a few organizations that support and sustain playwrights: The Dramatists Guild; New Dramatists in New York; the Eugene O'Neill Theater Center in Waterford, Connecticut; and most especially The Playwrights' Center in Minneapolis, which has served as my artistic home for eight years and has provided support, collegiality, security and inspiration to me, my work and the work of dozens of talented playwrights I've had the chance to know, teach, learn from and work with. I'd also like to thank the colleges and department chairs I've worked with over the years. Ruth Weiner and Ed Sostek at Carleton College in Northfield, Minnesota, and Sears Eldredge at Macalester College in St. Paul, Minnesota. There's nothing more invigorating for a playwright than working with eager, energetic, intelligent, talented and imaginative young writers.

Thanks to Lee Blessing, Marsha Norman and José Rivera for their wonderful interviews, as well as to the other writers and artists I consulted: Anthony Clarvoe, Bill Corbett, Barbara Field, Kent Stephens, Douglas Hughes, Ben Kreilkamp, Randy Latimer, Kira Obolensky, Tom Szentgyorgyi and Craig Wright.

But a special thanks is due two playwrights who have been great influences on my writing: Gram Slaton, who nagged and provoked me to write plays when I was living in New York and who critically and patiently took me through the endless drafts of my first scripts; and Phil Bosakowski, whose friendship and sly, wise, good humor delighted and sustained me from the day we met in 1990 until his death in 1994. His wife Gay will remember the night at the O'Neill when Phil gave me this bit of advice about a character in a play of mine: "It would be nice if he *did* something."

To all of them—and to my wife Lisa, who lives with every draft for the run of the show—my great and good thanks.

Table of Contents

Introduction

The best place on earth is in the back of a theater. It's the aisle behind the last row of seats. The space is a little narrow, and the carpet has worn a bit thin. It's called "the Playwright's Alley," and it's where the writer lives during the opening night of a new show. It's where a nervous and excited author shifts, paces, bites his nails and cheers like a fool while the actors onstage speak his words and perform his actions, moving the audience between the stage and that back row to laugh, cry and lean forward in delighted anticipation. There are hundreds of these alleys in the United States—from Broadway to Seattle, from the giant auditorium at Lincoln Center to the smallest ninety-nine-seat hole-in-the-wall in West Hollywood. It's the place where a writer sees his dreams and obsessions come true. "The Playwright's Alley" is a playwright's home.

The journey to that home is often a long and arduous one, filled with danger and disappointment. There are lonely hours at the typewriter and discouraging trips to the mailbox. There are frustrating attempts at rewrites and torturous hours in the rehearsal halls. There is the slim chance of greatness and the daunting prospect of disaster. But if you have talent, courage, determination—and the ability to grasp and manipulate the skills of this most demanding and rewarding profession—you can reach that glorious alley. Talent will out. You will find your home and fill the house.

I've been writing drama for ten years now, and I've had the good fortune to be produced by some of the finest theaters in this country: Manhattan Theatre Club, Yale Repertory Theater, Cincinnati Playhouse in the Park, Portland Stage, The Denver Center Theater Company, Florida Studio Theater, The Empty Space and dozens of others in cities like New York, Chicago, Los Angeles, Seattle and San Francisco. I've had a lot of luck, and I've made a good many mistakes. But I've learned from my mistakes, and I've written better plays because of what I've learned. One of the truths I've come to know is that there *are* rules that all successful playwrights live by. True, there are many sorts of plays and many sorts of rules—but a playwright has to believe in certain dramatic and theatrical principles, and my life in the theater has taught me the following:

I believe in audiences.
I believe in inspiration.
I believe in craft.
I believe in Aristotle.
I believe the first duty of any play is to interest, engage and delight its spectators.
I believe all plays are mystery plays.
I believe in the three-part structure.
I believe in beginnings, middles and ends.
I believe in strong stories with strong characters who want and need and act.
I believe in protagonists, antagonists, goals and obstacles.
I believe that concrete goals are stronger than abstract ones.
I believe in dramatic tension and suspense.
I believe we learn from the plays of the past.
I believe all good plays contain character/conflict/action/ideas.
I believe all good plays contain secrets, sex, love, money, power, ideas, the potential for crime, the possibility of death, and a sense of theatricality.
I believe all good plays are about human nature and the questions of our hearts.
I believe a playwright is a poet disguised as an architect.
I believe a play is crafted. A play is designed. A play is planned.

• • • • •

Playwrights receive a lot of rejection letters. It's part of the deal we make in exchange for the Broadway premieres, the rave reviews and the Hollywood offers that come our way when the world is just and bright. The most valuable letter I ever received from a theater came in the form of a rejection. The letter was a polite, personal one (as opposed to *personalized*—"Dear *JEFF HATCHER*, Thank you so much for sending *play title here*. We all felt it was a very *moving/funny/interminable* piece of theater."). The letter had lots of complimentary things to say about my work, but the penultimate sentence was one I'll never forget—nor should anyone writing for the theater.

"While there was much to recommend your script, in the end we did not feel *compelled* to produce it." (My italics.)

There is no other *good* reason to produce a play.

Why do commercial producers and nonprofit artistic directors produce a play? There are many reasons, but the best is because the play *compels* them. Because they *must* produce it. Because they *have* to. Because something in the playwright's voice and ideas and talent insists they do. Because their artistic souls will shrivel and die if they don't. A play should be produced because the producer couldn't put it down—and couldn't wait to get it on its feet in front of an audience.

Your goal is to write that play. Maybe you want your play to right a wrong or expiate a guilt or tickle a funny bone or change the world. Fine. But remember this question, one Dr. R. Elliott Stout, my theater professor at Denison University, had framed above his desk: "AND WHAT IS THE *AUDIENCE* DOING ALL THIS TIME?" David Mamet, who wrote such great plays as *Glengarry Glen Ross* and *American Buffalo*, once noted that the two hours an audience spends at the performance of a play is a lot to ask of a person's life. Count the hours spent in the dark by even the most infrequent theatergoer and by the time he reaches eighty-three years of age, you'll find he'd like a lot of those hours back. Our job in the theater is to make that octogenarian regret not one moment he's spent in the dark.

Think of the times you've gone to the theater at the end of a long, tense, tiring day. You got the ticket for some godforsaken reason, and as the clock ticks toward eight, you want nothing more than to leave the theater and get home as soon as possible. You look at the program and are horrified to find the production has not one but *two* intermissions. You won't be home until eleven or twelve. You look for the exit, but before you can make your move, the crowd grows silent, the lights go down, and you're trapped in your row. You know in your bones it's wrong to yell "fire." And then it's forty minutes later, the lights are up, the crowd is moving to the lobby, and all you can think about is how excited you are to find out what's going to happen in the second act. You go back to your seat well before the curtain goes up again because you don't want to miss a beat. Suddenly it's the second intermission, and you don't leave your seat this time because you're actually talking about the play with the stranger next to you. Then the lights go down again, and before you know it the curtain call is over; the actors have left the stage, and you're still applauding. You're still sitting in your seat. You don't want to leave the theater. And you're trying to remember the last time a play made you feel that way.

That's our job as playwrights. That's what we do. We *compel* tired people, who have every reason to leave, to stay in their seats. And love staying. And come back for the next one.

·····

These days it's tough for a new play to be produced in this country. Tough for experienced playwrights and more than intimidating for the struggling writer—the comer who keeps coming but never seems to arrive, or the novice without a church. But that's a challenge the talented, ambitious writer meets head-on. The tougher climate simply means our plays have to be better. So we'll make them better. We'll write the plays the audience stays for. We'll write the plays that compel.

This book can help you start writing plays that compel. It is not a how-to-get-produced manual or a history-of-the-drama text or a balanced overview of every kind of theater writing on this planet. It is a discussion of what *I think works*. It is a discussion of the questions I have to ask myself every time I think about writing a play, the questions any good playwright has to keep in mind when creating a character, planning a story, plotting a scene, or just hoping for magic to strike.

It is a book about craft. Plays are not about craft. But play*writing* is. Plays are about Character, Action, Conflict and Ideas. Plays are about Stories—how they're told and what they mean in our experience of the world. Plays are about Language and Images. Plays are about Imagination and Discovery and Recognition. Plays are about Emotion. Plays are about the Mind. Plays are about the intimate collaboration that takes place between the Stage and the Audience in Time and Space, in Sound and Light and the Senses. Plays are about the Human Heart.

What plays are "about" can't be taught. A writer has to have "it," whatever "it" is—talent, genius, something to say. But without the techniques dramatists have employed for over two thousand years, without a grasp of play*writing craft*—a grasp so firm it *must* become a reflex—talent can atrophy and die. Craft is the vehicle of talent and the imagination.

The first chapters of this book—on drama, theater, and the six elements of Aristotle—are designed to provide the foundation you'll need before you begin writing your play. After this, we'll move on to a discussion of where play ideas come from and how they find their dramatic and theatrical form. Next we look at structure and offer a three-part model for writing a play. This is followed by a chapter on dialogue. After that, we'll analyze a well-known classic play-script, Henrik Ibsen's *Hedda Gabler*. The back of the book is devoted to three interviews with writers Lee Blessing (*A Walk in the Woods*), Marsha Norman (*'Night, Mother*) and José Rivera (*Marisol*). We'll see what these playwrights have to say about the challenges they encounter in writing their own plays, offering advice, tips and tricks-of-the-trade. Each of the early chapters is followed by a series of exercises designed to underline the concepts and craft issues detailed in the text. The exercises are essential in developing the mind, muscles and coordination necessary to successfully construct and write stageworthy drama. They are exercises in tension and conflict; wants, needs, desires; theatricality; subtext; stage space; imagination; action; and ideas. They are intended to keep the writer in the right dramatic and theatrical frame of mind. And if they happen to lead to a *real* scene or play, all the better.

The ideas in this book come from various sources. They come from my experience of writing for the theater. They come from the classes I've taught and the students I've had the privilege to meet. They come from talking to other playwrights—successful playwrights, struggling playwrights, playwrights who have made a difference in my writing and my life. They come from over thirty years of attending plays in the theater. They come from studying scores of plays, many of which are referred to in this book as we analyze what playwrights do to create dynamic drama and exciting theater. There are hundreds of plays we could use for our reference, but for the sake of economy and concentration, we'll cite about a dozen well-known dramas from various eras that represent a wide cross-section of styles and approaches. Thus, you will find frequent references to the following plays: *Hamlet* by William Shakespeare, *Hedda Gabler* by Henrik Ibsen, *The Cherry Orchard* by Anton Chekhov, *The Front Page* by Ben Hecht and Charles MacArthur, *The Little Foxes* by Lillian Hellman, *Who's Afraid of Virginia Woolf?* by Edward Albee, *'Night, Mother* by Marsha Norman, *The Odd Couple* by Neil Simon, *Betrayal* by Harold Pinter, and *Six Degrees of Separation* by John Guare.

A class I've always wanted to teach would be one called "Plays We Like." It would consist of smart playwrights talking about the plays they've always cherished. We'd read the plays, discuss them, and I think we'd find that these great plays have a lot in common.

That's what this book is about. Finding the tools, methods and strategies held in common by plays we like, plays that work, plays that delight and move us. Finding the common threads and the constant factors in plays that appear, at face value, to be completely dissimilar. What is the common structural thread that connects *Hamlet* to *The Odd Couple*? What is the constant character factor in both *Hedda Gabler* and *Richard III*? What similar playwriting twist is found in both *The Front Page* and *Hedda Gabler*?

Well?

If I told you in the introduction, you wouldn't be compelled to read on.

And I wouldn't be a dramatist.

CHAPTER ONE

Drama and Theater

Before you begin to write a play, it's important to understand the medium for which you are writing and how it differs from other narrative forms, such as fiction and film. For all their similarities (character, story, etc.), plays, novels and films have divergent histories with various traditions and conventions, requiring unique talents of a writer. The essential formal distinction is this: Novelists write for the *page*; motion picture writers write for the *screen*; and playwrights write for the *stage*—a three-dimensional space encompassing live action performed by human beings. Writing for the stage demands an understanding of two fundamentals: the essence of drama and the nature of theater. In this chapter we'll define these terms and show the ways writers utilize drama and theater to create effective stage plays.

DRAMA AND STORY

The terms *drama* and *theater* are not interchangeable. Drama consists of characters in conflict and in action. Theater is both the arena for the action and the sensory experience of that action. Let's look at the definition of the word *drama*. It comes from the Greek *dran*, to do. To act. An action. In his *Poetics*, Aristotle defined drama as "an *imitation* of an action." Drama—written drama, performed drama—is the reproduction of people performing actions. People *doing*.

In drama, the actions of the play must cling together to form a story, *one action causing another*, adding up to some meaningful point that touches the thoughts and emotions of the audience. Good drama has an ordered narrative, often referred to as a plot, and plot can best be defined as the arrangement of actions that take place in a play. These plotted actions accumulate to tell the story in an arranged sequence. The plot of your play starts at the very last possible moment. The plot must begin near the entrance ramp of the greatest problem and the most exciting journey of your character's life. In your play, the characters must face their greatest test, their toughest battle. Why would you show the audience your character's second- or third-best story? Shakespeare showed us Hamlet's crisis involving the murder of his father, not his school difficulties at Wittenburg. Sophocles focused on the nightmarish day of Oedipus' downfall, not on the comparatively pleasant day he got married. Felix Unger and Oscar Madison did lots of things together, but in his comedy *The Odd Couple*, Neil Simon showed them *living* together, not going to a movie when they were still married to their wives. Your play tells your character's most interesting story. And the plot is taking place in present tense, right in front of us.

Is there a difference between story and plot? The scholar G.B. Tennyson, in *An Introduction to Drama*, recalls the British novelist E.M. Forster's distinction between story and plot: " 'The king died of grief and then the queen died,' is a *story*. 'The King died and then the queen died *of grief*' is a *plot*." (My italics.) As Tennyson points out, plot— planned, designed and executed by the playwright— utilizes the notion of *cause and effect* to shape and arrange events to tell a story.

Stories are humanity's way of understanding our lives and the world in which we live. When we try to comprehend an event—a marriage, a divorce, a war, a crime, the life and death of a human being or the rise and fall of a civilization—we tend to investigate and explain the events in terms of story. We ask the basic question: What happened? Then we ask: Why? Then we ask: What happens next?

Human beings ask questions every moment of the day, questions about the world, about people, about ideas. Life moves forward, and as it does we are constantly presented with one simple but resounding question: What are you going to do next? The stakes can be small or large: Should you cook dinner or go to a restaurant? Should your nation attack an enemy or seek a peace? And when we report on our lives— our questions, actions, decisions and answers—we see the events in a time sequence. "*This* happened," we say, "then *that* happened." And we see the actions in a causal chain that takes place in a linear movement through time.

An obvious example of linear, cause-and-effect dramatic action can be found in *Hamlet*. King Hamlet is dead long before the play starts. The play begins with the scene between the soldiers on the battlement. Then the ghost enters. Then the soldiers tell Prince Hamlet about the ghost. Then Hamlet meets the ghost of his father and learns about the king's murder by his uncle Claudius. This then causes Hamlet to vow revenge and scheme to catch his uncle. Then Hamlet runs rings around the opposing forces, including Ophelia, Polonius, Claudius, Gertrude, Rosencrantz and Guildenstern. Then the players arrive, causing Hamlet to come up with the idea of staging the play-within-a-play, which in turn causes Claudius to reveal his guilt. Then Hamlet kills Polonius, causing Hamlet to be sent to England. Polonius' death and Hamlet's disappearance cause Ophelia to go mad, in turn causing her death. Then Hamlet returns, causing Claudius to plan Hamlet's murder with the help of Laertes. Then Hamlet duels with Laertes, causing Laertes to stab Hamlet, in turn causing Hamlet to stab Laertes, causing Laertes to confess his guilt and accuse Claudius of plotting Hamlet's death, causing Hamlet to stab Claudius. Then Hamlet dies.

The story always moves forward, each action caused by a preceding action and in turn causing yet another action to follow. The arrangement of the actions is the plot of the story.

Ninety-nine percent of all plays have stories that move forward in time. Some plays have a story that covers many years; the British director Peter Brook's epic *The Mahabharata* and George Bernard Shaw's political satire *Back to Methuselah* depict events over centuries. Shakespeare's tragedy *Hamlet* and Lillian Hellman's family melodrama *The Little Foxes* take place over weeks and months. Noel Coward's comedy *Hay Fever* takes place over a three-day weekend. Some plays follow Aristotle's classical theory of the "unity of time," with all the play's actions taking place within a twenty-four-hour period. Examples include Sophocles' fifth century B.C. Greek tragedy *Oedipus*, Moliere's seventeenth-century French comedy about religious hypocrisy *Tartuffe*, nineteenth-century Norwegian playwright Henrik Ibsen's drama about the last day in the life of a tortured, tempestuous woman *Hedda Gabler*, and Edward Albee's savage early sixties party-play *Who's Afraid of Virginia Woolf?* And some plays—I call them Time = Time Plays—cover the exact amount of time it takes to watch the play; if the action takes ninety minutes, the play runs ninety minutes. Examples include Marsha Norman's *'Night, Mother* about a woman who announces to her mother her intention to commit suicide; Lanford Wilson's two-character love story *Talley's Folly*; and German writer Franz Xavier Kroetz's searing, wordless one-character play *Request Concert*.

Regardless of the *amount* of time a story covers (minutes, hours, days, years), most playwrights *organize* their stories in a forward-moving fashion. True, some writers construct stories as flashback or memory plays. Peter Shaffer's psychological mystery *Equus* and Tennessee Williams' delicate family drama *The Glass Menagerie* are stories narrated by onstage characters in the present about events that took place in the past, but when the narrator steps aside to show us what happened, the play's actions are depicted in linear forward-moving progression. The "present" narration of these plays is always understood to be a framing device. The majority of the action is depicted in linear sequence.

Some playwrights have written their plots in reverse order: Harold Pinter's love-triangle drama *Betrayal* and the Stephen Sondheim musical about friends and show business *Merrily We Roll Along* depict a sequence of events going backward in time. *Betrayal*, for example, begins with scenes taking place in 1977, starting with the last encounter between Emma and Jerry, the two lovers of the triangle. After this first scene we move *forward* to a tense encounter between Jerry and Emma's husband Robert, who is also Jerry's best friend. After which we move *backward* to Jerry and Emma's breakup two years before. Then we move *back* a year to the day Robert found out about Emma and Jerry's affair. Then we move *forward* about a week to a scene in which Emma finds herself unable to confess to Jerry that Robert knows. Then we move *forward* again to an awkward encounter between Robert and Jerry a few days later. Then we move *back* two years to a happier time before Jerry and Emma's affair was uncovered. By the end of the play we have reached the night Jerry first told Emma he was in love with her, an event that takes place seven years before the first scene of the play. That's the gimmick, and it's a great one.

Fewer dramatists employ a technique that depicts the often nonlinear nature of human experience and thought. We all know what it's like to have nonlinear ideas. Our thoughts, fantasies and memories may bounce around in our heads in various orders, and so some writers seek to depict that experience onstage. The plays of British writer Caryl Churchill, such as *Top Girls* and *Cloud Nine*, attempt this, as do those of the American playwrights Mac Wellman, Suzan-Lori Parks and Craig Lucas, among others. Events in a character's life may be *remembered*, *fantasized* and *depicted* onstage in a nonlinear fashion (A nonlinear sequence: *First* I remember my college graduation, *next* I fantasize about my high school graduation, *last* I imagine my own death), but these nonlinear scenes are used sparingly in theater. A playwright who writes an entire play in this manner can easily provoke confusion and boredom in his audience. Theater audiences may be entranced by stage depictions of nonlinear experience from time to time, but the shrewd playwright does not write an entire drama this way. The rule of thumb for nonlinear writing: A little goes a long way.

Experimenting with time structure can be liberating for the writer and entertaining for the audience. The audience may enjoy the "trick" of a nonlinear structure, but the primary questions they're asking are not structural ones but rather human ones: Where have the characters been? What are they doing? What are they going to do? What audiences crave in drama is an understanding of people and ideas through the forward-moving *connection* of incidents. David Ball, in his book for actors, directors, designers and writers, *Backwards and Forwards*, underlines this notion when he argues that a successful play may be read "backwards" action-by-action to see exactly how each action was affected by a previous one. This is a wonderful way to analyze a text.

The nature of a dramatic story lies in its *linkage* of one event or action to another. Sometimes the detailed events depicted do not, at first glance, seem to connect. A murder mystery, for example, might include an ostensibly extraneous scene that appears to have no bearing on the main plot, but in the end we realize it actually had great importance. In a good story, in good drama, everything connects. And in good drama, the connected actions are ones intentionally performed by strong characters.

Drama does not examine human beings in repose, at leisure. While many good plays often depict moments of joy, relaxation, even boredom, the majority of any drama has little to do with inactivity. Drama examines human beings in extremes. Under pressure. In trouble. Within conflict.

Good drama allows for *some* random acts to affect action. Weather, illness and accidental outside forces often change fictional events, just as they often change real ones. Hamlet *was* saved by a chance encounter with pirates after all, and in *Hedda Gabler* a character *happens* to find a precious manuscript in a gutter. But a shrewd playwright doesn't depend too much on coincidence. It's fine to allow your desperate hero to be held up in a rainy traffic jam *once*, or even upon arriving at his destination discover that his prey has just eluded him, but a play *filled* with traffic jams, last minute arrivals and sudden rainstorms suggests a world governed less by the actions *of* people and more by the accidents that *befall* people. And audiences go to the theater to see people act, not to see puppets be manipulated by cloudbursts.

In its highest sense, drama makes powerful statements about the human condition. It reveals truths about our world and ourselves, truths that rise out of characters acting under the pressure of conflict, need and desire. Remember the old saying: "If you want to find out what a person is made of, put that person under pressure." Good playwrights remember another old saying: "Always keep your hero in trouble." Putting a character under pressure and keeping that character in trouble will assure two things: that the audience will find out what the character is made of, and that the story will move forward.

In successful drama, conflict is incited, is developed via action and complications to a crisis, results in a climax, and comes to its resolution. So, for our purposes, let us redefine drama as: (1) People doing things, performing acts, to affect other people and cause other actions. (2) A conflict of people, ideas and wills that must result in a Resolution of the Conflict. (3) A contest between opposing forces. (4) Imitated actions that tell a story.

REAL-LIFE DRAMA, MYSTERIES AND DRAMATIC QUESTIONS

Is drama only found in theater? No. Drama can be found in film, on television, in fiction. Most important, drama can be found in real life. What is dramatic in real life? A war. An election. A divorce. A trial. A murder case. A courtship. An illness. A business deal. A love affair. In these examples, the drama is inherent to the situation. The opposing forces are obvious. The conflict is obvious. The dramatic questions are obvious. What isn't obvious are the answers.

One of my firm beliefs is that all plays are mystery plays. By "mystery play," I don't necessarily mean crime/murder mysteries such as Agatha Christie's whodunit *The Mousetrap* or Anthony Shaffer's *Sleuth* or Ira Levin's *Deathtrap*. Nor do I mean the religious "mystery plays" of the medieval period. What I mean is that all good drama is carried by mystery, by the questions posed in a play. Think of these questions as little hooks to pull the audience along. The audience leans forward to find out the answers to these questions. Even a casual look at many great plays, including *Oedipus, Hamlet, Hedda Gabler*—even

Neil Simon's comedy *The Odd Couple*—reveals a large number of mysteries posed by the playwright throughout the script; questions about riddles and parentage (*Oedipus*), murders and marriage (*Hamlet*), manuscripts (*Hedda Gabler*), and why someone is late for a poker game (*The Odd Couple*). The answers to these and other questions are dramatically revealed over the course of each play. In this sense, all great dramas are great mystery plays.

In Agatha Christie's *And Then There Were None*, we ask: Who will be killed next on Indian Island? Will anyone survive? And who is the killer? In Ben Hecht's and Charles MacArthur's *The Front Page* we ask: Will the tough editor Walter Burns get his star reporter Hildy Johnson back on the paper? Will someone discover the killer hiding in the rolltop desk? In Lorraine Hansbury's *A Raisin in the Sun* we ask: Will Walter Lee get his family to sell their house and move away to a better life? In each of these examples, certain key questions are posed by the predominant dramatic situation. These key questions can be seen as the dramatic spine of the play. A well-constructed play usually has one central dramatic question, a question that suggests a conflict of opposing forces. Examples: Which side will win the war? Which candidate will win the election? Will the jury return a guilty verdict against the accused?

But a play that is truly dramatic—especially a full-length (sixty-five minutes to three hours)—needs more than one question to keep the audience interested, engaged and involved. So sub-questions, inner-questions, side-questions, thematic-questions must be posed. Take our real-life dramas—the war, the election and the courtroom trial. What sub-questions can join the major one?

In our war play: Will a third army join forces to win a battle? Will the general be replaced? Will the weather aid the attackers? Will the spy reveal the troop movements? Will the infantryman find his courage? Will the captain lose the love of his fiancée? Will the diplomats arrive at an agreement before the assault? Will there ever be an end to war?

In our election play: Will the candidate use incriminating photos to smear his rival? Will his wife leave him? Will the campaign manager unify his staff? What was in the letter we saw the rival candidate read, then burn? Will a headline story change the nature of the political debate? Will it rain on election day? Is a democratic election the best way to instate men in power?

In our courtroom play: Will the accused tell the truth? Will the prosecutor use the phony evidence? Will the defense attorney stop drinking? Who is the mysterious woman who keeps lurking in the back of the courtroom? Will the corrupt judge rule in favor of the accused? Is Law the equal of Justice?

The critic and scholar Martin Esslin, in his book *An Anatomy of Drama*, describes these series of mysteries, these series of questions as "arcs," much like the arcs of a suspension bridge that keep the structure standing. Says Esslin: "Put in its simplest and most mundane terms, the basic task of anyone concerned with presenting any kind of drama to any audience consists in capturing their attention and holding it as long as required. Only when that fundamental objective has been achieved can the more lofty and ambitious intentions be fulfilled: the imparting of wisdom and insight, illumination and purging of emotion."

The best authors of the most successful dramas of the last two thousand years have understood that the cornerstone of dramatic engagement is suspense.

SUSPENSE AND PLAUSIBILITY

What is suspense? Look at the word. It's close to the verb "suspend." In architectural terms—and echoing Martin Esslin—one might think of a "suspension bridge"—the taut emotional/intellectual cable on which an audience member is suspended; it could be shown on a graph as a line of interest between a point of departure and a point of arrival. Think of these points as information. Consider these examples:

1. If an audience knows there is a disguised killer hiding in the drawing room, they are suspended between that information on this line of questions:
   - Who is the killer?
   - Will he kill again?
   - Will he be caught? In time?

   At the end of this line of questions are the answers:
   - John Doe is the killer.
   - No, he won't kill again.
   - Because he is caught before he strikes again.

2. If an audience knows that the married Bob and the married Betty are having an affair, they are suspended between that information on this line of questions:

- Will they be found out?
- Will the affair end?

At the end of this line of questions are the answers:

- Yes, their spouses discover the affair.
- No, their affair continues.

What is vital here is that the questions posed are worthy of the audience's time and attention. To insure audience engagement, keep the following rules in mind:

All your characters must compel the audience's attention. After all, what kind of audience members would go to the theater to watch a play about people less interesting than themselves?

All your dramatic questions must have high stakes. They must connect to an audience's concerns, be they intellectual, emotional or spiritual. After all, why would audience members care about a dramatic question they wouldn't care about in real life? The unraveling of the mystery must *matter* to the audience. In some cases, the audience must even *root* for an answer or an outcome.

The answer to a dramatic question—for the audience and the play's characters—is a *goal*. And characters in plays must pursue their goals.

Let's look at *Hamlet* again.

Hamlet is the main character. The major dramatic question of the play is this: Will Hamlet prove Claudius' guilt and avenge his father's death? The next most important questions are these: How will Hamlet prove this? And what precisely will he do when he does prove it? How will he overcome the obstacles Claudius puts in his way? Every time Hamlet acts to find the truth and solve the mystery, he comes into conflict with the other characters in the play. Their actions are designed to stop Hamlet from discovering the truth. His search for answers leads to conflict. And a conflict is the key human obstacle a character encounters as he acts to achieve his goal. The conflicts must also work hand-in-hand with the mysteries, or questions. Without conflict and obstacles, the answers to the questions will come too easily, the goals will be achieved too speedily, and the play will end too soon.

One should note that "Detective Hamlet" answers the question of Claudius' guilt two-thirds of the way into the script. For the remainder of the play, the questions are: Will Hamlet avenge the murder? When? How? Who will try to stop him? What obstacles are in his way? In drama, the best obstacles are always those presented by other characters.

If the stakes are high (the throne of Denmark), characters may be capable of doing *anything* to protect their secrets, their power, their wealth, their loved ones. And so, the detective (Hamlet) will come into conflict with the criminals (Claudius and his assistants). How should Hamlet proceed? What is the best, most entertaining and engaging way for Shakespeare to have his prince go after truth and vengeance?

First, let's try some actions Shakespeare did *not* have Hamlet perform:

1. Hamlet confronts Claudius about his suspicions immediately. Claudius denies his crime. Hamlet believes him. End of play.
2. Hamlet confronts Claudius immediately. Claudius admits to the killing and goes to prison. End of play.
3. Hamlet confronts Claudius immediately. Claudius kills Hamlet. End of play.

All of these variations are *plausible*. Shakespeare *could* have written his play this way. But what's the problem here? None of these optional actions are very *interesting*. They display little extended conflict. They suggest no more than one or two actions at best. They display Hamlet as a bumbling inquisitor, not a crafty investigator. They display his enemies as fools or brutes, not sly manipulators. A *Hamlet* populated by such characters would not be very engaging. They wouldn't fill an entire evening in the theater. Again, these alternative *Hamlet* plots *are* plausible, but—and this is a good rule to remember—*What is plausible is not always dramatic or interesting.*

Shakespeare planned a play that would extend the conflict, extend the dramatic questions, and extend the actions over the running time he needed—at that time in the Elizabethan theater, five hours. Shakespeare designed and built a suspension bridge. Shakespeare designed Hamlet as a man who would plot a strategy to catch the king. Hamlet is too intelligent to think the crafty Claudius will confess when confronted. So Hamlet uses the coincidence of the arrival of the players to lay a trap for the king. This plot takes time to detail in the play. The audience is often kept in the dark about Hamlet's plans, creating more suspense. The audience wonders if Claudius' spies will unearth Hamlet's plans. The audience wonders if Hamlet's plan will work. The audience wonders what the king will do when he sees the players' performance. One main question, many smaller questions. All of them important.

The film director Alfred Hitchcock, known as "The Master of Suspense," once described suspense as "the *addition* of information."

Hitchcock explained that if you show a group of men eating lunch at a table under a clock, and suddenly a bomb blows them to pieces, that's a surprise. Surprise is good, but its shock lasts just moments in the minds of the audience. If, however, in an earlier scene, you had added the information that someone planted a bomb under the table and set it to go off in three minutes, *then* when the men come in and start to eat, you've purchased at least three minutes of suspense. If you add the information that one of the men is a new father, you've raised the sympathetic stakes. If you add a scene where one of the men drops his fork, thus necessitating his looking under the table where the bomb is planted, you've created more suspense, more pressure, more hope and more drama.

Suspense—often misunderstood—means knowing more, not less about a situation. But the crafty playwright always holds back the most vital information and the final, most important answers until the very last moment.

DRAMA VS. THEATER

At the beginning of this chapter, we noted that while drama and theater are inexorably linked, they are not interchangeable.

Let's look at the definition of the word *theater*. It's derived from the Greek word *theatron*—a "place for seeing." Literally, then, the word refers to the "place," the structure for the performance. The entire building, or the stage itself. But theater is not simply a place. Theater is more than a setting for "seeing." To focus exclusively on theater as either a place or a vantage point for viewing would be to leave out the larger definition the term has taken on over the course of its history.

Theater is pretending, make-believe, dress-up games. Theater is "play." Theater makers and audiences have always understood the vital part make-believe plays in our lives and our societies. Every child understands the need to pretend. As children and later as adults, we *learn* through our pretending. We understand the roles of society, the minds of our fellow human beings, and our own hearts by trying on the costumes of others.

In its largest sense, theater is the human arena for our understanding of the human condition. It reveals human truth by *showing* that truth onstage. For over two thousand years, theater has thrown a powerful spotlight on the actions, shapes, sounds and meaning of existence. In theater, audiences gather to witness thoughts and emotions, shapes and sounds.

For our purposes, let us define theater in this way: (1) A place for seeing; (2) the stage itself, or auditorium; (3) the building in which a theater is found; (4) a theatrical company; and (5) the sensory appreciation of live performance.

This last definition, having to do with the senses, may be the most important for us to remember.

Is theater only found in the Theater? No. Theater can be found in real life. At a political convention. At a wedding. In a courtroom, at a party, at a riot or at a funeral. Places and events that bring people together in a *performance ritual*; events that, through their re-enactments, lend understanding to our lives. Events that include role-playing. Events that repeat themselves and gain meaning by repetition. In the theater, we gather to observe and involve ourselves in a ritual that is both completely familiar and completely new.

Theater takes place in that space—the mind, the senses, the imagination—between the stage and the audience. Theater is flair. Theater is life with quotes around it. Theater is a collective conspiracy on the part of the players and the audience. The audience "suspends its disbelief." For the duration of the performance, the audience will believe that Peter Pan can fly; that the events of an entire day can be depicted in two hours; that a male wearing a dress is actually a woman; and that two men holding sticks in front of their faces are actually prisoners behind bars.

Theater is a place where—because it's live, taking place right in front of the audience—we know anything can happen. Theater takes place in the present tense—characters performing actions *now*; good theater is not about what *has* happened or what *will* happen, but what *is* happening. If drama involves an audience with characters, stories and ideas, then theater is a "show" to dazzle that audience. Drama is the steak; theater is the sizzle.

The first time prehistoric man put an ostrich feather in his hair and danced around in front of his friends, that was theater. The first time he asked a friend to help him show how he battled an ostrich in conflict, how he finally defeated his foe and reached his goal, that was drama. In time, these performances became necessary to their audiences. They celebrated their society, explained their people, depicted adventures and explored ideas. These performances honored their gods and celebrated their harvests. Eventually, they required organization, planning and rehearsal.

When you're writing a play, you must keep *both* a sense of the theatrical and a sense of the dramatic. But with which should a play-wright begin? Drama or theater? The initial impulse for a play can come from either, but for a play to succeed, that impulse must be firmly grounded.

Plays are about people.

Start with Character.

We'll return to character in the next chapter, as part of the six elements of Aristotle. For now, consider the subjects discussed in this chapter and work on the following exercises.

EXERCISES

1. Make a list of dramatic actions, actions you've witnessed or experienced from real life. Actions such as a fistfight or a marriage proposal or a business maneuver. Then develop your list by answering the following questions: Who performed the actions? What did the actions tell you about the person who performed them? Were the actions part of a larger context, a larger situation? What did the actions tell you about that situation? About the world? What ideas about people, life and the world strike you when you contemplate the meanings of these actions? Write down your answers to these questions next to the corresponding dramatic action.

2. Select one of the actions from above. Write it down. What earlier action could have precipitated this action? What reaction could follow it? You're not writing a play here, but you are identifying actions that have the potential for dramatic action linkage.

3. Recall an incident from your past, one that had a profound effect on you, changing the course of your life. Write the story of this incident in "Once upon a time" fashion, like a fairy tale. Write it down in a few sentences or paragraphs. When you've finished, identify the actions that took place in the story. What actions caused these actions and in turn caused others? How did you use actions to tell the story of this incident? Did you tell the story in linear sequence, or was there a reason to tell some parts of the story out of sequence? What role, if any, did chance, coincidence, accident, fate, the weather or dumb luck play in the story?

4. Find a story in the news—a story still ongoing (an election campaign, a war, a murder trial, a custody battle, a fight between the president and Congress). What are the conflicts, large and small, inherent to the story? What dramatic questions surround the story? What is at stake for the "actors" in the drama (politicians, defendants, parents, children,

people)? What are all the possible outcomes to the conflicts? What will the struggles and their outcomes tell you about the people involved and our world in general once the conflict is concluded? Write down your answers. Make the thoughts concrete.

5. Choose a theatrical event from real life—a ritual activity well-known to you, such as a wedding, a funeral, a court case, etc. What do *you* define as theatrical about the event? What do you learn from people and society when you partake in or witness that event? What actions occur every time one of these events takes place? And what parts of the event lend themselves to a specific dramatic, theatrical experience onstage? Answer each of these questions in a few sentences.

CHAPTER TWO

The Six Elements
of Aristotle

Aristotle's theory of drama, his *Poetics*, was written over two thousand years ago. Aristotle was writing primarily about classical Greek tragedy in the fifth century B.C., but his blueprint for a play is as useful now as it was then. Most successful plays still follow Aristotle's dictates and include his six elements. Keep them in mind as you write your play. The six elements are translated variously from the Greek as

action or plot
character
thought or ideas
language, diction or verbal expression
music or song
spectacle, image or visual adornment

For our purposes we will choose the following definitions but alter Aristotle's order:

character
action
ideas
language
music
spectacle

Most playwrights today believe in the primacy of character. Aristotle did not. He believed plot, or action, was the most important aspect of the play. In one large sense, he was right. When viewed from the perspective of the audience, the plot *is* the most important aspect. When an audience recalls a play, what stays in the mind more than anything else is *what happened*—and that's the plot, the action. The audience perspective is absolutely vital to keep in mind, but the composition of a script by a playwright does not necessarily follow the same order as in its viewing and appreciation by an audience. An audience may remember the actions first, but the playwright must start with *character*.

CHARACTER

Remember one of our simple rules from the previous chapter: All your characters must compel the audience's attention. While it's been said that audiences often go to the theater to see reflections of themselves, they don't go to see *duller* reflections of themselves.

A compelling character can be a king or a carpenter, a monster or a marriage broker. The title the character wears doesn't matter. Interest is engendered by what a character *does*. The most interesting character in your play is the person with the greatest needs, the biggest problems, and the greatest potential for action. She may be seductive, funny or flawed. He may be courageous, cruel or kind. The first test is yourself: Does your character interest *you*? They have to fascinate you. So an initial question you should ask yourself is, What kind of people fascinate you in real life?

What Makes a Character Compelling?

Your aim is to create characters an audience wants to spend time with. Your aim is to create heroes, villains, and every complicated variation of human nature in between—people your audience will want to join on a journey, root for, gasp at, pity and boo. Passive characters are never interesting. Playwright Marsha Norman, in her interview at the end of this book, says that the most interesting characters are those who "take control of their own lives." In most plays, that control is hard-won. It is the result of struggle.

Most characters who compel our attention and interest are sympathetic. But an audience isn't fascinated only by good-guy heroes. Other great characters found in the history of drama include "The Villain" (Claudius in *Hamlet*; Roy Cohn in Tony Kushner's *Angels in America*); "The Love Interest" (a girl if it's Juliet or Ophelia; a boy if it's Romeo or *The Glass Menagerie*'s Gentleman Caller); "The Friend of the

Hero" (Horatio in *Hamlet*); "The Catalytic Character" who comes into the plot at a key moment to act as a springboard for a new development or action (Polonius, whom Hamlet accidentally murders, in *Hamlet*; the sickly Horace Giddens on whose heart condition so many financial futures depend in *The Little Foxes*); "The Comic Relief" (the porter in *Macbeth*); "The Messenger" (every Greek play ever written); "The Surprise, or Deus Ex Machina" (the disguised witness in Agatha Christie's *Witness for the Prosecution*; "The God Who Saves the Day at the Last Minute in a Greek Tragedy"); and scores of minor characters.

What is the key relationship between the audience and a character? Identification. Audiences want characters who will take them on a journey both foreign and familiar. Characters in situations the audience recognizes—births, courtships, marriages, affairs, divorces, illnesses, battles, professional struggles, deaths, financial and family crises. Characters who act out and personify the hopes, dreams and ambitions of the audience. Characters who are the audience's agents in the fictional world of the stage, acting out our desire for romance, for revenge, for retribution, for control.

A strong character must define herself early in a play if the author wants to hook an audience's interest. Oscar Hammerstein II, the great lyricist and playwright who collaborated with Richard Rodgers to create such landmarks as *Oklahoma!*, *South Pacific*, and *The King and I*, said that the lead character in a musical always has to sing an "I Want Song" within the first twenty minutes of the show. The "I Want Song"—or "The 8:15 Number"—is usually the second song in the show. It defines the character's needs and wants. In the Stephen Sondheim/Jule Styne/Arthur Laurents musical *Gypsy*, the "I Want Song" is Mama Rose's "Some People," the song that details Rose's ambitions for her daughters and for her own career in show business. It's the song that tells us who she is, where she's been, and where she wants to go. In the Frank Loesser/Abe Burrows/Jo Swerling musical *Guys and Dolls*, the "I Want Song" is "Oldest Established," introducing the gambler Nathan Detroit who has to find a hideout for his next craps game. And in the landmark hit *A Chorus Line*, the "I Want Song" is "God, I Hope I Get It"—the opening number of the show that introduces the dancers who desperately "need this job."

Of course the "I Want Song" isn't just found in musicals. It's really the "I Want *Moment*." In Shakespeare's *Richard III* it's the very first soliloquy or monologue: "Now is the winter of our discontent made glorious summer by this son of York." The speech describes Richard's wounded ego, his warped wit, his intelligence, and his ambition to become king. In *Hamlet*, it's Hamlet's Act One, Scene Two soliloquy that begins "O! that this too too solid flesh would melt." It's this speech that depicts Hamlet's pain, anger and resentment at his mother's marriage to his uncle Claudius—and Claudius' usurpation of the Danish throne—so soon after his father's mysterious death.

When one character's "I Want" comes up against another character's "I Want," you have dramatic conflict. In musical terms, the two "I Want Songs" clashing together creates disharmony. In August Wilson's *The Piano Lesson*, the constant refrain is "I want to sell the piano!" followed by "Well, *I don't* want to sell the piano!" In *The Odd Couple*, it's Felix Unger's "We have to have a neat home" butting up against Oscar Madison's "I like being a slob." So while a character can be interesting because of her background, her psychology, her humor, her way of talking, the most interesting thing about a character is what she wants, how badly she wants it, and what her actions will be to get it.

Interest is generated both by the audience's familiarity with the character's goal and by the actions the character performs to achieve that goal. Are Hamlet's goals familiar to the average audience? I'll admit there aren't many of us who can identify with the plight of a Danish prince. Few of us have witnessed our mother marry our uncle after our father's murder, nor lost our own chance at becoming king. And we seldom bump into the ghosts of our relatives on castle battlements. *But* we *all* know what it's like to engage in internecine battles within a family; we all understand jealousy, betrayal and injustice; and although there aren't real ghosts in real life, aren't we all haunted by the recollections of lost loved ones to whom we wanted to speak one last time, and to whom we wanted to prove something? Few of us *are* the villainous *Richard III*, but many of us are ambitious; many of us want a better job, a promotion, a chance to shine in power. In Tennessee Williams' *A Streetcar Named Desire*, Blanche DuBois' desperate need to hold onto the illusion of her family plantation at Belle Reeve in the face of battered reality may be foreign to many audiences, but the desire for a lost home, the desire for protection, the desire for grace and beauty is one shared by every human being.

Are there some goals that are better than others? Sure.

Concrete goals are always better than abstract ones. What are some of the things characters in great plays want? Sex, money, power, love, a jewel, a key, an answer, a job, a fortune, a crown, revenge, truth, justice. Which of these are abstract goals? Which are concrete? Abstract goals are not *tangible*, they cannot be material. They are concepts. They are important and worthy of a character's desire, but they have no stage presence. Concrete wants/needs/desires/goals are *tangible*. You can hold them in your hand, touch them, feel them, see them.

But, you argue, isn't the pursuit of justice a greater goal than finding a bagful of money? Not in drama. Drama takes place in the land of the concrete. But, you argue, Hamlet wanted justice, Hamlet wanted revenge. Aren't those abstract goals? Yes, but Hamlet's desire for justice and revenge was not generalized; Hamlet's desire was specific: to prove Claudius a killer and then kill him. That's very concrete. Goals like that are the best kinds of dramatic goals: concrete goals (prove Claudius is a killer, then kill him) moving the play's action and depicting the play's characters, with big abstract concepts (justice, revenge) standing behind them. To write a character who just generally wants justice is to write a character who grasps at the air.

A brilliantly drawn villain like Regina in Lillian Hellman's melodrama *The Little Foxes* certainly has abstract goals, but all of her actions, her dramatic wants are about *specifics*. She wants money, control of the family business, a new husband, a new city to live in, and she wants her daughter to stay with her. These are concrete wants and goals, but they are connected to abstract ideas about love, sex, resentment, revenge, power and the needs of Regina's sick, hungry soul. When Regina famously sits by and watches her husband Horace suffer a heart attack—watches him as he pleads with her to get the medicine that may save his life—Regina has a concrete desire: to kill her husband. She *allows* his death. She does not act. What she does *not* do becomes the most violent *action* in the play.

Positive goals are better than negative goals. For example, you might want to write a play about a philosopher who is trying to disprove the existence of God. To disprove God may seem like a fascinating goal, but there are problems with it. Does the problem have to do with religion? No. It doesn't have to do with disproving *God*; it has to do with *dis*proving. It's negative. Its dynamic is less magnetic, both for the character and for the audience. In our "disproving God" example, the goal is weak because:

- it is abstract and amorphous;
- it is, by definition, impossible to prove a negative;
- it is difficult to depict in concrete dramatic terms.

But, you say, Richard III has negative goals. Wrong. Richard III has nothing but positive goals—to "get" the crown. True, he's a villain, he *kills* people along the way, but *his* goal, from *his* point of view, is a positive one.

Active goals are better than reactive goals. If your character's primary goal is to escape, to run away, you have a weak goal. From Shakespeare's *As You Like It* to the movies *North by Northwest* and *The Fugitive*, drama has often depicted characters in flight. But if your character is running away from something, he must also be running *toward* something. Running away is reactive. Running toward is active. That's why movie heroes on the run from the law (reactive goal) are also trying to prove their innocence and find the real culprit (active goal). "Will our hero be caught?" *and* "Will our hero catch the real killer?" is more interesting than simply "Will our hero be caught?"

To gauge a character's level of compelling interest, you'll need to know that character well. I'll make the argument that the best, most organic and safest way to develop characters would be to create detailed biographies, backgrounds, psychology for the character *before* writing or outlining the play. Once the playwright understands what her character will or will not do under a multitude of circumstances, only then can she proceed to construct a story based on the character's actions.

One surefire way of assuring an audience's interest in your character is to make him or her likable. Even a glancing look at the history of great dramatic characters will tell us a few basic points that should be remembered by every dramatist:

- Most memorable dramatic characters are likable.
- If they aren't likeable *in a traditionally understood way* (more below), they're passionate or witty or magnetic.
- If they're villainous monsters, they're monsters with charisma.
- They *do* great things (greatness within context, of course).

Likability is tricky. It's not the same as being "nice." For example, we like Richard III. Why? He's a killer, to be sure. He murders his entire family to get the English crown. He even has two little boys smothered in a tower. But he's been bruised by life (that humpback, that deformed hand), and we pity him. He's obviously the most intelligent political thinker in the court, so we sympathize with his wounded sense of justice. He's witty. He's funny. He's charming. And—this is vitally important— he does extravagant things and gets away with them. We wish we could too. Sure. We like Richard.

In *Hedda Gabler* we like Hedda. Why? She's cruel to her husband, her in-laws, her old school friend, her lover, *everyone*. But, like Richard III, she does things we wish we could do. She fights against constraints. She bucks the claustrophobic world in which she lives. Most important, Hedda desires beauty and passion—the fully lived, fully experienced world of love, intellect and fire. What audience member hasn't desired that? Sure. We like Hedda Gabler.

Character in Action

When you're sure you have an interesting character, your next step is depicting this character to your audience. "Action is character," goes the old saying, "as character is action." They cannot be separated. For example:

Character is action—A man conditioned by his upbringing to cut corners, look for easy ways out and be greedy steals a suitcase full of money. The kind of character determines the action.

Action is character—A man steals a suitcase full of money; therefore we conjecture he may be the kind of man conditioned to cut corners, look for easy ways out and be greedy. The action determines the kind of character.

A fictional character is depicted onstage by the evidence of that person's actions. The audience acts as a detective. The audience looks for clues to understand a stage character, just as they look for clues to understand a real person. There are three ways to display your character onstage:

1. What a character says about herself.
2. What other characters say about her.
3. What the character *does*.

All three are useful ways of depicting character. But is one of these more important than any of the others? Yes. Number three: what a character does. If I hear a man *say* he is honest, and I hear his friend say he is honest, I may well surmise that he is honest . . . until I *see* him steal a suitcase full of money. His actions prove him dishonest, despite what he says or what others say. To stoop to a cliche: "Actions speak louder than words."

Aristotle identified the main character, the hero of the tragedy, as the protagonist. In its various Greek definitions, a protagonist is the "carrier of the action"; an actor who plays the first part; the chief personage of the drama; the principal character in the plot; one who contends for a prize; a combatant; an *actor*. Break up the word: Pro—to be "for" something; Agonize—to "struggle." To struggle for something.

In classical tragedy, the protagonist was a high figure—a king, a prince, a royal personage: Oedipus, Hamlet, Othello. He was a noble figure with a tragic flaw—pride, jealousy, ignorance. He fought against great odds (events, people, nature, the gods) and was eventually destroyed by them. In a contemporary play, the main character need not be a good person, but the protagonist's problems, goals, intelligence, charms and weaknesses must be worthy of our interest and our time.

Most great plays have one strong protagonist, but some great plays have two, three, four or more strong, active characters working toward their goals. For example, Terrence McNally's Tony Award-winning *Love! Valour! Compassion!* concerns seven gay men who spend an entire summer together. Each of the men passionately pursues his own goals. In one sense, every character in your play is the protagonist, with strong goals and a rich, complex personal history. If you think of the protagonist as "the ball carrier," or a football player, and if you think of your play as a football game, then the point from one end zone to the other side's goalpost is the trajectory of your plot. Your protagonist(s) must get the ball across that goal line. The other characters are there to help or, in most cases, to hinder. The job of everyone playing against the protagonist is to stop his progress down the field, tackle him, confuse him, and take the ball away. How the ball carrier plays the game determines the kind of player he is.

When you think about your plays and the characters who people them, you probably think in terms of lead characters and supporting characters. This makes sense. Hamlet is a lead; Ophelia, Polonius and Claudius are supporting characters. In *Hedda Gabler*, Hedda is a lead; her boring husband Tesman, her lover Eilert Lovborg, and the sardonic Judge Brack are supporting characters. In *The Odd Couple*, Felix and Oscar are leads; the poker buddies and the Pigeon sisters are supporting characters. You've probably heard the old saying "There are no small parts, just small actors." Let me share one of my favorite theater anecdotes to illustrate a point. It involves the first New York production of Tennessee Williams' *A Streetcar Named Desire*, starring Jessica Tandy, Marlon Brando, Kim Hunter and Karl Malden, in addition to a number of actors in smaller parts. The roles of Blanche DuBois and Stanley Kowalski are obviously the leads; in a classical sense, Blanche is the active protagonist (a bruised soul seeking shelter), and Stanley is the active antagonist (a magnetic brute jealously guarding his invaded territory). But there were ten other actors in that play, portraying neighbors, drinking buddies, others. One of these ten actors played "the doctor," who, with his nurse, comes to take the shattered Blanche away to the sanitorium in the last minutes of the play. It's a tiny part, no more than a line or two. It is the doctor to whom Blanche says the famous line, "Whoever you are—I have always depended on the kindness of strangers." One day a friend bumped into this actor on the street. The actor told his friend that he was in a new play by Tennessee Williams. The friend asked the actor what the play was about. The actor said, "It's about a doctor who comes to take a woman to a sanitorium."

This is a very telling story. It's funny, of course; a story about an actor's ego. But it's illustrative of how an actor *should* think of the character he's playing. It's also illustrative of how playwrights might think about *all* their characters.

Characters in Conflict

What do your characters consist of? Wants. Needs. Desires. Sure, but what else? Fears. Phobias. Addictions. Weaknesses. How smart are they? (Smart is always better than dumb.) How shrewd? How clever? How devious? How charming? How funny? How ethical? How practical? How malleable? How pathetic? How willing are they to *negotiate*? Some playwrights and teachers refer to all dramatic conflict as negotiation. What will one character do or say to get something from another character?

I'll argue that the reason many plays fail—even ones written by talented writers—is because the author hasn't given her characters

1. Strong enough goals,
2. Difficult enough obstacles,
3. *Talents* and *opportunity*.

Why do I stress "talents" and "opportunities"?
Take Hamlet. Hamlet is very intelligent. He's clever, witty and

ingenious. He pretends to be mad so that he may spy on the court and arouse less suspicion. These are talents. But Shakespeare also gave him opportunities—the arrival of the players is such an opportunity. It's happenstance that they arrive while Hamlet is conducting his clandestine investigation. But their presence at Elsinore gives Hamlet the idea to stage the play that will "catch the conscience of the king." When Hamlet is later sent to England via ship with Rosencrantz and Guildenstern, the audience knows what Hamlet does not: that Rosencrantz and Guildenstern carry a letter from Claudius to the English king ordering Hamlet's execution upon arrival. Hamlet is smart enough to find that letter, open it, and change its contents so that it will order Rosencrantz and Guildenstern's execution instead of his own. But that's not enough. Shakespeare also provides Hamlet with the opportunity he needs—an attack on the ship by pirates. Hamlet escapes onto the pirate's ship, and Rosencrantz and Guildenstern sail on to England and their doom.

The successful playwright knows how to combine her character's skills with a judicious sprinkling of opportunity. A smart playwright won't overuse either of these, however. A protagonist who has a successful strategy for every obstacle is a combination of Einstein, Superman and James Bond. And a playwright who tosses in nick-of-time opportunity after nick-of-time opportunity to save her hero courts accusations of contrivance. As you plan your play, you have to keep asking yourself: What *should* happen? What *could* happen? As each obstacle is overcome, does a new obstacle rise up in the protagonist's way?

The protagonist's enemy is the antagonist, the "opposer of the action." The antagonist is anyone or anything that tries to stop the protagonist, take the ball, or get in the way. A good antagonist is as powerful or more so than the protagonist.

• A good antagonist is a strong villain—Claudius in *Hamlet*.
• A good antagonist is a loved one—George and Martha in Edward Albee's *Who's Afraid of Virginia Woolf?*
• A good antagonist is fate—in classical Greek tragedy, a god.
• A good antagonist is society—the oppressive and corrupt community of Henrik Ibsen's *An Enemy of the People*; the ancient city of Thebes in Sophocles' *Oedipus*.
• A good antagonist is weather—the draught in N. Richard Nash's *The Rainmaker*.

• A good antagonist is chance, luck, circumstance—a random act; a mad sniper who kills the hero's friend at a key moment in the play is acting as an antagonist.

• A good antagonist is oneself—Hamlet's inability to kill Claudius when the villainous king is praying; Hedda Gabler's fear of scandal; Shelly Levene's foolish braggadocio that destroys him at the conclusion of David Mamet's *Glengarry Glen Ross*.

Use all these potential antagonists. But the *best* antagonist is always another character. Why? The heat generated by the conflict between human beings can't be matched by the heat generated by a person and an object, a person and nature, a person and an abstract concept. Recall from your own experience the battles you've fought with friends, family, rivals. Now recall battles you've fought with broken-down cars, snow and contradictory philosophical theories. There's no contest.

A writing exercise I use to teach this point involves a conflict between two characters in a locked room. The two characters must do battle over an object that is of value to one or both of the characters. The object might be valuable in and of itself (a sack of money, a diamond ring, a famous painting); it might be valuable for its information (an incriminating letter, a secret report, a tape recording); it might be valuable for personal or sentimental reasons (a photograph, a diary, a souvenir). Each character must *act* to win possession of the object.

In a recent class, I encountered three versions of this scene. In the first, a young woman and an old man battled over a painting hidden inside the bedroom wall of the old man's house. In the second, a spurned lover and his landlord argued over a love letter. In the third, two women fought over an article one of them wanted to have published in a newspaper. In each case, the exposition was handled deftly; the characters were drawn in strong, clear strokes; the revelation of the object was organic and natural; and the conflict was joined early. But each writer fell into a similar trap. Once the conflict was joined ("I need to get that painting"; "Let me see that letter"; "You can't publish that article"), the character who *most* wanted the object *gave it up to the other*—usually after saying as little as, "I don't really *want* to give it up, but . . . oh, all right!" Just when the scene threatened to get interesting.

The first question I ask these writers is: "When did you feel the air go out of the scene?" In other words, when did the dramatic tension slacken? It slackened rather quickly. The next question I ask is: If *you* were the character, and *you* wanted that painting, that letter, that article, would *you* give in so *early* and so *easily*? Wouldn't you use every strategy at your disposal? Wouldn't you lie, steal, commit murder if need be? Often the writers respond to this question in the following manner: "Well, it's *just* a painting/letter/article."

"Just" is the one word you must *never* use when referring to your writing and your characters. "Just" is a small word. A weak word. A shrug. It means you have no confidence in the magnitude of your object and its value. It means you have a half-hearted approach to your characters. There is no "just" in *Hamlet*. In a "just" play, characters achieve their goals easily, or they shrug them off. In *Just Hamlet*, Hamlet doesn't bother with the ghost's order for revenge. He goes back to school at Wittenburg and becomes a classics major.

This is what *dull, lazy, weak, unimaginative* protagonists do. Dull, lazy, weak, unimaginative characters cannot propel action forward, cannot pursue their goals against obstacles, and cannot carry the ball down the field. And they certainly can't make an audience want to come along for the ride.

Protagonists and antagonists alike, your characters are stand-ins for yourself and your audience. Remember: We go to the theater to be entertained and to understand our world. What better guide to this world than characters who make us want to join them? It doesn't take a genius to tell the difference between a likable character and an unlikable one; between a witty woman and a dull one; between a vital, active man and a placid one. Audiences want to connect to the characters onstage. The majority of memorable stage characters are successfully rendered because the author of the play created a *person* who loves, desires, fears, commits crimes, seeks joy, knows sadness, and acts with every fiber of his being. Characters in plays are stand-ins for the audience, striking back at oppressive structures in life—society, morality, events, other people. We all want to be extraordinary. So create characters who do extraordinary things.

The extraordinary can be saving the universe. It can also be giving an old enemy a second chance. It can be a duel to the death or a decision to go on a date. Many onstage acts are ostensibly minor but, in context, resoundingly major.

A character is best seen in motion, in action, in change and evolution. Contrary to some opinions, all successful stage characters do change, as do all people. Change fascinates. "Change is," as Oscar Wilde said, "the only sure thing." If a successful character does *not* change, that character's will to maintain a status quo must be equally fascinating.

How the dramatist displays a character in motion and moving toward change is shown through dramatic conflict and action.

EXERCISES

1. Create a character. A protagonist. Perhaps it's a character based on a real-life person, perhaps it's one you've imagined. In one to two pages, write a brief biographical sketch of this person. You are creating a fictional character, but don't be afraid to base this character on a person or persons from real life. Maybe the character is you. Maybe it's someone you hardly know. Choose the character's birthdate, birthplace, and where the character grew up. Choose the character's family, social and economic background. Next describe a few key events in that character's life—deaths, winning the lottery, childhood scars. Now look at your biography. Is it interesting enough? Could the events and actions you've imagined be altered to create a *more* interesting person? Is there any hint of that rebellious spirit so much in evidence in Richard III or Hedda Gabler? Revise the biography. Play with different possibilities, different actions and events. Has your biography brought your character to a point in his or her life where a potential high-pressure crisis is suggested? The kind of crisis that could start a play?

2. Create a concrete goal for your character. A want. A need. A desire. Just one. Concrete, not abstract. Write it down.

3. "Character is action; action is character." Create an action that tells us what kind of person your character is. (Example: A young boy steals a purse from an old lady.) Write the action down. Is the action connected to a concrete goal? What does it show you about your character? Does he get what he wants? Or does he run into an obstacle?

4. Create an antagonist for your protagonist. Although we noted that an antagonist can take many forms, for this exercise make the antagonist another person. Create another biography. Rework your biographies in a way that will bring both your protagonist and your antagonist together into the same room or space. Now rework the action from exercise number three. Place both characters in the same action. What happens when both people are aware of the concrete goal? Define the conflict in one sentence.

ACTION

Plot is the arrangement of actions designed to tell the story of a play. The simplest way to describe any plot is to list every action of the play, starting with the first moment and moving to the last. Plot, as we have noted before, depends on tension and suspense, created by the playwright's organization of actions and information and by the playwright's posing of questions. In constructing an effective, intriguing plot, a playwright must create, prolong, subvert and satisfy audience expectations.

In literary theory, this arrangement of actions is called the "strip tease." While one doesn't want to emphasize the sexual aspect of performance more than is necessary, it's important to note that theater and sex, drama and romance, share certain aspects: There is initial interest; followed by a development of attraction; followed by an involvement with the subject; followed by the setting of a goal; then a pursuit; with obstacles to overcome; generating suspense and tension (all enjoyably frustrating); finally ending in success and satisfaction.

This is a gross oversimplification of the parallels, but a dramatist who does not see the similarities between sex and drama will probably not make the connection between a lot of life experiences to art. It's amazing to note the number of real-life activities and experiences that resemble drama, in shape, in sequence, in their expectations, suspense and satisfaction. Plots are constructed to re-create this sense of experience along recognizable lines, whether or not the audience is consciously aware of the parallels. On an unconscious level, plots are a working out of life patterns, patterns based on the experiences and expectations of human beings. Sex, eating, sports, war, trials, birth, even the aging process.

Our youth is exposition; who we are, where we are, when we are, what we are going to do. Our maturation—for most people 75 percent of their time on earth—is the conflict and rising action. Who among us does not expect that the great middle period of our lives (from our late adolescence through retirement) is fraught with questions, tensions, conflicts, tests, failures, resolve, successes, climaxes and understanding? Our old age is resolution—when conflicts, for the most part, are resolved, and we make our peace with the world. If we see life as having this shape—or at the very least *desire* this shape, *crave* this order from our chaotic lives—then it stands to reason that playwrights will design plots along the lines of that perceived shape.

Actions vs. Activities

It's easy to confuse effective dramatic action with activities. Activities are the dramatic equivalent of busy-work. They may *look* like actions (a fistfight) and they may *sound* like actions (a shouting match), but if they don't cause a reaction, then they're not actions. A dramatic action is an act performed by a character which in turn causes another character to perform yet another action. Good drama builds a chain of such actions from the beginning of the play right up to the end. If the fistfight doesn't lead to anything, it's not an action. If the shouting match doesn't change anyone, it's not an action. But if the fistfight prompts one of the characters to plot his revenge, or if the shouting match causes one of the characters to leave her home, they're vital dramatic actions.

Plots and Subplots

Can a play have more than one plot? Yes. But be careful here. In his Poetics, Aristotle wrote about the "Unities." One of these is the "Unity of Action," meaning that a good play has one central plot, one dramatic through-line. Good drama needs a solid spine to hold it together. But many plays also have one, two, three or four subplots. It's risky to write a play with lots of subplots; too many plotlines can make a play blurry and confusing. The dramas of Anton Chekhov contain multiple plotlines, but there's always a *central* plot to bring all the other lines of action together. In *The Cherry Orchard*, it's the sale of the estate. In the nineteenth-century French farces of Georges Feydeau, we may see numerous mistresses, gigolos, hotel clerks, maids, detectives, furious spouses and errant gendarmes—each pursuing his own goal—but in the end they all intertwine and connect at the central love-triangle, the most important plotline of the play. Subplots are best observed in larger canvass plays with a greater number of characters—Shakespeare, Ben Jonson, Richard Brinsley Sheridan, William Congreve, Kaufmann and Hart, and many American musicals.

We know what the function of a main plot is. It is an arrangement of actions designed to tell the story of the play. As we'll detail more fully in the chapter on Structure, the plot propels the characters forward from inciting incident to point of attack, posing dramatic questions, prompting goals and obstacles, leading to complications, taking advantage of other actions, surprises, revelations and reversals, as the characters move through the play to a crisis, and then race forward to the climax.

The function of a subplot is twofold:

1. To provide a separate and much smaller plot with its own forward action, moving toward its own climax and conclusion;
2. To provide dramatic and thematic resonance to the main plot.

A perfect example is *King Lear*. The main plot concerns Lear's decision to divide his kingdom into three parts. In doing so, however, he demands that his three daughters profess their love for him in court. His evil daughters Goneril and Regan praise him effusively, but his beloved daughter Cordelia refuses to acquiesce to his grandiose wish. Infuriated, Lear banishes her, and his kingdom is instead divided between Goneril and Regan. Eventually Lear is stripped of his army, and escapes into the wilderness as Goneril and Regan plan a battle against Cordelia who has returned to rescue Lear. At the climax, the armies converge, and Lear dies cradling the dead body of his beloved Cordelia in his arms.

The subplot involves Lear's prime minister, Gloucester. Gloucester's legitimate son is Edgar; Edmund is his bastard, born to another woman. Edmund manages to convince Gloucester that Edgar has plotted to kill him. Edgar flees to the wilderness disguised as "Poor Tom," a madman. Gloucester is captured by Goneril, Regan and Edmund; he is blinded by them, and thrown into the widerness—where he is found by "Poor Tom." The blind Gloucester doesn't know that this "madman" is his son. But Edgar protects his blind father until Gloucester's death.

Obviously, the *themes* of the subplot—rejection, forgiveness, parents turned against children and children against parents—complement those of the main plot. What's *most* important, however, is that the action of the Gloucester subplot *connects* with the Lear main plot and propels it forward. Here's how:

- the bastard Edmund joins forces with Goneril and Regan;
- Goneril and Regan capture and blind Gloucester;
- Gloucester and "Poor Tom" meet Lear during the storm;
- after Gloucester's death, Edgar tosses aside his "Poor Tom" disguise, battles the villainous Edmund to the death, and leads Cordelia's army to victory.

The subplot takes up approximately one-fifth of the action of *King Lear*. The main plot takes up the rest. The plots are brought together not only to make a thematic point, but to drive the action toward its climax and conclusion. A subplot must *assist* the main plot. It must *help*.

In *The Front Page*, for example, the main plot concerns Walter Burns trying to get Hildy Johnson to stay on his newspaper long enough to write the story of the Earl Williams escape. But early in the play the villainous sheriff and mayor are alone onstage in the jail's press room. Williams has just escaped, and the police are gunning for him. The mayor wants to make sure Williams is killed. Then a man enters. His name is Pettibone. He has a message from the governor. It is a reprieve for Earl Williams. The mayor can't let this reprieve be delivered. So the two corrupt officials send the simple, sweet-natured Pettibone off on an "assignment"—to visit a "house," a bordello the mayor controls. Pettibone trots away, not knowing that his visit will cause the reprieve to arrive too late. This is a short scene, a page or two. Very soon thereafter we return to the action of Walter Burns and Hildy, the rest of the reporters, and the love story of Hildy and his fiancee. Earl Williams shows up in the press room, and Hildy hides him in a rolltop desk. The police arrive. Williams is discovered and taken off to be hanged. The mayor and the sheriff think they're about to put Walter and Hildy in jail.

And then Mr. Pettibone—drunk, but still reeking of civic duty—returns to deliver the reprieve and announce that he can't be bought! Walter and Hildy realize what's happened and turn the tables on the sheriff and the mayor. *The Front Page*'s Pettibone subplot, while taking up very little time in the play (two or three pages), has returned to connect with the main plot and it has changed everything. Pettibone's two entrances are fortuitous actions, both of which propel action. In the second entrance, his return saves Walter and Hildy's skins, saves Earl Williams' life and saves the day. It's a wonderful example of an efficient and beautifully used subplot.

Think of a subplot as an action that runs parallel to the main plot and then zooms forward, changing its angle, to enter the main action near its end. A subplot, although experienced sequentially (Example: A Lear/Fool scene, followed by a Gloucester/Edmund scene, followed by a Lear scene, followed by a Gloucester/Edgar scene, etc.), is a little like a service road that runs along a major highway and then suddenly feeds into the traffic.

A CHOICE OF ACTIONS
Characters in plays, just as do human beings in real life, have choices. And the choices our characters make, like the choices we make in life,

define character, propel further action, and lead to conflict and resolution.

What is important is that a character's choices—inevitable, fatal, foolish, crafty, wise—be believable. How many times have you heard audience members say of a moment in a play, "That didn't make sense" or "That wouldn't happen" or "He wouldn't do that"? Audiences bring their experience of the world to the theater. They compare the theater's "mirror up to nature" to their own reflections. When you're constructing a plot, you must consider the plausibility of your characters' actions in the light of your audience's comprehension of real-life human behavior. You must also consider these actions in light of the audience's understanding of the characters you've already created, given the history and circumstances you've assigned them.

A man may be a perfect husband, a good father, a benevolent citizen, but he kills his brother. Why? A hardened criminal may lie, cheat, steal, even kill; but he is arrested while escaping from a burglary one night when he stops to save a woman from a burning building. Why? A meek housewife may obey her husband, speak only when spoken to, and bake cookies for twenty-four hours a day, but she starts a prostitution ring. Why?

At first glance these character sketches might not seem to fit the actions described. The biographies don't match the actions. But history, psychology and biography tell just part of the story. Circumstance tells us the rest. The perfect husband knew his brother was abusing his girl-friend; the girlfriend wouldn't go to the police; the husband couldn't prove anything, so he killed his brother before he could kill his girlfriend. The criminal saw the woman in the burning building and thought she was the most beautiful woman he'd ever seen. The housewife needed money, had no training, no experience, no other way to get it. One day a man offered her money for sex; she saw a way to get the money.

These are elementary examples. For a more sophisticated one, let's look at *King Lear*. Why *necessarily* does Lear banish Cordelia? Cordelia stood up to him, but can't a father put his hurt feelings aside and forgive? What *circumstances* does Shakespeare provide to make sense of Lear's rejection of Cordelia, this infamous, irrevocable, foolish, tragic action?

- Lear is old.
- Lear is a king.
- Lear is prideful.

- Lear is a widower.
- Lear expected Cordelia to say something else (never underestimate what a character will do when flustered, when surprised).
- Lear made the announcement of the division of his kingdom in court, in public, and Cordelia's rejection of him was a public rejection, humiliating Lear.

Take one of these circumstances away, and Lear *might* have forgiven Cordelia. A younger Lear might have been less needy and intolerant. A Lear who was not a king would have had less to lose or give. A Lear who was not prideful would have cared less. A Lear with a wife might have listened to a wife's counsel. A Lear satisfied by Cordelia's response would have had no reason to banish her at all. And—in what I think was Shakespeare's genius stroke—a Lear who announced the division of his kingdom privately would never have been embarrassed so publicly and hence would never have needed to display his power immediately.

Take a key circumstance away, and Lear's rejection, his brutal action, doesn't make sense. Take the action away and there is no dramatic problem, no dramatic question, no potential for mystery, tension, suspense, expectation. Take all that away and you have no play.

A good plot is filled with dozens of actions, performed by characters with wants and needs. Their actions create further actions as the characters attempt to overcome the obstacles placed in their way. All these actions must be moving in the same direction. There is usually one main plot, one major dramatic question. There may be subplots—lesser questions and actions performed by the main characters and the minor characters—but they are all vehicles moving toward the same destination. They may take different routes at different speeds, but the point of arrival is always the same.

EXERCISES

1. Using the two characters you sketched in the previous exercises, and including both the goal the protagonist desired and the obstacle the antagonist supplied, decide which of the two combatants wins the conflict. Now write down the story of this conflict in no more than three pages. Write it down as a short story or synopsis. Write down what happened before the conflict took place, write down what happened in the scene of the conflict itself, and write down what happened in its aftermath.

2. Now write the story again, but this time trim the story to its essential actions. What parts of the story are necessary? What parts are not? Start the plot as late into the story as possible. Remember: The plot of *Hamlet* starts long after the murder of the king, but very soon before Hamlet is set on his quest for revenge.

3. Now write the pared-down version of the story along the lines of the "strip tease." Initial Interest; followed by a Development of Attraction; followed by an Involvement With the Subject; a Goal, a Pursuit, Obstacles to Overcome, Suspense and Tension; finally Success and Satisfaction. If you can, great. If you can't, rework the plot until it follows this "strip tease" form.

4. What choices did you make available to your characters? Did the characters choose plausible actions? What guided their choices? What were their personal qualities, attributes and flaws? What were their strengths and weaknesses? Would their choices be interesting to an audience in a dramatic sense? List the characters' qualities on paper. List the options. List the choices. Do they connect? Do they seem plausible? Are they interesting? If so, great. If not, revise.

5. Using our *King Lear* example, list the circumstances you created to facilitate maximum conflict, tension and action. Could the circumstances and the actions lead to further dramatic actions? List the potential further actions.

IDEAS

When Aristotle wrote about a play's idea, he was referring to what we now more often call "theme," the abstract issues and feelings that grow out of the dramatic action. In her book *A Room of One's Own*, the novelist Virginia Woolf called this the "nugget"—something of value a person takes home from an artistic experience and puts on the mantle. As playwrights, we want to move our audience, to change or deepen their thoughts and feelings, to give them something to remember. Jon Jory, the artistic director of Actors Theatre of Louisville, has said that a talent he looks for in playwrights is the ability to make metaphor from ordinary human events.

There are big play ideas, and there are small play ideas. A big idea might concern "the ends of ambition," as in *Macbeth*, or "racism" in Anna Deavere Smith's *Fires in the Mirror*. But there are other ideas within these plays. Ideas about war, magic, fate, children, politics and marriage permeate *Macbeth*. Ideas about religion, perspective, the decline of New York City, the media, revenge and justice permeate *Fires in the Mirror*. All successful plays contain big and small ideas.

Ideas, however, don't in themselves make a play successful. "War is bad" is a nugget, to echo Woolf. But a good play and a bad play can have the same nugget of an idea. It is not the quality of the idea that matters most, but rather the quality of the ideas as depicted by the actions of the play.

Even more basic, especially for beginning playwrights, is the question of which should come first, the ideas or the story. There's no right answer to this question.

If you happen to come up with a theme first (war is bad), the act of writing the play will be a working out of this theme. If this is the case, you are most likely the sort of writer who will intellectualize an idea, *then* articulate that idea in dramatic actions. If, on the other hand, you decide on the actions of the story first, you're most likely the sort who follows inner instincts, inner voices, and an innate dramatic sense. If you're talented and gifted, the actions will often lead organically to the thematic idea, whether you're conscious of it or not.

I don't believe Shakespeare sat around trying to come up with a play that would encapsulate his thinking on the subject of ambition and after a long period of diligent research and strenuous planning came up with something called *Macbeth*. Nor do I believe he blithely stumbled upon the story of a Scot's murderer, wrote a blood-curdling thriller, and then looked up, surprised, as if to say, "Why, I had no idea my crime story would turn into such a fascinating dissertation on the subject of ambition!"

Maybe some great playwrights start with the great thematic idea, but the truth is that good dramatists have a nose for an exciting story that has the potential for exciting ideas.

The anecdote about how Peter Shaffer came to write *Equus* is famous. The playwright was driving through the English countryside with a friend. The friend mentioned a story he'd heard: A stable boy had blinded six horses in a remote English village. No one ever discovered the reason for the mutilation, but it shook the small community in which it happened. Shaffer's friend died soon thereafter, and he was never able to verify the story. But he knew he'd just heard a great idea for a play. When Peter Shaffer heard that story he knew he had the makings of a play with a great mystery, strong characters, a forward-moving story and terrific theatricality. He also saw the potential for a play of *ideas*—ideas about passion, intellect, madness, sex, religion and the human spirit.

A playwright connected to her imagination, her intellect and her environment gathers many disparate stimuli and makes them into a play. Playwrights get their ideas from their observations of the wider world, their observations of the people around them, and their observations of their own souls—their own concerns, convictions, fears and desires.

Something that is painfully true about drama and theater is that the limits of stage time (one hour, two hours, even five hours) and the length of a play text (75-150 pages) do not lend themselves to a multitude of ideas. The novel—especially the Big Novel of Charles Dickens, Leo Tolstoy, James Joyce and Norman Mailer—has a lot more room for ideas. The dramatist must make the most of the little time and space he has. He must be economical. He must choose the most important ideas and leave out the rest. The smart dramatist knows better than to throw everything *and* the kitchen sink into the idea pile.

The best plays come from ideas that are

- personal/societal/spiritual concerns of the playwright
- personal/societal/spiritual concerns of the audience
- best shown through dramatic action

There two ways to articulate an idea in a play:

1. Characters state the idea overtly—in speeches, in dialogue, either to other characters or directly to the audience. This is the direct, rhetorical approach.

2. Actions depicted in the play make the audience think of the idea. This is the Character + Conflict × Action = Ideas approach.

Of these two, always choose Number 2. This is not to say that the playwright can't speak directly to the audience. Sometimes characters come downstage, look out over the footlights at the audience and simply talk. But there is a strategy to these direct-address approaches. When will an audience be most receptive to this kind of rhetorical speech?

• At the beginning of a play, when everything is new and an audience is at one of its highest states of awareness and attentiveness (see the opening of *Equus*);

• Following a large action, when an audience needs a "cooling off" and is receptive to a rational means of understanding (see the choral reportage that tells the story of the Rumanian revolution in the middle section of Caryl Churchill's *Mad Forest*);

• Preceding a pending, expected action, when audience anticipation is highest (see the prebattle St. Crispin's Day speech in Shakespeare's *Henry V*);

• Between a vital question posed and a vital answer delivered, when an audience leans forward to discover the solution to a mystery or a central dramatic question (see Agatha Christie's *Witness for the Prosecution*, Robert Bolt's *A Man for All Seasons*, and, yes, *Hamlet*);

• At the end of the play, when an audience is seeking the final summation (see the last speech of Wallace Shawn's disturbing political play *Aunt Dan and Lemon*).

So, yes, there are strategic points in a script where the shrewd playwright can place rhetorical speeches and deliver ideas. But I will make this argument: An audience will *always* listen more carefully and become more *personally involved* with an idea when it is presented *dramatically.* It is one thing to *hear* a psychiatrist in a play say "Sometimes it's better to leave a person with her delusions than it is to cure her." It is another to *see* her

• Try to *Cure* her patient
• *Fight* the delusion
• *Cure* the patient
• *Witness* the light go out of the patient's eyes
• and *Reverse* the painful results of "sanity"

It's the show-don't-tell principle. Remember: An audience is a detective. They look for evidence, and they believe what they can see. What they can see are the actions. The best way, then, to convince an audience of your ideas is to give them ideas embedded in the action, developed by the action, and understood in the action.

If you spoon-feed your audience too much, they become lazy, less interested, and less receptive to your ideas. Playwrights often forget one of the actors in the drama—the audience. The audience has goals too: to understand, to comprehend, to make sense of what is happening onstage. There is a direct dynamic with the audience, and a dynamic requires points of tension, push and pull—like isometrics. This muscular dynamic requires work. And an audience likes to work in the theater. They like to try to figure out things; they look for clues ("Match wits with Inspector Hamlet!"). They'll listen to characters expound directly, and by extension they will listen directly to the playwright. But if the audience senses, even unconsciously, that it isn't doing any work, that there isn't an active role for them to play in their relationship with the play and its ideas, then an audience doesn't really know why it was invited to the show in the first place. Underline the word "unconsciously" here. I don't think audiences are very cognizant of this dynamic or their need to work in the theater. But the dynamic exists, and the playwright who ignores it throws her ideas out into the wind.

Sometimes characters debate ideas, as they do in the plays of George Bernard Shaw, but there are always personal dramatic stakes. The outcome of a debate on war and munitions-making may affect a marriage, as in Shaw's *Major Barbara*. When the idea is worked into the fabric of the dramatic action, when the stakes involved are human stakes, then the ideas are not simply bumper stickers tossed from the stage. The ideas are blood and flesh and fire and oxygen, the fuel of characters who are in the process of making discoveries about the world, their fellow creatures and themselves as a result of their thinking and their acts. In these instances, debates *are* human actions.

Meaning is best articulated in the minds of the audience who have witnessed the events and reached their own conclusions. It is this joined activity that the playwright and the audience embark on that makes the journey and the discovery worthwhile. Theater is often referred to as a collaborative art. And in this question of ideas, as in many others, the playwright should remember that her most important collaborator is her audience.

EXERCISES

1. What ideas are important to you as a playwright, as an artist, as a human being? Make a list of some of these ideas.

2. Do any of these ideas connect to any of the dramatic actions you developed in the previous exercises? If so, write down the action that would display one of these ideas. If not, find an action that does. Write that down.

3. Look at the actions you developed in the previous exercises. The actions tell you something about your characters. But what do the actions tell you about the world in which the characters live? Do the actions you choose say anything about life, love, mortality, youth, politics, race, or a thousand other subjects? If not, consider other potential actions that might engender these kinds of ideas. Write the various actions and ideas

on paper. How many different actions can depict the same idea? How many different ideas are inherent in a single action?

4. Now turn one of your ideas into a short scene. Use two characters, your protagonist and your antagonist. Put them in conflict. Make them do battle over something tangible (an object, a decision, a concrete goal). Dramatize the idea (war is bad, charity is good, suicide is defensible) without ever mentioning the idea in words. Let the actions speak for themselves.

LANGUAGE

Language refers to what is *spoken* onstage by the actors in a play. Most of a play's action and meaning is articulated through language, what a character says, how a character speaks. Aristotle wrote about language as "tone, imagery, and cadence (sound)." He argued that its power lies in its many incarnations onstage—as verse, metaphor, strophe, antistrophe, jest, rhyme and epigram.

The language of a play is often discussed as if it were separate from character, plot and ideas—as if the audience could understand character, plot and ideas without a play's language. With very few exceptions, every action depicted in a play is depicted through language. One could even say that, in drama, language *is* action. Even stage actions that ostensibly take place without dialogue—a kiss, a duel—either follow language that refers to the action or precedes language that results from the action.

When an audience member leaves a successful play like *Hamlet* and is asked about what she recalls of the play, she will most likely note two things: memorable events and actions—"when all those Danish people got killed at the end"; memorable dialogue—"To be or not to be."

Good dialogue tells the audience what it needs to know—the time period, background, setting and style of a play—but above all, good dialogue creates an event, changes the dynamic of the plot, and alters the characters' lives. It is action-oriented. It has a subject and a predicate, and it emphasizes the verb. An active verb is dramatic. Good dialogue is language *doing*. Good dialogue is both expressive and economical. In most plays, it must shift tenses constantly:

- It must deliver *exposition* (what has happened).
- It must depict *action* (what is happening).
- It must promise *future action* (what may happen).

Present tense action-dialogue is informed by the past and in turn informs the future, all the while seeming natural to the character's speech, psychology and education. The following quote from Lillian Hellman's *The Little Foxes* is a fine example of this past/present/future kind of dialogue:

REGINA: I'm smiling, Ben. I'm smiling because you are quite safe while Horace lives. But I don't think Horace will live. And if he doesn't I shall want 75% in exchange for the bonds. And if I don't get what I want I am going to put all three of you in jail.

A well-drawn character with language specific to that character will *never* sound like another character. Diction, grammar, word choice and syntax are all clues to character. Good dialogue identifies the character of its speaker. Even without their characters' names printed on the page we would recognize a key line of dialogue spoken by Richard III or by Blanche DuBois from Tennessee Williams' *A Streetcar Named Desire* or by Ricky Roma from David Mamet's *Glengarry Glen Ross*. Which of them said, "Now is the winter of our discontent"? Which said, "I have always depended on the kindness of strangers"? Which said, "All train compartments smell vaguely of shit"?

Have you ever done this? You're reading a play. The dialogue sounds less like the writer has *listened* to his characters than *assigned* lines to them. The names are not memorable, so you find that you keep paging to the front to check the character list to try to keep them sorted in your mind. If the play has a list of the original actors, maybe you start trying to hear their voices to help make the distinction. Still you can't figure out who's saying what. But, you argue, onstage that won't be a problem. We'll see and hear the dialogue coming out of the actors' mouths. True. But neutral-sounding dialogue—generic dialogue—has a flattening effect on an audience. When all the characters sound alike, a dullness sets in. Dialogue must not only move action, it must define character.

EXERCISES

1. Return to the situation you established in the earlier exercises. Maybe you've already thought about some of the things the characters might *say* to get what they want. Maybe not. After all, if a character's goal is to steal a bag of money, pulling a gun and grabbing the cash might be the quickest, most effective means. But write a scene that doesn't depend on physical action or props. Put two characters in conflict

over an object—a jewel, a diary, a letter, a photo, whatever. What can each character *say* to the other to get the object? Be clever. Be imaginative. What could your protagonist say to get what he or she wants?

2. Look at your dialogue. Did you use active verbs ("Give me that letter or I'll strangle you")? Or did you rely primarily on descriptive passages emphasizing nouns and adjectives ("That letter reminds me of a long-lost love, like a memory of a delicate flower")? As we discussed in this section, active verbs are what drive the best dialogue. Look at great lines and passages from famous plays. Find the verbs within the sentences. You'll be amazed at the number of active verbs writers use and how the verbs provoke actions and reactions on the part of other characters. If your own dialogue seems to lack active verbs, rewrite your scene to include them as much as possible.

3. Write a one-page scene of dialogue in which every exchange regarding the conflict contains a verb. (Example: "I want you to *give* me that letter." "Only if you *leave* this room." "Not unless you *turn* your back first.")

MUSIC

When Aristotle wrote his *Poetics*, music was an integral part of the classical Greek theater. The dialogue of the time was not spoken but rather sung. Music has always played a major part in the theater—as song, as music for dance, in opera, in musicals and as incidental music. Remember when we defined theater, in part, as the sensory appreciation of live performance? Music has great power in our lives. We respond to music in physical, emotional and intellectual ways. Music feeds the human spirit, and the smart playwright includes music to the sensory experience of his play. Many of Shakespeare's plays contain songs. *Hamlet* includes the eerie song Ophelia sings before her death. *Othello* has Iago's devilish drinking song.

Vaudeville, burlesque, melodrama (literally "melody" and "drama" folded together) kept music a part of the theater well into the early twentieth century. The piano player situated in his pit or off to the side of the rehearsal hall is a staple theatrical image. The great musicals of the Broadway stage started early in the century with George M. Cohan. But it was with the landmark 1926 production of Jerome Kern's and Oscar Hammerstein's *Show Boat* that the modern American musical was born. *Show Boat* was the first "book-musical"—a musical that alternated between songs, dance numbers and a written, dialogue-driven plot. The genius of *Show Boat*, however, was that its music and lyrics *also* moved the story. Songs like "Can't Help Loving That Man of Mine" and "Old Man River" were not only beautiful melodies with moving lyrics that depicted the lives of the characters, they also constituted actions that moved the story. Oscar Hammerstein's work on *Show Boat* revolutionized the American musical theater.

Music still plays a large part in the contemporary theater, and not just within the traditional "musical." Many playwrights explicitly include music in their "nonmusical" plays—the haunting melody Arthur Miller required for *Death of a Salesman* comes to mind, as do the incidental score Richard Peaselee composed for the Peter Brook production of *Marat/Sade* and Christopher Durang's *The Marriage of Bette and Boo*.

There are many dramatic ways to represent music onstage:

• Hedda's last trill at the piano, the trill that so annoys her husband George and her rival Mrs. Elvstead, before she shoots herself at the end of *Hedda Gabler*.

• The eerie whistling of the killer in Emlyn Williams' thriller *Night Must Fall*.

• The "ta-rum-ta-rum" Masha and Vershinin hum to each other as a kind of lover's code in Anton Chekhov's *The Three Sisters*.

• The pulsating, scatological chant that punctuates the end of the first act of Caryl Churchill's satire about greedy financiers, *Serious Money*.

Unfortunately, as we move deeper into the twentieth century it's fair to note that most plays do not include music. Nonetheless, Aristotle's fifth element shouldn't be dropped from the list. In fact, we can stretch the definition of music. We can stretch it to include *sound*.

Language is about the words. But the sound of those words can be musical. A line from *Othello* ("She loved me for the battles I had fought, and I loved her that she did pity them.") sounds beautiful to the ear— its cadence, its combination of vowels and consonants, its balance— devoid of its intellectual and emotional meaning. The active sound of typewriters in Ben Hecht and Charles MacArthur's newspaper comedy *The Front Page* or the clamp of horses' hooves in *Equus* or the sinister tap of a golf putter on a frightened man's glasses in Sam Shepard's *True West* all have a musical sense. Strategically placed sound can have tremendous theatrical effect.

One of my most memorable theatrical experiences took place at the Guthrie Theater in Minneapolis in 1979. In Barbara Field's adaptation of nineteenth-century Russian playwright Nikolai Gogol's satire of love and courtship *Marriage*, a bachelor played by Peter Michael Goetz had a habit of petulantly kicking a wall. His kicks had an odd rhythm. At the end of the play, his fiancée is waiting for him at the wedding banquet. The audience knows the bachelor has run off. What we hear on the sound system is the rapid clip of his horses' hooves as they gallop away. The rhythm of the hooves is the same as his odd kicks heard earlier in the play. The Guthrie's sound system was sensurround—in-the-round— and the audience heard the hooves gallop around them, as if the horses were circling the house, torturing the weeping bride. And at the end of the play, in a marvelous coup de theatre, all the champagne corks on the wedding banquet table popped off together, at once, on cue.

One more example: Silence can be musical.

Look at the plays of Harold Pinter and study his precise arrangement of pauses and silences. The impact of what is *not* heard—like an expected action that does *not* take place—is often as theatrical and dramatic as what *is*.

In the theater, as in life, audiences need music. Imagine our lives without it. A baby falls asleep to a lullaby. A teenager cries along with a love song. An old man hums a tune from a half-remembered symphony. A percussive rhythm makes a woman leap to her feet and dance.

Music is a vital part of the human experience, just as it remains a key ingredient of Aristotle's six elements. And the playwright who ignores the impact music provides in terms of vitality, melody, mood, and elucidation of character and action ignores what is often the very spirit and soul of a theatrical/dramatic experience.

EXERCISES

1. Go back to your dramatic situation. What opportunities for music are afforded you by this situation? Could either of your characters sing? Or play an onstage instrument? Is there a band nearby? An orchestra? A radio? Could someone whistle or tap out a rhythm on a table?

2. If you could include music in your scene, what function would it perform? Would it tell us about the time period or setting? Would it create mood? Would it be an action? How might you use a song to perform an action? Maybe it's a love-affair code like the one Chekhov used in *The Three Sisters*. Maybe it has an emotional effect, like "As Time Goes By" does in *Casablanca*. Maybe it's used as an irritant, something to provoke another character. Write a scene involving

conflict. Write in a cue for music. Make it depict the setting or time period. (Example: "We hear the sound of a radio broadcast of 1930s dance music.") Now write a scene where an onstage instrument is played for dramatic effect. Now write a scene where a character sings all or part of a song to provoke an action on the part of a second character.

3. What sounds lend themselves to your scene? Think of the setting. Think of props. Almost any object can have a dramatic sound if placed within the proper context. How can sounds be used by a character to achieve goals? Write a scene that utilizes everyday items (shoes, pencils, bottles, buckets of water, etc.) that can have an aural impact. How could a character use the sounds these objects make to provoke another character?

SPECTACLE

In Aristotle's time, spectacle referred to what was seen onstage, and what was seen onstage in fifth century B.C. Greece was often spectacular—lead players wearing masks and robes, the sweep of the Chorus. Big stuff. But it's easy to confuse the concept of spectacle with that of bigness. Let me define spectacle this way: It's whatever looks neat onstage. Some examples:

• The Greek Chorus majestically entering the stage in *Oedipus*.
• The swordfight at the end of *Hamlet*.
• The intricate, moving, mechanical stage designs that Inigo Jones created for playwright Ben Jonson's seventeenth-century Stuart court plays, or "masques."
• The first time "real" furniture appeared onstage in Restoration comedy when a playwright attempted to make eighteenth-century London audiences identify with the social and material aspirations of his characters; a love seat in Richard Sheridan's comedy of manners *The School for Scandal* may have had the same spectacular visual impact in the 1700s that the famous helicopter does in the today's musical *Miss Saigon*.
• A dance number from the musical *Guys and Dolls*.
• A puppet show.
• A box that transforms itself into many things in the course of a play (see Shel Silverstein's comedy *The Box*).
• A single match lit in the darkness in Bill Corbett's nightmarish political satire *Motorcade*.

Remember the sensory definition of theater. Spectacle makes the audience say "Wow." A big wow or a small one—it's all context. *Miss Saigon* is a big musical filled with big visual moments—marches, dances, onstage cars, etc. *Miss Saigon* needs something as big as its famous helicopter to make an impression. Because the show has challenged itself and upped-the-ante, its spectacle impact demands a grander scale. It's the same with the falling chandelier in *The Phantom of the Opera*.

On a bare stage, spectacle takes on a different meaning on a different scale. Trevor Nunn's famous eight-hour version of the Royal Shakespeare Company's *The Life and Adventures of Nicholas Nickleby*, adapted by David Edgar from Charles Dickens' novel, utilized every theatrical trick in the book. Actors "played" animals, children and soldiers. Actors "played" a stagecoach. Actors "played" a wall. That's spectacle.

Sometimes spectacle is achieved by a small gesture. In the premier production of Bill Corbett's *Motorcade*, two actors portrayed dozens of characters in a small midwestern town. The sight of two gifted impersonators changing character before our very eyes—by just a shift in body-language, an alteration of expression, a lowering of voice and flick of rhythm—was spectacle enough. But at one point, the lights lowered to darkness and one of the actors, Corbett himself, struck a match. The effect—the scrape of the match, the spark, the flash of blue, then the tiny ball of yellow and red as the pinpoint of fire illuminated Corbett's devilish transformation into one of his more diabolical characters—was stunning. Aural. Visual. Dramatic. Spectacle.

Props such as the match are often useful in creating stage spectacle. Guns, swords, pens, flags, letters—all have a power onstage. Sometimes a prop has a dramatic purpose as well as a theatrical/spectacle purpose. The latchkey that is used in Frederick Knott's *Dial "M" for Murder* is dramatic because its use by Tony Wendice in the play's final moments proves Tony's guilt. Tony had earlier lent the key to the hired murderer. And it's theatrical because we *hear* the key enter the lock, and then *see* Tony enter the flat, key in hand. In Elizabeth Egloff's romantic drama *The Swan*, a woman and a man toss a full beer bottle back and forth a number times, but they don't spill a drop. The spectacle comes from our knowledge that this is happening live, and that the actors could drop the bottle. It's not a movie; there aren't any retakes. The "live" aspect of such an action lends the bottle toss its spectacular quality.

Spectacle can be about the human form and the physical/spatial relationship onstage between human beings. Remember: Always show instead of tell. What will an audience think if a man says he hates the woman he is arguing with and *then* grabs her hand and kisses her? The physical action will counteract the verbal expression. Physical gesture in theater can be as grand as a wave of actors doing battle onstage in Shakespeare's *Henry V,* and it can be as small as a woman reaching out a hand towards her husband in J.B. Priestley's *An Inspector Calls.* In the right dramatic and theatrical contexts, both gestures are huge. That wave of soldiers and their patterns of battle will determine the fate of nations and the futures of many characters we've grown to care about in Shakespeare's play. That woman has been depicted in *An Inspector Calls* as an icy, imperious grande dame; when she is forced to reach out for her husband, we see in her gesture the desperation, the fear, and the tender need beneath her armor. Spectacular.

Because spectacle is primarily a visual element—framed action, as it were—it's important that you study visual depictions of dramatic scenes. Look at models and drawings of famous theater designs. Look at photographs of nineteenth and twentieth century stage productions. Look at paintings that render dramatic characters, settings and actions: religious paintings, family portraits, representations of historical events—battles, executions, picnics, marriage proposals, surrenders and last rites. Spectacle is vital to an audience's senses, as sight is to a person's comprehension and enjoyment of the world. It is seeing, and spectacle is most firmly connected to the concept of the theater as a place for seeing.

EXERCISES

1. Imagine the stage picture you've created for your confrontation scene, the one between your protagonist and antagonist. What possibilities exist for spectacle? Could there be a violent disruption of the stage picture? Could something explode onstage, be destroyed onstage, come through a wall, turn the set upside down? Could something be constructed onstage? Could there be a dance? An embrace? A fight? Write the scene with this in mind.

2. Think in terms of props again. What do they lend themselves to? Imagine a waving American flag, or a spinning full-length mirror, or a book catching fire. Write your scene with one prop used as an instrument of dramatic spectacle.

3. Think in terms of the body. What can the body do by itself—

without props—that has visual force and meaning onstage? Can the body transform itself into another person or object? Can it be shaped onstage, like a sculpture? What actions can be depicted by the body? What meaning can be derived from the actions? A crippled girl "dances" in Peter Nichols' *Joe Egg*. Actors pretend to be horses in *Equus*. A crazy minister gets on the floor and acts like bacon frying in Christopher Durang's *The Marriage of Bette and Boo*. Write your scene with the transformative nature of the human body in mind; make the body do something spectacular.

PUTTING ARISTOTLE TOGETHER

The great plays of Western drama employ all six of Aristotle's elements. There is a constant handoff of elements, often many working together at a single moment. I'd like to detail one famous example of a dramatic scene that employs all six elements at the same time to great dramatic effect. It is at the end of *A Doll's House*, Henrik Ibsen's famous 1879 play about Nora, the "little bird" of a housewife whose involvement in a blackmail plot finally results in a discovery of her own power and possibilities, which in turn causes her to leave her husband, Helmer. Here are the last lines and stage directions of *A Doll's House*.

HELMER: This is the end then! Nora, will you never think of me any more?

NORA: Yes, of course. I shall often think of you and the children and this house.

HELMER: May I write to you, Nora?

NORA: No. Never. You mustn't do that.

HELMER: But at least you must let me send you—

NORA: Nothing. Nothing.

HELMER: But if you should need help—?

NORA: I tell you, no. I don't accept things from strangers.

HELMER: Nora—can I never be anything but a stranger to you?

NORA: (*Picks up her bag*) Oh, Torvald! Then the miracle of miracles would have to happen.

HELMER: The miracle of miracles?

NORA: You and I would both have to change so much that—oh, Torvald, I don't believe in miracles any longer.

HELMER: But I want to believe in them. Tell me. We should have to change so much that—?

NORA: That life together between us two could become a marriage. Goodbye. (*NORA exits*)

HELMER: Nora! Nora! Empty! She's gone! (*A hope strikes him*) The miracle of miracles—?

(The street door is shut downstairs.)

Curtain

Did you find the six elements? Let's take them one by one:

Character—The moment *defines* Nora. Her decision to leave Torvald—a shocking moment in both the history of drama and the history of gender politics—is a turning point for her character, the culmination of all her previous history and actions, and a launching pad for the person she will be for the rest of her life.

Action—Nora's departure is the key action of the play. Nora's act changes not only her own life, but the lives of her family. It is the result of all of the play's previous actions, and no other acts on the part of any of the characters will ever be the same because of it.

Ideas—Shocking then and still startling today, Nora's exit is a philosophical rallying point for a discussion of the role of women in modern society. What is a wife? What is a family? What duties and responsibilities do husbands and wives have to each other? And does the act of one woman—the act of one Nora leaving her Torvald—have a societal impact greater than her simple exit would suggest? Does it create repercussions in the audience? No idea engendered by any of Ibsen's other writings was ever as impressively wrought, discussed, debated and dramatized as Nora's exit.

Language—Ibsen was never known for his flights of rhetoric. In terms of language, he was probably the least indulgent of the great playwrights of the last one hundred years. His characters say what they need to say, no more, no less. Sometimes the power of language lies in its dramatic simplicity. "Goodbye" is a simple word. We say it every day, dozens of times, to friends, family, associates, acquaintances and strangers. But it is in context that "goodbye" has such power. In the context of this scene, "goodbye" has a finality that seals the end of Nora and Torvald's life together. A relationship changes, a marriage ends, a world is revolutionized in Nora's simple "Goodbye."

Music—There is no actual music in *A Doll's House*, but in it we do find one of drama's most indelible sounds: the sound of the door closing.

Like the word "goodbye" the sound of that door shutting behind Nora imparts a finality to the scene, to the play and to the characters. The thud of wood, the cold snap of a deadbolt is the final beat of a heart. The sound of that door closing—its weight, its wood and steel—tells us a lot about Nora's will, her strength, and the kind of world she's rejecting.

Spectacle—Here, too, we return to the image of departure. Look at the onstage picture Ibsen has drawn. We see a comfortable, middle-class home complete with a Christmas tree. Everything about the image suggests safe domesticity. And then the wife leaves. It is a powerful image of departure. How many times have you seen someone you love walk away from you, perhaps never to come back? How many times did your heart break at the leaving? A hole exists where there was once a person, movement, color. The person has gone, and the picture is changed forever. Onstage entrances and exits have great power. An entrance begins an action, introduces a story, ushers in a character who may change the onstage world as we know it. A stage exit can suggest a person moving away to accomplish a great offstage task. It can also suggest a person being taken away in shame as the result of actions that have taken place before our eyes. The last image of *A Doll's House* is a visual summing up of all the previous dramatic actions and previous visual images that have come before it.

Ibsen could have dispatched Nora from the stage in any number of ways. She could have left Torvald a letter. She could have decided to leave but stayed one more night. She could have avoided the word "goodbye." She could have slipped out a window, leaving behind no sound at all. Each of these options would have been plausible. But they weren't as interesting. They weren't as dramatic. They weren't as theatrical. By combining all six elements at this crucial climactic moment of his play, Ibsen assured his audience a maximum experience, maximum impact. He assured his audience a conclusion they would never forget.

The ending of *A Doll's House* reminds us of the power of Aristotle's six elements when woven together at the conclusion of a play in a memorable and satisfying whole. One does not want to be too prescriptive, but it's amazing how powerful a dramatic, theatrical moment becomes when the elements are all working together in an organic movement.

Read the plays you love, plays that have the power to excite the senses and engage the mind. And track the ways the playwrights have woven the six elements into the drama, into the theater. Chances are you'll be amazed by how many of them are actively in play at every moment.

EXERCISES

1. Look over your previous exercises. Sift through the various character-driven actions, images, sounds and ideas you've sketched. Some of what you've come up with for a few of the exercises may fit with other parts of the exercises. More won't. Go back to square one. Look at your two characters, the protagonist and the antagonist. Are they the people you want them to be? Are they interesting? Do they have strong needs? What about that goal for the protagonist? Is it the right one? Look at your setting, your dialogue, the sounds and images you selected. Think about it all very carefully.

2. Now. Start again. Create a short scene that employs all six of Aristotle's elements, in much the same way that Ibsen does for *A Doll's House*. You don't have to follow his method, point by point. Be imaginative. Your scene can take place in a middle-class living room or on the dark side of the moon. Your characters can be a husband and wife or two talking hot dogs. Whoever they are, create a dramatic situation. Create vibrant characters with goals; put them in conflict; energize their language through action verbs; find visual and aural complements; engender ideas through the action. It may take a few false starts and run to a few pages, but work through the exercise until you've got it. It's exciting to activate all the theatrical elements at your disposal when writing drama.

CHAPTER THREE

Space, Time and Causality

In college, my theater professor Elliot Stout gave me a bit of advice I'll always remember. "If anyone ever comes up to you at a cocktail party and says, 'What *is* reality?' just reply, 'Reality? Why, space, time and causality.' "

This was German philosopher Immanuel Kant's eighteenth-century definition of reality. While Kant's definition is only one way of looking at reality, his space/time/causality model works extremely well for drama and theater. What's most useful is that for each of the three parts of Kant's definition there is a double meaning. The word means one thing *within* the play and in the reality being depicted; it means something else in regards to the theatrical depiction of that reality *onstage*.

SPACE

Within the reality of the play, "space" refers to the rooms, landscapes and settings of the play's action. The castle battlements of *Hamlet*'s Elsinore, the drawing room of the Tesman household in *Hedda Gabler*, the desert wilderness of Samuel Beckett's *Waiting for Godot*. In terms of the performance, "space" refers to the actual stage where the actors perform.

Obviously, these are not the same. The stage is always representing the play's reality. Sometimes the stage is designed to appear just as the room or the desert or the battlement would. The director and the designer provide a realistic depiction of the setting that, save the absence of the "fourth wall" where the audience sits, looks just like the real thing. This realistic approach reached its zenith at the end of the nineteenth century. Castles, gardens, racetracks, ships, forests, factories all were realistically depicted at great cost and with great impact. To this day, most productions keep more than a foot in this realistic world. Within the last thirty years, apartment living rooms, kitchens, writers' studies, offices, even mountains have been successfully rendered onstage in full realistic mode. An audience is thrilled when they see a set that so painstakingly represents a reality they know (the middle-class kitchen in Willy Russell's *Shirley Valentine*) or have never even dreamed about (the munitions factory of George Bernard Shaw's *Major Barbara*).

By contrast, in a nonrealistic mode, reality can still be depicted in numerous ways. Here we must acknowledge the contract signed between the audience and the theater. It is the "suspension of disbelief" that audiences allow when watching a play. The audience allows that there is no fourth wall. The audience allows that events that usually take many hours, days, weeks, months or years (dinners, meetings, trials, investigations, wars) will be depicted onstage in stage time that will amount to no more than two or three hours. The audience allows that the visual elements that depict a scene can be rendered as powerfully by one or two suggestive scenic elements as by full realistic depictions. An English sitting room could be rendered by a full realistic set, or it could be rendered by one Queen Anne sofa. An office might be rendered by a full realistic set, or it could be rendered by a desk and chair. A garden could be rendered by a full realistic set, or it could be rendered with a single trellis. In the suspension of disbelief an audience member says to herself, "If they *say* it's a garden, I'll *believe* it's a garden, even if I can see that it's just a trellis on an empty stage." The audience is willing to play along. It's part of the fun.

This kind of scenic shorthand is so common today and so effective that sometimes the suggestive scenic element is not even an onstage set or prop. Sometimes it's just a word. In Shakespeare, we find numerous courts, throne rooms, battlements, beaches and blasted heaths. Seldom is there a mention of a particular piece of furniture unless it's vital to the action (Desdemona's bed, or the arras behind which Polonius hides). Shakespeare was very crafty about these things. The setting notations in the script are never more than "A Room in the Castle." What often defines these rooms is the language, the dialogue. If the king and queen are holding court and the dialogue suggests a royal setting, it stands to reason that we are in the court. The audience doesn't *need* the thrones, the banners, the trappings.

As a playwright, ask yourself this question: How might you depict a realistic setting for one of your plays? How about a hospital nurses' station? First ask yourself what is dramatically essential. What furniture or props do your characters really *need*? Only when you have determined what you need onstage for your characters to act and move the plot forward can you decide how to represent it.

But, you argue, isn't that the job of the designer or director? True, some directors and designers can solve problems of set and staging, but you want to write plays that are stageworthy, and the more you can do in the writing to suggest solutions and create ideas, the better.

The nurses' station. How to depict it:

Realistically: A full set with all the walls, doors and hospital gadgets

One or two suggestive scenic elements: A swivel chair and desk

One scenic element: A counter with a sign on it that reads "Nurses' Station"

One hand prop: A hospital clipboard

By costume only: An actor in a nurse's uniform

By dialogue only: MAN: "Excuse me, ma'am, is this the sixth-floor nurses' station?"

See how quickly you can reduce the necessities?

In today's theater, realistically reproduced settings are found primarily in one-set plays, like Felix and Oscar's living room in Neil Simon's *The Odd Couple* and Jessie's kitchen in Marsha Norman's *'Night, Mother*. More and more, stage design—especially when dealing with multiple settings—requires a nonrealistic approach. Part of the move toward nonrealistic depictions comes from the expense involved in designing and building huge realistic sets, and the playwright who ignores the financial realities of producing a play today is blindsided by his own ignorance. It is important to remember that realistic depictions of reality were primarily a nineteenth-century addition to the theater, an addition that has dominated much of the twentieth-century theater we know and love. Prior to the nineteenth-century, stage designers and playwrights were much less concerned about making things onstage appear real. Eighteenth-century Restoration comedies took place in front of flat drawings of rooms and outdoor settings. The sixteenth- and seventeenth-century staging of plays by Shakespeare and Moliere often took place out of doors on wooden planks, with only the occasional table or chair brought in when necessary. And no Greek dramatist ever spent any time worrying about what Oedipus' taste in throne room furnishings was like. A Greek drama took place on a stage that would remind us more of a Gospel concert at the Hollywood Bowl.

Realism is relatively new to the theater. And those playwrights who require realistic sets today stick to one or two. The rule of thumb: If the action requires a set, make the set realistic. If the action doesn't, allow for a lot less. Examples of necessary set pieces would include the office door behind which the real estate salesmen are taken to be interrogated in *Glengarry Glen Ross*, the locked room where the woman is held captive in Jane Martin's abortion-rights drama *Keely and Du*, and Oscar Madison's kitchen wall in *The Odd Couple*. Why is that wall necessary? Because Oscar throws a plate of linguini at it. No wall, no crash.

Space onstage can be theatricalized as well with two or more scenes taking place at once. A play like Craig Lucas' haunting comedy *Blue Window*, which concerns a group of alienated New Yorkers, operates on multiple spatial levels at one time: two or more scenes taking place onstage at the same time but representing actions that take place in different locales. This technique is most commonly seen in musicals. One thinks of the first-act ending of Stephen Sondheim's *A Little Night Music*, in which all the characters sing about the "weekend in the country" they're about to embark on. The characters are understood to be in their separate homes as they read their invitations, but the audience sees them downstage at the footlights together. It is a stage convention. It is also delightful in its theatricality.

One of my favorite memories from my early theater-going was seeing a production of Neil Simon's *Barefoot in the Park* by the Steubenville Players in my hometown. If you know the play, you'll remember that in the first act the young married couple has just moved into their Greenwich Village fifth floor walk-up apartment. The apartment is a disaster, but the young wife sees it as a challenge. The first act ends. The audience takes its intermission. When they return to their seats and the lights come up, there is a gasp in the audience, followed by applause. The formerly shabby apartment has been transformed into a beautifully decorated home.

Why does the audience applaud? Two reasons: (1) They are applauding the character of the wife, her imagination, talent and hard work. (2) They are applauding the set changeover planned by the designer and carried out by the crew during the intermission. They are applauding what took place behind the curtain. They love the idea that while they were at the intermission bar, all this activity, this *transformation*, was taking place. They *know* it's supposed to represent the efforts of many weeks, but they also know the truth: that it was all a matter of careful planning and stage tricks—panels that revolve, carpets that fit easily into place, fixtures that snap into the set's fake walls. They are applauding the *reality* depicted and the stage conventions used to depict it. It delights them. And in this example of realism, it was the playwright, Neil Simon, who provided the words on the page that created this delight.

There *are* plays, however, that seemingly require realistic settings (offices, apartments, bedrooms), but allow for and lend themselves to great flexibility in the design. Tony Kushner's award-winning *Angels in America* requires over a dozen sets as varied as Roy Cohn's townhouse, Washington restaurants, a Brooklyn apartment, a federal courthouse men's room, a Salt Lake City backyard, a deserted Bronx street corner, a hospital room, Central Park and the North Pole. On Broadway, with a huge budget, these settings were rendered as realistically as possible. In fact, the Broadway production actually included an iceberg for the North Pole scene. But a close look at the script shows that it is not necessary to be quite so realistic. With the exception of Roy Cohn's desk with its complex phone system, most of the scenes can be staged without any pieces of furnishing—yes, even the North Pole. More often than not, Kushner's dialogue furnishes the setting.

So, in this question of space, the key points to remember are these:

- Require only those scenic elements that are absolutely necessary.
- Know that audiences love the completeness of a realistic set.
- Know they also love the nonrealistic theatricality of "let's pretend."
- Multiple realistic sets are almost prohibitive in the contemporary theater.
- Economics often require a scenic imagination that is liberating to the writer.
- Never say, "Let the design people worry about that."

TIME

Within the reality of the play, "time" refers to the time it takes to perform the realistic action depicted in a realistic manner. A war in *Macbeth* or Shaw's *Saint Joan* might take place over months or years. A trial, such as those in Agatha Christie's *Witness for the Prosecution* or Aaron Sorkin's *A Few Good Men*, takes at least weeks to complete. A late-night party such as the one depicted in Edward Albee's *Who's Afraid of Virginia Woolf?* takes four, five or six hours. In terms of the performance, "time" refers to the number of minutes it takes to watch the performance—the playing time.

These are not necessarily the same amounts of time. While there *are* some plays we call Time = Time plays, in which the time it takes to perform the realistic action (real time) is exactly the same as the time it takes to watch the performance (playing time), most plays are not written this way. Even Greek classical tragedy—which obeyed Aristotle's "unities" of time, place and action—"compressed" time.

Let's look at the unities for a moment.

* Unity of place—all the events take place in a single setting.
* Unity of action—there is one central action in the play.
* Unity of time—all the events take place in a single twenty-four-hour time period.

Even in this ancient scheme, there was room for theatricalization. True, there may be one action in *Oedipus* (the hero's attempt to end the plague of Thebes), and true, the action takes place in a single setting (the royal court); nonetheless, the events of that twenty-four-hour period take far less than twenty-four hours to perform. These events and this time period were compressed into just a few hours of stage time.

Very few contemporary dramatists write Time = Time plays, but we would all be well advised to try our hand at one. It's a demanding form that tests many different kinds of dramatic muscles. Marsha Norman's *'Night, Mother* comes immediately to mind. The play is a two-character one-act, performed without intermission, which makes sense in a Time = Time play, given that *real* time has no intermissions. But even here we have to acknowledge Norman's compression of time. Events that would take place over many hours in real life somehow take place in the neat confines of ninety minutes when depicted in her play. This, as Alfred Hitchcock once defined drama, is "life with the dull bits cut out." The trick is to make an event *seem* as if it could take place in less time than it really does.

In Anton Chekhov's Russian comedy about writers, actors and lovers, *The Sea Gull*, an offstage dinner party is begun and completed within about seven minutes. In Maxwell Anderson's thriller about a homicidal little girl, *The Bad Seed*, a three-minute cocktail hour is made to seem longer by the refrain of "Freshen that drink?" In David Mamet's *Glengarry Glen Ross*, a policeman is ostensibly interrogating a group of salesmen behind a closed door, but his "thorough" interrogation of each man can't possibly last more than twelve minutes each.

It's a trick—one the audience plays along with. The audience allows for an acceleration of action as part of the suspension of disbelief. As long as the compression of time is not *too* accelerated—so accelerated as to appear ridiculous—the action of the play will not seem to rush by at too rapid a pace. The audience *wants* the playwright to cut out the dull bits. Fifty-five minutes of onstage action *can* seem to represent an entire dinner party (*Blue Window*) or a stockholders' meeting (Jon Robin Baitz's *The Substance of Fire*) or a political debate (David Hare's *A Map of the World*), all of which are events that would take hours to enact in real life. What the playwright must keep in mind, however, is that no matter how willing the audience is to suspend its disbelief, they do expect the shape of the scene to follow the shape of the real event. The cocktail party may take only minutes, but it had better follow the form of introductions, offers of drinks, refills and the like. The courtroom battle may not take months to play out as it does in real life, but the audience expects to see the opening arguments, the questioning, the cross examinations, the summations and the verdict. The stockholders' meeting may be over in moments, but the audience wants to know who owns what percentages, what is at stake, who's on whose side and they want to see the vote at the end.

A five-second pause onstage feels like an eternity. Time elongates onstage, so playwrights are always compressing action. Since Shakespeare's time, audiences have been well acquainted with the notion of a scene beginning "five months later," or in Ibsen's day, "the next morning," or in the comedies of the 1930s, "a few minutes later." Audiences can make that leap and make it comfortably. And, as in scenes that take place in multiple settings on the same stage, time can be fluid onstage. A character may go back in time or forward. A character may relive a past moment in the present. Historical events may hurry by in seconds. The audience's contract with the stage allows all this and more.

The greatest danger onstage is that time may seem longer than it really is. In most cases the playwright doesn't want an audience to think they've been in the theater longer than they have. We all know what it means when someone says that a thirty-five-minute first act "seemed to go on forever." It means not enough happened. There weren't enough actions, followed by reactions, followed in turn by new actions to hold the audience's interest. That's how time elongates. If the actions are moving forward and the suspense is properly generated, the hours pass like minutes.

So, in this question of time, the key points to remember are these:

- Require only those dynamic actions that are absolutely necessary.
- Know that audiences love the completeness of a Time = Time play.
- Know that they also love nonrealistic, fluid, theatricalized stage time.
- Audiences "agree" to the artificial compression of action and time.
- Onstage, thirty seconds of nothing is an eternity.

CAUSALITY

Causality is an entirely dramatic concept, not a theatrical one. Causality refers to *why* events or actions occur. But when I say "why," I don't necessarily refer to a twentieth-century psychological concept of "why." In this context "why" means "what actions cause other actions to take place?" It's a question of dramatic dynamics, of falling dominoes. Causality is closely related to the dramatic concepts of goals, obstacles and linkage. To more fully understand this linkage of actions, let's examine a situation established in a play and find its dynamic causal relationships. The causal relationship is directly connected to the idea of goals, obstacles and actions.

In *The Changeling*, a seventeenth-century Jacobean revenge tragicomedy written by Thomas Middleton and William Rowley, we meet Beatrice, engaged to Alonzo but in love with his younger brother Tomazo.

Goal: Tomazo and Beatrice are in love with each other and wish to marry.

Obstacle: Beatrice is betrothed to Tomazo's brother, Alonzo.

Solution action: Beatrice and Tomazo plot to kill Alonzo.

Further obstacle: Neither can perform the murder without courting suspicion.

Solution action: They hire DeFlores, Beatrice's servant, to kill the brother.

Further obstacle: DeFlores will only commit the murder if Beatrice allows him to have intercourse with her after the murder.

Solution action: Beatrice acquiesces to DeFlores' wish.

Action: DeFlores murders Alonzo.

Payoff: Beatrice allows DeFlores to make love to her.

Complication: After having sex with DeFlores, Beatrice falls in love with him.

. . . and then the play gets *really* interesting.

Can you track the causal effects, the falling dominoes? Experiment with causality. Track the plot of *Hamlet* and change an action performed by Hamlet, by Gertrude, by Polonius, by Claudius. Change one of their actions and the play changes. It no longer runs on toward the famous climax we all remember. See how unsatisfying those alternate actions and conclusions are when you change them.

Make sure the causal actions in your play link up. Nothing frustrates and infuriates an audience more than to follow a play and miss an important step. An audience can sense a playwright trying to patch together actions that were never meant to join. That's what makes them ask the question, Why did *that* happen?

Do yourself a favor. Be like the child who constantly tugs at his parent's hand asking over and over again, "Why?"

So, in this question of causality, the key points to remember are these:

- Require only those dynamic actions that are absolutely necessary (just as you did with "time"); skip the unimportant actions.
- Remember that audiences hate it when playwrights skip essential causal steps.
- Always make your actions link.
- Track your actions from the beginning of the play to its end, and vice versa.
- Focus the linkage of events on the constant exchange of your character's goals, obstacles and actions. Of every action ask the question, Why?

And always pull out Immanuel Kant at a cocktail party.

EXERCISES

1. Select an event that either happened to you or that you caused to happen. Make it an event you know well, one that contains human dramatic conflict. Understand its setting: Did it take place in one space or many spaces? Understand its time frame: Did it take place in one

continuous length of time, or did it take many hours, days or more? What caused the event to come about? What action did you perform? What happened after? Write down the key factors in the event.

2. Now imagine the scene onstage. What do you need to show the event? Start with space. What is the fully realistic version of the set? What is the suggestive version? What is the version that needs only dialogue to depict its setting? Write down your conclusions.

3. Next, focus on time. Do you show the event in Time = Time? Or do you compress time? Will you show the event in a series of scenes? Will you go backward and forward in time? Will different *depicted* time frames exist onstage in the same *stage* time? Experiment with all the possibilities. Take a dramatic situation of conflict and write the same scene in at least three different ways: (a) Time = Time, (b) compressed time, and (c) multiple time frames.

4. Find the causal links in the action. If the central action was your decision to run away from home at the age of ten, find the links that run backward and forward from this action. Why did you run away? And what happened after you ran? Using the model from *The Changeling*, list the problems, solutions, actions and reactions until you have found the starting point and the concluding point of the central action.

5. "Five places in four pages." The stage is bare. You have one to five characters at your disposal. In four pages, take your audience to five completely different locations. You may use one hand prop or rolling piece of scenery (grocery cart, toy wagon, wheelchair, etc.) per location to help suggest the scene. You get extra points if you use *no* props or scenery, depending entirely on dialogue.

6. "Five time periods in four pages." The stage is still bare. You have one to five characters at your disposal. In four pages, take your audience to five completely different time periods. You may use one hand prop or costume per place to help suggest the time. Again, you get extra points if you use *no* props or scenery, depending entirely on dialogue.

CHAPTER FOUR

Getting the Great Idea and Turning It Into a Play

P eople always ask playwrights, "Where do you get your ideas for your plays?" The simple truth is that there's no rule of thumb for getting play ideas. Writers get play ideas from history, from current events, from overheard anecdotes and from personal experience. They have to keep their artistic antennae up to pick up signals from their world and their own concerns. It's not the quality of the idea that makes a good play, it's the quality of the *dramatization* of the idea. Still, there are a few guidelines you might consider when you're rummaging around whatever psychic box you keep in the basement for your ideas. Here are a few:

• A play idea that suggests conflict is better than one that doesn't. "My mother's funeral" is a play idea. It suggests a situation, but it doesn't suggest dramatic conflict. However, "Two daughters battle over an estate at their mother's funeral" suggests both situation *and* conflict.

• A play idea that suggests a journey of change on the part of its characters is better than one that doesn't. "Two daughters battle over an estate at their mother's funeral" suggests situation and conflict. But "Two daughters battle over an estate at their mother's funeral, resulting in one of them deciding to leave her loveless marriage" suggests situation, conflict and journey.

• A play idea that suggests theatricality is better than one that doesn't. "Two daughters battle over an estate at their mother's funeral, resulting in one of them deciding to leave her loveless marriage" suggests situation, conflict and journey. But "Two daughters battle over an estate at their mother's funeral, resulting in one of them deciding to leave her loveless marriage when the ghost of the mother speaks to them from her coffin" suggests situation, conflict, journey and theatricality.

The real gold in a good idea is seldom found in the initial spark. It's found in the dramatist's *development* of the idea. Of course, there are some play ideas that lend themselves to successful development more readily than others, like Peter Shaffer's play *Amadeus*, about the rivalry between the composers Mozart and Salieri. The play was based on historical fact and on the famous rumor that Salieri had poisoned Mozart. The situation (the existence of Mozart and Salieri in Vienna in the eighteenth century), conflict (two composers vying for power in the same court), journey (Salieri's movement from complacency to envy) and theatricality (music, costumes, etc.) all rose organically from Shaffer's initial idea. But a good play can come from any idea. As a dramatist you have to cultivate a nose for recognizing an idea's potential for development as absorbing drama and exciting theater.

There is such a thing as subject matter that, by its very nature, is more intriguing than others. David Mamet's powerful and highly controversial *Oleanna* is gripping, in large part, because of its subject matter (political correctness, sexual harassment, the battle between men and women). *Oleanna* was written and produced right after the Supreme Court confirmation hearings involving Judge Clarence Thomas and his former assistant Anita Hill. The subject already had the nation in thrall, and then along came *Oleanna* to capitalize on it. *Oleanna* was produced all over the world. It is one of Mamet's most successful—and divisive— plays. But during that same period, there were lots of plays written on the subject of political correctness, sexual harassment, and the battle between men and women. The majority of them were bad. The difference lies in Mamet's talent, in his treatment and development of the idea. Subject matter can only take an audience so far. A play about uncovering the identity of Jack the Ripper will grab an audience even before the lights go down in the theater. But after that initial adrenalin jolt, powerful subject matter must *earn* its grip on an audience. Once the playwright has hooked the audience, the play itself, not the subject, must carry it through.

Playwrights get their ideas for plays from many different sources:

• From history: Shakespeare's tragedies and histories came from earlier chronicles and sometimes earlier plays. Robert Bolt's *A Man for All*

Seasons came from the sixteenth-century histories of Sir Thomas More and his battle with Henry VIII. Robert Sherwood's *Abe Lincoln in Illinois* is based, in part, on the record of Lincoln's early court cases.

• From contemporary news stories: John Guare's *Six Degrees of Separation* came from an article about a scam in *The New York Times*. Lee Blessing's *A Walk in the Woods* came from reports of an unofficial meeting between U.S. and Soviet arms negotiators in Switzerland. And Anna Deavere Smith's monodrama *Fires in the Mirror* came from the media coverage of the Crown Heights incidents.

• From their work and surroundings: Ben Hecht and Charles MacArthur got *The Front Page* from their experience as newspapermen. David Mamet recalled his time working in a questionable real estate office to write *Glengarry Glen Ross*. Willy Russell's *Educating Rita* came from his own background as a hairdresser and night-school student.

• From their thoughts about politics and society: Caryl Churchill's *Cloud Nine* and *Mad Forest* reflect her concerns with, respectively, sexual/gender politics and the Rumanian revolution. Tony Kushner's *Angels in America*, William Hoffman's *As Is*, Larry Kramer's *The Normal Heart* and Paul Rudnick's *Jeffrey* are all derived from the playwrights' concerns regarding the AIDS crisis. And Arthur Miller's *The Crucible*, although based on the Salem witch-hunts of the seventeenth century, was his notable response to the 1950s McCarthy witch-hunts.

• From themselves, their families and friends: *Hedda Gabler* is based on a number of people in Henrik Ibsen's wide circle of friends and contemporaries. *The Odd Couple* came from Neil Simon's recollection of visiting the apartment of his fastidious brother Danny and Danny's sloppy room-mate Roy. Alfred Uhry's *Driving Miss Daisy* was based on his memory of his white grandmother and her black chauffeur.

The idea for the play could have come from a premise, a moral, a message; it may have come from an anecdote; it may have come from a person; or it may even have come from an overheard conversation or an imagined scene, a preoccupation or obsession.

At the end of this chapter you'll find a few exercises concerning how to find and develop play ideas. For now, remember that your play idea can come from any number of sources. In fact, the great idea for your play will probably come from a *combination* of sources; the best play ideas always do. But if the initial idea for the play doesn't lend itself to conflict, journeys and theatricality—indeed to all of Aristotle's six elements—something essential will be missing. And if the idea doesn't connect directly with *you*, it probably won't connect with an audience. You always need to find the *person* inside your play.

I learned this playwright's lesson the hard way. My first two full-length plays were comedies. They were funny. They contained ideas. But I hadn't thought about the person inside the play. There was no "me" in my first two (unproduced) plays. The person inside the play is always the writer.

Your play, no matter its source or influence, must spring from a feeling or belief that you value deeply, be the play a searing political statement or a rollicking comedy. Sometimes the connection will appear obvious to you. If you go to your grandmother's funeral and you witness your mother and your aunt arguing over their inheritance, the familial strife—that complicated combination of love, resentment, memories and need—may be so palpable that when you sit down to write the play you're fully conscious of the connection you've made between the idea and yourself. Sometimes the connection is unconscious. Many playwrights talk about the magnetic pull some ideas have for them, realizing only after they've written the play how connected the idea was to one of their own deeply held concerns. Your first step in developing the right ideas for your plays should be to find out what topics and subjects interest you.

When your dramatic skill unites with an idea that has meaning for you, something breaks through. *My* breakthrough came during a long weekend in 1986 when I was visiting the home of a woman I'd known in college. Her father was the headmaster of a private school outside New York. Friday night there was a cocktail party with faculty members and parents. Saturday morning I rose early and made coffee in the kitchen. There was a rattle at the back door. I looked out and saw a figure in a worker's smock emptying the garbage. I recognized the man's face, but I couldn't place it. Something was out of context.

My friend's mother came into the kitchen. "Who's that?" I asked. "Oh, that's Ashton," she said. "You met him last night."

Ashton was a teacher at the school, a charming man with no independent income of his own. He had been married many times, and his alimony was "killing him." Because he made so little money, Ashton had been forced to take on additional jobs to make ends meet. At first he'd kept these jobs a secret, but one night the headmaster and his wife had gone to a party in a nearby town and discovered Ashton working as a bartender. Since then Ashton's moonlighting had become known to his colleagues and students, and they accepted his odd jobs as just another part of his life. But I noticed that the headmaster's wife did not attempt to greet Ashton, nor did he knock on the back door, although it was obvious we were inside. There had been a mutual, unstated agreement that when Ashton was at school, he was part of the group—a peer—but when he was doing one of his odd jobs, in his gray smock and gloves, he was invisible.

I had a play idea.

It would work within a recognizable form—a cocktail party comedy. It would contain conflict—personal, social, even philosophical. It would be a play with a journey, with a character who changed before the eyes of his friends, and in turn changed their lives. It would be a social commentary, because it would deal with issues of money and class and privilege. And I would find ways to make it theatrical. Most important, I had found an idea for a play that connected with *me*:

• I was twenty-eight years old. I had been writing plays for three years. I was afraid of failure. If I failed as a playwright, how would I survive in the world? Would I have to find other work? Physical work? Manual labor? Would nonintellectual work save me or destroy me?

• I had never been handy. Not with tools, not with mechanical things. I couldn't fix a car. I couldn't even open a tin can. I felt I was not—as Chekhov has his pedant scholar Serebrekov protest in *Uncle Vanya*— "a practical man." What would I do if I was forced to start functioning in the practical world?

• I was fascinated by the subject of social class. It's not often discussed in the United States, but a class system exists. How did a person survive a descent from one class to another? How did one's friends react? What did one's friends do?

• This was 1986. There was much talk about the failure of liberal "Great Society" programs and the futility of trying to change personal behavior by experimentation and engineering. The debate raged between the left and the right in journals, magazines, books and public forums.

I jotted down on a piece of paper what the play would be about: class, failure, the salvation of work, social engineering, friendship and its limits. I titled the play *Neddy*.

REMEMBERING THE SIX ELEMENTS

Before I even began to outline the play, I started writing down its six Aristotelian elements in a notebook: character, action, ideas, language, music and spectacle. I started with one page per category. You may come up with dozens of important thematic ideas, reams of great dialogue, terrific scenes, stunning stage image after stunning stage image—all floating around in your notebook. But very quickly you're going to realize that nothing goes anywhere—not an idea, not a joke, not a scene—without focusing on character.

So start with your character page. You actually may write *lots* of pages for this one. List the characters who might people your play. Who are they? What are their wants and needs? How do those wants and needs connect to the ideas and situations you're considering? You don't have to write extensive biographies for your characters, but you do have to know what they'll *do* in certain circumstances. You have to know what they'll do under normal circumstances, and you have to know what they'll do under extraordinary circumstances. A good play will combine both kinds but lean towards the extraordinary. That means that characters under pressure, pushed to extremes, may behave in surprising ways. Like the mother whose adrenalin gives her the power to lift a car off her child, a character in extremes may be capable of unsuspected heroics and unspeakable crimes under the right pressurized circumstances.

When I was sure that the characters and situation would hold interest—for me and for an audience—I wrote down the play's story in brief descriptive form:

> A penniless prep school teacher goes to a party one night and announces to his friends that he has just been abandoned by his wealthy wife. Despondent, he asks for help from his close circle of friends. They loan him money for a while, but they fear they're simply supporting his depression and sloth. Then, one of them, Ned's best friend Allen, a sociology teacher, decides the best way to help is to give Ned odd jobs, so that he can earn his own money and feel good about himself. Ned takes on these jobs, with great misgivings and grumblings. In the course of raking leaves, cleaning gutters and painting bathrooms for his friends, he sees a different side of his colleagues, as they all try to negotiate this change in relationship. Then Ned has an epiphany. He realizes he *can* use his hands. He *can* fix things. He has talents he never knew he

possessed. He becomes a dynamo, going into overdrive. Suddenly Ned is everywhere, doing everything. And he's bothering his friends, especially with his new assurance and his constant exhortations to better themselves in similar ways. In a key scene, Ned's practical advice is not listened to, and one of the characters is humiliated. Ned is made the fall guy for a school disaster. Allen and Ned confront each other, and a choice must be made. Stand by Ned, or let him fall. Allen doesn't have the courage and integrity to support his friend when his peers are telling him to cut Ned off. Allen rejects Ned. Ned leaves the school and starts his own handyman business. In the end, the other characters gather at Allen's Christmas party, a party Ned would normally be invited to. There is a rattle of steel. Allen goes outside and discovers Ned with his garbage can. Allen gives him a tip. Ned takes it. When Allen returns to the party and is asked who was outside, he says simply: "The garbage man."

This is a quick synopsis of the story. The final version of the plot was much more intricate. A lot happens in *Neddy*, involving all the characters. But this synopsis was the strong spine of the story. And it all came together rather quickly. A play idea that has drama, theater, and the playwright's personal concerns at its very core, falls into place faster than half-formed or ill-considered ones. So does the play's story and its plot.

Although I focused on character for *Neddy*, I still kept notes on the other elements—images, dialogue, sounds I might use when I came to write the actual first draft. Remembering the "space/time/causality" theory, I considered *Neddy*'s theatricality: There would be no single setting, but many settings defined by dialogue and small hand props. Some scenes would take place simultaneously on the same stage. There would be music—the sounds of students singing in chapel choirs, innocent voices in an environment that would begin to darken. There would be spectacle: a man in an empty house laying dinner for a wife who's left him; a man carving an assembly line of Halloween pumpkins onstage in front of the audience; a man giving a convocation speech at a chapel as the school's ancient light and sound system fail; and, last, a man alone carrying a garbage can across a stage as his friends celebrate Christmas inside.

Once you have plenty of notes for all six categories, you are ready to outline your play. Many playwrights, including me, use what is called the "French scene" method for outlining. This method enables you to know very clearly which characters are onstage during which actions. A French scene refers to a new configuration of actors onstage. Whenever a character enters or exits the theatrical space, that's a new French scene. The name comes from French rehearsal practices. It's a way of knowing which actors to call for which blocks of rehearsal, and it's used by stage directors to this day. It includes the setting; all entrances and exits; who is onstage together at any given time; and what key actions take place in the scene.

Here's what a breakdown in French scenes might look like:

Act One, Scene One
John and Mary's living room

1. John/Mary
   John tells Mary he's leaving their marriage
   Mary pulls a gun on him

2. Mary's father Joe enters
   John/Mary/Joe
   Joe tells Mary her lover Frank is at the door
   Mary gives Joe the gun
   Mary tells Joe to keep John in the room

3. Mary exits
   John/Joe
   Joe gives John the gun

My French scene outline of *Neddy* took a few weeks. Yours might not take as long, but spend as much time as you need. Even if the work seems tedious, it's time well spent, because you're giving your play its foundation and spine. You'll make mistakes in your outline. I know I did. A writer can't help that. But like a good architect who would never dream of starting a building until every detail had been worked out in blueprint form, a good playwright is better advised to work out the story on yellow legal pads before he ever gets near a keyboard. Isn't it easier to change a few pages of notepaper than it is to change an entire play once it's been laboriously typed up as a 120-page script?

There were false starts and wrong turns in my outline for *Neddy*. I had to keep remembering the principle of "action verbs." Remember our discussion from chapter two: "I *love* you" is an action verb. "If you *leave* this room, I'll *call* the police" are action verbs. "I *confess*" is an action verb. What were my characters *doing* to each other? What were their actions and reactions? What were the stakes? Were the characters smart, clever, resourceful? Did they make good combatants? Could they strategize? Were they funny? Were they likable? Sad? Could the audience identify with their hopes and aspirations? Their wants and needs, their rebellious natures, their pettiness and crimes? And were the actions part of a larger whole—did every action underscore the ideas of the play, illustrate the ideas I wanted the audience to "get" when the final curtain dropped? All those musings about class and money and work and friendship—were the actions linked to those ideas?

Once I had an outline that told the story in action verbs, I tracked the dramatic progression of each of the six characters. Did each character have a story? Did each character's story satisfy the audience's questions about the characters? Did the characters all perform actions? Were their actions all organic to their histories and to the situations I had devised for the plot? And were all the characters' actions moving towards the single most important action of the play, the final climax involving Neddy?

If I found snags—a character whose line of actions seemed to weaken, a character whose story seemed to fade away, a subplot that took the play off its major course—I went back to the yellow legal pad again and thought some more. You have to ask yourself two vitally important questions about characters' actions:

1. What *would* they do?
2. What *could* they do?

Sounds simple, but it isn't. What a character *will* do is based on the background you've given him combined with the situation you've put him in. What a character *can* do is *anything*. How interesting can your character be—how bold, how mysterious, how enthralling and entertaining—and still be true to the person you have created? In rethinking your character, you may sometimes change the background and circumstances so that he may perform actions more vital to the story; you may also eliminate some individually terrific actions because, regardless of how stunning they might seem in and of themselves, they do not follow the very sound character background and well thought out circumstances you've settled on.

Must a character be consistent in all her actions? Audiences look for character consistency, but contradictions are part of human nature. What's more important is to create characters whose actions, no matter how supposedly inconsistent, are *understandable* in a dramatic context, given their psychology and the set of dynamic, dramatic circumstances the playwright has devised. You can surprise your audience by revealing that a sympathetic character has done a terrible thing, or that a villian has a softhearted side. But make that surprising revelation comprehensible.

I made some of these mistakes writing my outline, so I reworked it again. And again. Sometimes your first idea for a scene or an action *is* the best idea. And a lot of the time it isn't. Nor is your second idea. Nor your third. I would advise not starting the actual writing of the play until you really think you've got the story the way you want it. Clear. Strong. Comprehensible. And powerful. With as much complexity and meaning as the actions can display. *Then* begin to write.

As you begin your first draft, the temptation is to know vaguely where you're going and hope inspiration will strike along the way. *Avoid this temptation.* As screenwriters know, and as their guru Syd Field says in his own screenplay texts, it's a little like driving your car into the wilderness: If you know where you're going, if you know your destination ("Know your ending!" admonishes Syd Field), your journey has purpose and you can find wonderful things along the way. If you don't, you may make some wonderful, surprising discoveries while sightseeing, but you're just as likely to get lost, run out of gas, and get stranded in a desert.

Anthony Clarvoe, who has written such U.S. regional theater successes as *Pick Up Ax*, *The Living*, and an adaptation of *The Brothers Karamozov*, once told me that a writer has a lot of control *before* he starts to write and a lot of control *after* he's written but not much control *while* he's writing. A dramatist sits down at his typewriter or computer or legal pad and consults his outline. He starts to follow the map he's drawn. It's hard to get started. It's thick, heavy work just getting the first stage directions on the page. The first line of dialogue is like knocking down a wall at Fort Knox. But he does start. And then the words come. And something he didn't count on starts to happen. Characters say things he hadn't expected. They're wittier or angrier or do things he hadn't thought of. They want to go to different, more exciting places than he'd imagined. And that's tremendous. It may change things about his outline, but he has to be open to that—open and critical at the same time. Successful writers depend on this kind of inspiration. It's what we live for. It's what makes the hard spade work that came before really sing. Call it inspiration, call it a trance, but hope for it, pray for it.

Of course sometimes characters say other things you hadn't planned on. Sometimes they're *duller* and decide to go to *less* exciting places. You know what you do then? You stop writing. When the characters start talking like people in the grocery store, your creativity has had it for the day.

When I finished the first draft I noticed something. *Neddy* contained the ingredients my friend the playwright and teacher Gram Slaton had taught me were found in every great play:

Goals, Conflicts, Obstacles and Actions. (Ned's desires conflicting with the others')

Tension and Suspense. (What would happen to Ned? To the group?)

Secrets. (Four of the characters had secrets revealed)

Sex. (At least three of the characters were having affairs)

Love. (All of the characters were in love)

Money. (Ned's problems stemmed from a lack of money)

Power. (The power of the school; class power; economic power; personal power)

Crime. (Characters lied and stole)

Death. (Neddy threatens suicide)

Ideas. (Themes about class, failure, growth and responsibility)

Theatricality. (Multiple time frames; multiple spatial uses; spectacles of fire and color and light)

By focusing on the essential dramatic elements, I had taken the idea I got that morning in the headmaster's kitchen and turned it into a play.

EXERCISES

1. Read a newspaper. *The New York Times*, *The Washington Post*, a small-town daily. Find and list at least three stories that suggest play ideas, ones that grab you and connect with your own ideas or interests.

2. Write each idea on a separate piece of paper. Write down the idea in terms of "situation" first: (a) "A young man is killed in a hold-up"; (b) "A senator resigns"; (c) "A television star is acting in a local small-town summer theater."

3. Now write down a potential conflict—either one described in the story or one imagined by you—for each situation: (a) "The young man's killer was his partner in crime"; (b) "The senator was being blackmailed by a rival"; (c) "The television star's ex-wife now lives in the town."

4. Now write down a character's journey: (a) "The killer decides to turn himself in"; (b) "The senator admits to an affair he had with his campaign aide rather than capitulate to the blackmailer"; (c) "The television star falls in love with his ex-wife and tries to get her back."

5. Now create theatricality in each idea: (a) "The murder of the young man is remembered and re-enacted onstage from various witnesses' points of view, each time appearing as a different set of actions"; (b) "The senator's press conference where he admits to the affair takes place on one side of the stage, while a scene depicting his lover's attempt to swallow sleeping pills takes place on the other"; (c) "The television star tries to keep his wife from leaving the theater audience while acting onstage, switching the lines of the play so that he can propose to her."

CHAPTER FIVE

Structure

E arly in this book I wrote that a playwright is a poet disguised as an architect. It's my way of saying that a playwright must learn to apply structure to her ideas and inspirations before an audience can appreciate the gifts she has to share with them. A work of art can be structured in many ways. A painter may structure in terms of color and composition. A sculptor may use dimension and proportion. A poet may use rhyme, sound, image and meter. Every successful artist must develop a structure that carries the weight of the work's idea, but *only* playwrights devise a structure that is designed to keep people happily in their seats. As Craig Wright, a talented playwright whose comedy *The Big Numbers* premiered at the Philadelphia Festival for New Plays, once told me, "A bad painting is just a bad painting. But a bad *play* you have to *sit through*."

My experience writing *Neddy* taught me a number of lessons. Some had to do with personal and artistic issues (put yourself in the play), but the majority of the lessons had to do with craft. And the most vital craft issue a playwright can master has to do with structured action. As we discussed in chapter two, action is a crucial element in all plays. Through action we develop character and move the story. To prove to yourself the importance of action, try the following experiment. It requires a good deal of reading, but no terrific playwright was ever hindered by her knowledge of the great plays that have come before. Use the following plays:

Hamlet by William Shakespeare
Hedda Gabler by Henrik Ibsen

Uncle Vanya by Anton Chekhov
The Front Page by Ben Hecht and Charles MacArthur
The Little Foxes by Lillian Hellman
The Glass Menagerie by Tennessee Williams
Dial "M" for Murder by Frederick Knott
Who's Afraid of Virginia Woolf? by Edward Albee
'Night, Mother by Marsha Norman
The Odd Couple by Neil Simon
Betrayal by Harold Pinter
Cloud Nine by Caryl Churchill
Joe Turner's Come and Gone by August Wilson
Six Degrees of Separation by John Guare

Get the plays from a bookstore or a library. It'll take you a few days to read them. Don't be impatient to get to your writing. Starting at the beginning and reading through each play to the end, write down every action, everything the characters *do* that is the result of one action and in turn causes yet another action. David Ball, in his book *Backwards and Forwards*, argues that the only true dramatic action is one that is linked in just this way. Actions that are not linked are just activities—busywork.

List the actions scene by scene. You don't have to be elaborate, but you should note the important actions in detail. Use the French scene model from the previous chapter. You'll find very early on that the exercise is primarily about verbs—action verbs—physical actions and language actions. A woman firing a pistol at her husband is an action. So is telling him she's pregnant. Each action will provoke a reaction. Using the plays listed above, what do you think you'll find? Plays with four actions? Ten? Twelve?

Try one hundred. Try more.

THE POINT OF ATTACK AND THE INCITING INCIDENT

Keeping in mind that every entrance and every exit can constitute an action, you'll be astounded to discover the large number and great variety of actions found in successful plays. Once you've written your long list of actions, you'll also be able to identify the divisions between the beginning of the play and its middle, and between the middle and the end. The first division will be an action or short sequence of actions that constitutes the point of attack, the launching pad for the play. In

Hamlet, it is the Ghost's "assignment" to Hamlet. In *Hedda Gabler*, it is the announced arrival of Hedda's great love, Eilert Lovborg. In *Dial "M" for Murder*, it is the husband's spoken desire to have his wife murdered. In *The Odd Couple*, it is Oscar's insistence that Felix move in with him. One of the key ways of recognizing a point of attack is that all the actions following the point of attack are a *direct result* of the point of attack; without the point of attack, the kinds of actions found in the beginning of the play would go on forever. In *Hamlet*, the Danish court would have proceeded as Claudius had wanted it to. In *Hedda Gabler*, Hedda would have remained Tesman's wife. In *Dial "M" for Murder*, the murderous husband and his wife would have stayed together. In *The Odd Couple*, Oscar would have continued to live alone. The point of attack is the first action that changes everything.

The action that creates a point of attack can have its origins in the past, what some playwriting teachers refer to as the inciting incident. Usually the inciting incident is an event that took place before the action of the play began. In *Hamlet*, the inciting incident is King Hamlet's murder, the action that leads to the ghost's encounter with his son. In *Hedda Gabler*, the inciting incident is Hedda and Eilert's affair. In *Dial "M" for Murder*, it is the husband's realization that his wife could divorce him, taking her wealth with her. And in *The Odd Couple*, it is the fight between Felix and his wife. We never see the scenes of these "back-stories." More often than not, an inciting incident is reported rather than depicted onstage. And most inciting incidents are reported at or very near the point of attack. In *Hamlet*, the ghost's revelation of his murder comes just a few lines of dialogue before he orders Hamlet to avenge his death. In *Dial "M,"* the husband's certainty of his wife's infidelity is revealed a page or two before he details his murder plot. In *The Odd Couple*, the story of Felix's broken marriage is told a minute or two before Oscar offers Felix his apartment.

A smaller number of plays have an inciting incident that isn't revealed until late in the play. In *Hedda Gabler*, the effect of Eilert Lovborg's return is strongly felt long before anyone onstage explains why—even before Eilert appears. Because of the odd way Hedda acts when she hears Eilert's name, we may suspect there is a history between Hedda and Eilert. His name is first mentioned in Act One. Soon thereafter, Hedda sends him an invitation to come to her house (point of attack). However, it is not until Act Two, almost a half hour later in stage time, that we realize Hedda and Eilert were once romantically involved. In the case of *Hedda Gabler*, the point of attack is in the right place, but the revelation of the inciting incident is kept from the audience (remember suspense?) until much later, until just the right moment.

Only you will know best how to build this moment into your play. In *Hamlet, Dial "M" for Murder* and *The Odd Couple*, the playwrights placed the revelation of the inciting incident close to the point of attack. This was for maximum effect and efficiency. Efficiency is very important in getting your play started. You don't have all the time in the world, especially given the fact that, unlike the five-hour *Hamlet* and the three-hour *Hedda*, most plays written today are over in ninety minutes to two and a half hours. You have less time to get the car started. You have minutes, never more than a half hour.

But sometimes the revelation *must* be postponed. In *Hedda Gabler*, Ibsen keeps the Hedda/Eilert affair a secret not just for suspense, although the suspense is great. When you read the analysis of *Hedda Gabler*, look at who's onstage when it is revealed that Eilert Lovborg has returned. Of the people onstage, only Hedda knows about their affair, and there's absolutely no one to whom she would want to reveal it. Not Tesman, her husband. Not Thea Elvstead, the woman now in love with Eilert. Hedda—and the audience—has to wait for Eilert to arrive before the inciting incident (the affair) can be revealed. What's wonderful is that the story of the affair comes out between the two people most directly affected by the information: Hedda and Eilert when they are alone, looking at Hedda's honeymoon pictures.

Even plays that seem, at first glance, to be constructed along less Aristotelian lines, like Harold Pinter's absurdist comedy of menace *The Caretaker*, and Craig Lucas' *Blue Window*, eventually provide the audience with a revelation of the pasts of the characters in a way that informs the present action and moves that action forward. In *The Caretaker*, Aston's long second act speech about his incarceration in an asylum is such a revelation. In *Blue Window*, the inciting incident—a terrible accident that resulted in death and injury seven years earlier—is not revealed until the last minutes of the play. Placed early or late, these scenes act as revelations of inciting incidents.

Martin Esslin, in *An Anatomy of Drama*, writes that most dramatic structure is based on the question, What's going to happen? This is true, both for the central dramatic question of a play (Will Hamlet revenge his father's death?) and the lesser ones along the way (Will Hamlet outwit Rosencrantz and Guildenstern? Will Hamlet be executed in

England? Will Hamlet drink the poisoned wine?). But Esslin also notes that one of the major questions of contemporary theater is not so much, What's going to happen, but rather, What's going on? Some plays have mysterious actions, actions that seem not to have causes or effects. Audiences—detectives all—watch the play to discover the reasons behind these puzzling actions. And a good deal of contemporary theater can be enjoyed and appreciated for its evocation of mystery. But most successful plays *do* provide the answers to their mysteries at some point, even at the very end. The important thing is not to reveal too late. An audience may be enthralled by a point of attack without a clear inciting incident, but they're going to lean forward to find out what that incident was. You may decide to withhold the information regarding the inciting incident to prolong the suspense and tension. But like the joke-teller who takes too long to get to the punchline, the playwright who prolongs the revelation until too deep into the play is simply using delaying tactics, and the audience will grow weary and finally tune out. By the time you reveal the inciting incident, it may be too late to matter. If you have selected an inciting incident but choose *never* to reveal it to the audience, you may be sacrificing both clarity and satisfaction. A play may be a strip tease, but it's got to be more strip than tease.

THE CLIMAX

Now. You have a notebook full of actions for all of the plays mentioned above. You've written down the actions in French scenes, in sequence. You don't need to make notations on motivation or meaning. These are successful plays. Motivation and meaning are there. Just write down the actions: the nouns and the verbs; the subjects, verbs and objects ("Mary shoots John"). You've found dozens of actions. You've identified the inciting incident and the point of attack.

The next major division to look for is the climax. It comes late in the play. The climax is that action or sequence of actions that resolves the conflict. In the climax, the major combatants come to blows. The protagonist meets his antagonist(s) for the final battle. The central dramatic question is answered. There is a win, a loss or a draw, although audiences prefer plays with winners and losers, not draws.

The climax is fairly easy to identify. One of the key ways of recognizing a climax is that all the actions *following* the climax are an acceptance of the situation derived from the climax. After the climax, there are no more major actions to be performed. The central dramatic question has been answered. The conflict has been resolved, happily or unhappily. In *Hamlet*, the prince finally kills Claudius; a few pages or minutes of minor actions remain, but the key question has been answered. In *Dial "M,"* the murderous husband is caught; the only action that remains is the inspector's telephone call to police headquarters. In *Hedda Gabler*, Hedda shoots herself; only four lines remain as Tesman and Judge Brack react to her death. In *The Odd Couple*, Felix moves out, and Oscar goes back to living alone, wiser about friendship.

On rare occasions, a climax is followed by a surprise action. This usually happens only in comedy. Famously, Ben Hecht's and Charles MacArthur's *The Front Page* reaches its climax when the newspapermen, Walter Burns and Hildy Johnson, hand over the convict to the authorities, save him from hanging, escape arrest themselves, get the big story to publish in their paper, and make amends between themselves.

Walter, the editor who doesn't want to lose his star reporter, tries everything to keep Hildy. But in the end, Walter realizes Hildy wants to leave the newspaper business for love. So Walter gives Hildy his blessing. He even gives Hildy his prized gold watch, as a kind of "diploma." Hildy thanks Walter, as he and his fiancée leave the press room to take the train to New York. A moment passes. Walter picks up a phone and dials.

WALTER: Duffy! Send a wire to the Chief of Police at La Porte, Indiana— That's right—Tell him to meet the twelve-forty out of Chicago— New York Central—and arrest Hildy Johnson and bring him back here. Wire him a full description. The son of a bitch stole my watch!

It's the most famous last line in the American theater. But it's not the climax. The climax came when the central dramatic question was answered, when the two men came to their understanding. Walter's comic punch line could be said to be the point of attack for a whole new play that was never written, with the entirety of *The Front Page* as its inciting incident.

Again, this kind of surprise twist tends to be found in comedy, not in drama. In drama, such last minute reversals can seem melodramatic or even unintentionally humorous. But convincing surprises *can* occur at the end of a drama. Let's look at a similar surprise from a noncomic play: *Hedda Gabler*. Hedda's final confrontation is with Judge Brack, the man who is blackmailing her into having an affair with him. It seems the climax has been reached when the judge presents Hedda with a fait accompli. It looks like he's won. The audience may think the climax is over. And then Hedda shoots herself, a shocking moment in the modern theater. We realize the conflict wasn't quite over; Hedda managed to escape Judge Brack's clutches, even at the cost of her own life. Our protagonist had one more trick up her sleeve, one more move in her strategy. The final move.

THE MOMENT OF TRUTH

So. You've found the point of attack and the climax. You have discovered that prior to each play's point of attack there have been just a handful of real actions. You have also discovered that after the climax there are even fewer real actions. What's interesting is what you've found in the middle: actions, reactions, complications, surprises, reversals.

Dozens or hundreds.

Now, the moment of truth: If you've already written a play, or if you've just outlined a play, do the same exercise with your own work. List the actions French scene by French scene. What have you discovered? If you're like me, you were probably shocked to discover that the play you'd written or planned to write had about one fourth the number of actions that Shakespeare, Ibsen, Frederick Knott, Caryl Churchill and Neil Simon put in their plays. This is not to say that the play with the most actions wins. But *all* successful plays use many cables (actions) to support the suspension bridge (plot). Nine times out of ten, a less experienced playwright finds that she doesn't have more than a few real, effective, change-making actions in her whole play. This is a problem. So what do you do? You give up, right? Or you try to comfort yourself by saying, "Well, *my* play isn't a driving machine, it's the sort of play where nothing much happens, but, uh, it's a character study, right, and it deals in mood, and the talk is pretty interesting, and . . ."

Forget it. Don't be proud of the fact that your play isn't a driving machine. Work hard to make it one.

Don't say, "Uh, well . . . nothing much happens in Chekhov!" One of the most damaging criticisms over the past hundred years is the kind that suggests that "nothing happens in Chekhov." That's not true. An *extraordinary* amount happens in Chekhov. Characters profess love, seduce each other, buy and sell property, shoot themselves, shoot others and abandon loved ones. True, unlike *Hamlet*, there are no wars in Chekhov's *The Cherry Orchard*, no stabbings, no poisonings, no pirate attacks. But *The Cherry Orchard* is no less dramatic. It's always a question of degrees, a question of context. An action takes on dramatic power and importance not because of the size of the action itself, but because the action has importance and power within the story being told.

PLANNING YOUR PLAY

All right. You've studied these plays. You've written down their actions. You're now ready to apply the lessons about structure and actions you learned from your reading and outlining. You have a good idea for a play and you've developed its dramatic potential. You've taken notes for the play focusing on the six elements. You've experimented with your ideas by using the exercises from the end of chapter four. Take out your legal pad again. You're ready to outline.

Not every playwright likes to do this. Many talented writers think that preplanning and outlining hinder their creativity. If some writers believe they can successfully pilot their way through a play without knowing where they're going before they start or planning their route, fine; I admire them. I wish I were as talented or lucky. I need an outline of the play's actions. And the plays I've written after I've outlined the actions have always been better plays, more successful plays, and more readily *produced* plays than the ones I've written blindly with only a few impressions and some crossed fingers to guide me.

Three Movements

In outlining your play, you'll want to refer to your study of the great plays and their chains of action. You've already identified their inciting incidents, points of attack and climaxes. You have most likely noticed something else important about all play structure. Every successful play works in three movements—a beginning, a middle and an end.

This may seem elementary, but I can't stress more to emerging playwrights the importance of orchestrating dramatic events into this three-part structure. The most successful plays have a structure that, when analyzed, exhibits three distinct and clearly delineated movements, and the playwright who ignores this structural ground rule does so at great risk.

You'll note I'm avoiding the use of the word "acts." While many plays have been written in three distinct acts with two breaks for intermissions, for the purposes of this book, I think it's wiser to proceed with an overall sense of the three movements, or sections, or parts, rather than acts. Why? To talk in terms of acts tends to make us think of traditional blocks of continuous stage performance that then stop for a firm division, curtain, or other punctuated interval. For now, it's more important to grasp the larger shape of the three-part structure than it is to focus on where to place the intermissions. We'll discuss placement of intermissions in chapter seven, "Great Middles."

Plays might have one, two, three, four, even five "official" acts, but *every good play embodies three distinct movements*, adhering to the following very rough outline:

Part One (15-30 percent of the play)
Start of play.
Introduction of characters, place, time, setting or exposition.
Introduction of the primary inciting event.
Initial point of attack or primary conflict.
Introduction of the central dramatic question.

Part Two (50-75 percent of the play)
Character(s) embark on journey/struggle/search for answers/goals.
Conflicts with other characters, events, circumstances.
Character(s) reassess situations, respond to obstacles and challenges,
plan new tactics, succeed, fail, attack, retreat, surprise and are
surprised, encounter major reversals (rising action).
A crisis is reached.
Characters embark on an action that will resolve the crisis and lead
inexorably to the conclusion.

Part Three (5-25 percent of the play)
The major characters or combatants engage in a final conflict
(climax).
The character(s)' goal is achieved or lost.
The central dramatic question is answered.
The actions suggest the themes or ideas of the play.
Following the climax is the resolution, in which a new order is
established.

End of Play

The first section (exposition and point of attack) is constructed to orient and excite the audience, praise its expectations, raise its sugar and adrenalin levels and wake them up. And so, ghosts appear in first sections (*Hamlet*). Murders are plotted (*Dial "M" for Murder*). Old lovers return after long absences (*Hedda Gabler*). Convicts escape (*The Front Page*). A woman announces that she is going to commit suicide (*'Night, Mother*). Two men are found in bed by an Upper East Side couple (*Six Degrees of Separation*). A fussbudget is thrown out of his apartment by his wife (*The Odd Couple*).

The second movement is designed to alternate raised tensions with relief of tension. The second movement, the middle, is your longest section. Pace yourself during it; a continuous rise in tension is exhausting, so the shrewd playwright follows a fast scene with a slow scene, a violent scene with a funny scene, a romantic scene with a scene of intrigue. The body, the mind, the senses require this constant handoff of mood and tension. Predictability and repetition are deadly to drama, so the second movement of the play is a complex mechanism designed to keep the mind engaged for what in most plays is a full hour or more, including the intermission (hence, the need for a cliffhanger first act curtain). And so, in second movements, princes pretend to go mad and plot ways to trap a killer (*Hamlet*). A murder goes awry and the plotter has to maneuver into a more ingenious strategy (*Dial "M" for Murder*). An old lover loses his manuscript, and it is hidden and destroyed by the woman who loves him (*Hedda Gabler*). The convict hides in a reporter's rolltop desk as the other reporters and policemen are kept on a wild goose chase (*The Front Page*). The mother tries to convince her daughter not to take her life (*'Night, Mother*). The Upper East Side couple search for the boy who came to their home and try to find out why he chose them to prey upon (*Six Degrees of Separation*). The fussbudget's messy best friend invites him to live with him, and various conflicts ensue that will hinder their friendship (*The Odd Couple*).

The third movement is designed to raise audience expectation yet again, just when their energies might have flagged. In a contemporary full-length play, the audience has probably been sitting still for a long time. Sugar levels may be dropping; adrenalin may be in short supply. A gauntlet must be thrown to excite the senses. This is what is often referred to as the crisis. Something happens that will change everything for the characters. Someone will win, someone will lose. An end is in sight. And so, the prince is challenged to a duel (*Hamlet*). An inspector thinks he's found the means to ensnare the killer (*Dial "M"*). The lover is killed, and there are incriminating circumstances that lead to a blackmail plot (*Hedda Gabler*). The convict is found and the reporters are arrested (*The Front Page*). The mother admits her daughter has reason to kill herself but still tries one more time to prevent her action (*'Night, Mother*). An innocent young man kills himself because of the mysterious intruder who then calls the Upper East Side couple to beg their help (*Six Degrees of Separation*). The fussbudget and the slob nearly come to blows, and the fussbudget disappears (*The Odd Couple*).

It is in the third movement of the play that your characters embark on their final conflict and reach the play's climax. You have raised expectations. You have taken the characters and your audience on a journey. There have been changes and surprises and complications and maneuvers. The search, the quest or the journey must end. The conflict must be resolved. And so, the prince kills his uncle and is himself killed (*Hamlet*). The wily murderer is foiled by his tiniest mistake (*Dial "M"*). The woman commits suicide rather than submit to blackmail (*Hedda Gabler*). The reporters are saved from prison, and the editor and his star writer seem to come to an understanding (*The Front Page*). The mother tries to save her daughter, but fails; her daughter shoots herself (*'Night, Mother*). The Upper East Side couple try to save the boy, but they are too late (*Six Degrees of Separation*). The slob and the fussbudget decide to remain good friends, but not roommates (*The Odd Couple*).

These are not *all* happy endings. There is death. There is separation. There is failure. There are complications even at the resolution of the conflict. But happy endings or sad, the audience's satisfaction is achieved. The central dramatic questions have been answered. Characters have been depicted in action. People have changed. A journey is complete. The human spirit has been affirmed—in light, in darkness, in complexity and with reverberations. A story has been told.

GREAT PLAY STRUCTURE IN REAL LIFE

I'm always fascinated by the fact that stories in real life often resemble the pattern of good play structure. Of course, there's another way to write that sentence: "I'm always fascinated by the fact that good play structure tends to follow the pattern of fascinating real-life stories."

Take Watergate. It has a strong character as its central *Protagonist*— Richard Nixon. An intelligent, troubled and complicated figure. He is worthy of scorn, hatred, pity and admiration.

It has a number of very strong *Antagonists* (some of which are, as we know, protagonists in their own private plays): Woodward and Bernstein, Ben Bradlee, Judge Sirica, John Dean, G. Gordon Liddy, the tapes, the Constitution of the United States, Congress, Nixon's own complex psyche and many more.

It has a strong *Inciting Incident* or *Back-Story*: Nixon's desire to win the 1972 election and punish his enemies leads to the formation of the secret burglars, or "plumbers" unit.

It has a great *Point of Attack* in its *Great Beginning*: the apprehension of the burglars at Democratic Headquarters on June 17, 1972, the action that necessitated the cover-up, the details of which ended up on Nixon's secret tapes, the revelation of which finally forced him to resign the presidency.

It has a wonderful *Great Middle* filled with goals, actions, obstacles, complications, surprises and reversals: the White House cover-up; the investigation taken on by the police, the FBI and the press; the attempts—many successful, many not—by the White House to halt the investigation, bribe witnesses and destroy evidence; the confession of burglars and White House aides to Congress, the *Washington Post* and Judge Sirica; the Senate hearings and the surprise revelation that the Oval Office taping system existed; the attempts by prosecutors, the press and Congress to retrieve the tapes; Nixon's legal maneuvers to stop them from getting the tapes; the partial release of some tapes, including the one with the famous eighteen-and-a-half minute gap; the House Judiciary Committee's vote to impeach Nixon; the Supreme Court's decision that ordered Nixon to hand over the tapes; and the "smoking gun" revelation, discovered on a June 21, 1972 recording, that Nixon approved "hush money" to the Watergate burglars.

And it has a great *Climax*: Nixon's August 8, 1974 resignation.

Not to mention the terrific *Subplots*: Spiro Agnew's fall, Martha Mitchell's descent into madness, and the struggles of Woodward and Bernstein.

There are other political scandals and other great characters in American political history. Why does Watergate in particular lend itself to a dramatic story? The characters had everything to win and everything to lose—all of them: Nixon, his aides, the reporters, the *people* of the United States. The characters had talents and flaws in great and equal measure (good protagonists have good antagonists). There were sudden opportunities provided by life and fate: the security guard who *happened* to find the taped door-lock at the Watergate complex and the *accidental* discovery that Nixon *taped* his conversations. There were outer conflicts and inner conflicts (Nixon vs. the Congress; Nixon vs. the Press; Nixon vs. the Supreme Court; Nixon vs. His Staff; Nixon vs. Himself—his fear, his anger, his frustration, his pettiness and his foolishness). And the characters didn't give up until they had won or knew they had lost.

It's all incredible. It's all organic. And it's all true. With plots as good as Watergate in *real* life, we playwrights have to keep on our toes when we're structuring our imaginations.

The successful authors of the plays we know and love have found that the three-part structure not only facilitates the telling of a story on stage, with the traditional notion of beginnings, middles and ends; it also follows the biological patterns of the human body. Keep in mind that since the days of ancient Greece, plays have been performed either in the afternoons following the lunch period, or in the evening, after the dinner period. This is commonly considered a time of rest, relaxation, naps, siestas—sleep. Biologically, the body is primed for unconsciousness. The organization of a play's events, actions, characters, and other points of interest, then, must be organized to fight the soporific nature of the viewing period. So the construction of a play is designed in a three-part structure, in large part to serve the needs of the human senses.

If I seem to be suggesting that the assemblage of a play is a conscious attempt to offset the effects of eating and the drowsiness that comes with the digestive system, don't take me too seriously. It's not that biologically scientific. But it's amazing that the traditional arcs of story-telling and the traditional plotting of successful plays follow a pattern that is so conducive to the inner workings of the human mechanism. In drama's best, organic fashion, the natural storyteller follows her instinct and uses her knowledge of the theater and dramatic technique not to *affect* a biological response, but rather *because* she is so attuned to her own rhythms, to the rhythms of audiences, and to the very rhythm of life. She can't *help* but write that way. A grasp of the three-movement structure of story is vital to the dramatist's craft and the audience's needs.

As you plan your play using the three-movement structure, remember that while I may be emphasizing detailed script analysis and extensive outlining, this structural approach will eventually function for your writing like physical memory, like tying a shoe or riding a bicycle. Once learned, understood and practiced, the three-part structure becomes part of your dramatic discipline. For now, however, our bones and muscles still need some limbering. So let's examine each part of the three-movement structure more closely in the following chapters, Great Beginnings, Great Middles and Great Endings.

EXERCISES

1. In one to three pages of prose, write a story from real life or one you imagine. Now start looking for its three movements. Are they already there? Is there a beginning that contains an inciting incident and a point of attack? Is there a large middle section with conflicting forces? Is there a climax followed by resolution? Play with the story, reworking it a few times until this shape emerges.

2. Once you've identified this three-part structure to the story, rewrite it in three to six sentences. This is reductive, true, but it will boil the key actions and characters down to their essentials. It will tell you which actions and characters are most important to *you*. (Example: *Hamlet*. *Movement One:* The ghost of King Hamlet appears to Prince Hamlet, telling him that Claudius murdered him and exhorting Hamlet to avenge his death. *Movement Two:* Hamlet attempts to prove Claudius' guilt by pretending to be mad and by staging a play that closely resembles Claudius' murder of King Hamlet. Hamlet gets his proof but kills Polonius by mistake and is sent to England to be executed. *Movement Three:* Hamlet escapes his execution, returns to Denmark and is challenged by Polonius' son Laertes to a duel. Claudius plots with Laertes to kill Hamlet. Instead, Laertes is mortally wounded, as is Hamlet. Laertes confesses to Hamlet, implicating Claudius. Hamlet kills Claudius. Hamlet dies.) Again, many other actions—and deaths—take place in *Hamlet*. But this tells the essential story.

3. Now isolate all the verbs you used in the three sentences. How many of the verbs were actions performed by people to get what they wanted? Did they affect other people in the story? Did they cause further actions to take place?

4. Outline the play idea you've developed according to the plan we discussed earlier in this chapter. Then expand the outline in more detail, using the French scene method.

CHAPTER SIX

Great Beginnings

Every play teaches its audience *how* to watch it *as* they watch it. As a play begins, it instructs its audience how to comprehend its journey and its world. If the play *says* it is a comedy, the audience will agree to comprehend it as a comedy. This comedy cue is referred to as "giving the audience permission to laugh," usually within the first minute or two of the action. If a play *says* it is a serious drama, then a serious dramatic experience will be expected, and that permission to laugh will most likely be delayed and granted less often. The beginning of a play is where you plant the seeds for everything to come. Guns displayed in the beginnings of plays often go off at their ends. Character flaws depicted on page five become running gags for the next 115 pages. It's like loading a revolver in preparation to fire it. A good play carries all of its details with it as it moves from its beginning to its conclusion.

Within the first few minutes of a well-constructed play, the audience must learn:

- the central characters (Who are they? How many?)
- the foreshadowing of the central dramatic action (What's the plot? What do the characters want? What's in their way?)
- the tone (Serious? Comic?)
- the style (Naturalism? Realism? Restoration?)
- the design—setting, sound, light, costume (A real bedroom? An abstract unit set? A bare stage?)

These factors create the world of the play. Most plays *stay* within the world established in their beginnings. A sudden break from that world or a wandering from the established action is apt to throw the audience off the track. If you subvert the expectations you've established early on, you'd better have a good reason. Imagine an *Odd Couple* that suddenly changes its plot so that Felix catches an incurable disease. Imagine a *Hamlet* that suddenly has Hamlet telling jokes to the audience.

In writing a play today, you have approximately ten to fifteen minutes to set space, time, tone, situation, most major characters and the central issue of the drama. If these central points are not elucidated early on, your audience will lose focus quickly and become frustrated in their attempt to understand and enjoy the play. Aristotle describes this in the *Poetics*: "In the first act set forth the case." And a dramatic "case," like a case in a court of law, requires evidence and information. This detailing of information vitally important to the audience's understanding and enjoyment of the play is called exposition.

EXPOSITION

Exposition tells the audience what has happened, what is happening, and what may happen next. Exposition can be communicated in a number of ways:

- Through dialogue between characters onstage
- Through monologues spoken by one character to either an unseen character or directed toward the audience
- Through stage action
- Through design elements (sets, lights, sound, costumes)

Most exposition, however, is accomplished by dialogue. There are two ways of communicating expositional information to the audience via dialogue:

1. Representational exposition
2. Presentational exposition

A representational depiction of reality is an attempt to make an onstage dramatic scene appear as if it were happening in much the same way it would in real life. In a representational play, the onstage characters behave as if they are unaware of the audience's presence. A representational play behaves as if unaware of its own artifice. The actors stay "in character" as characters. The onstage characters assume a real fourth wall separates them from the audience. The play pretends it is not a play.

A presentational play depicts reality *within* the frame of a theatrical presentation. It knows it is a "show." In a presentational play, the characters do behave as if they are aware an audience is watching. Soliloquies, asides, direct-address, even audience interaction underline this kind of presentation. The actors are saying, in effect, "We are presenting a play to you. We are not pretending to be real. We know you're out there."

Let's look at a few examples of representational exposition. Arguably, it is much more difficult to write exposition in representational theater. You want to suggest place, time and character relationships. You need to move the story's conflict along as well, and propel the action forward. When striving for a naturalistic effect in an opening scene between two old college roommates who were once rivals for the same woman's affections, it would be ham-handed to have the expository exchange go like this:

BILL: It certainly is good to see you, Tom, my old roommate.
TOM: I feel the same, Bill, even though we used to have affection for the same girl.

Why doesn't this exposition work in a representational, realistic scene? Because people don't talk like this in real life. So what do you do? You look for the code words that suggest place, time and relationships:

BILL: Who was the guy who lived down the hall from us?
TOM: The big fat one from Nebraska?
BILL: Right. Lowest GPA in the freshman class. Ginnie used to tutor him.
TOM: Yeah. Ginnie.

(Pause)

BILL: Sorry, sore subject. You still hear from her?
TOM: No. (*Beat*) You?

The first representational exposition example is crude and simplistic. The second is subtler and more dramatically effective. By using code words that refer to college ("GPA," "freshman class," "tutor," "down the hall"), the playwright will lead the audience to a conclusion: that these two characters were college roommates. By mentioning one name, "Ginnie"—a name that causes a momentary halt in the conversation—the playwright can not only add further information but also suggest the possibility of a love triangle between two men and one woman. What's useful, as well, is that this past triangle, this past offstage conflict, might become part of a present onstage conflict as well. A past action may influence a present action. The old rivalry over Ginnie might come back.

When using code in writing exposition, the playwright must seek out the words, phrases, and points of reference endemic to the place, situation, action and characters involved.

An audience hangs onto exposition that has to do with the dramatic questions posed by the play. An audience hangs onto exposition that has to do with conflict, with action, with mysteries. To that end, the *best* kind of exposition is deeply worked into the fiber and muscle of the drama. And dramatic exposition is best displayed in active, forward-moving exchanges spoken by characters who need to tell information to other characters who need to know, especially when the information is part of ongoing action, mystery and conflict.

In Anton Chekhov's final play, *The Cherry Orchard*, the character of Lopahkin begins his speech about the declining fortunes of the estate on about the tenth page of the first scene. He is delivering vital information to the audience. If we don't understand the central situation, we won't be able to enjoy the rest of the play. But the audience isn't the only group that needs to know. Lopahkin needs to tell because other characters onstage need to know. Madame Ranevskaya has just returned from Paris, and she must be informed about the dire straits in which her orchard now finds itself. Lopahkin is "in character" in this expository speech because Chekhov has made him the kind of big-talking man who likes to orate in front of groups. And the conflict is that the characters onstage during his speech, the characters who most need to understand the information he is imparting, don't want to listen. Lopahkin, as a character, has a need. This need is frustrated by other characters onstage. There is a conflict. So he must act. He speaks.

LOPAHKIN: Your brother here, Leonid Andreich, says I'm a boor, a moneygrubber, but I don't mind. Let him talk. All I want is that you should trust me as you used to, and that your wonderful, touching eyes should look at me as they did then. . . . I wish I could tell you something very pleasant and cheering. (*Glances at his watch.*) I must go directly, there's no time to talk, but . . . well, I'll say it in a couple of words. As you know, the cherry orchard is to be sold to pay your debts. The auction is set for August twenty-second, but you need not worry, my dear, you can sleep in peace, there is a way out. This is my plan. Now, please listen! Your estate is only twenty versts from town, the railway runs close by, and if the cherry orchard and the land along the river were cut up into lots and leased for summer cottages, you'd have, at the very least, an income of twenty-five thousand a year.

GAYEV: Excuse me, what nonsense!

LYUBOV ANDREYEVNA: I don't quite understand you, Yermolai Alekseich.

LOPAHKIN: You will get, at the very least, twenty-five rubles a year for a two-and-a-half-acre lot, and if you advertise now, I guarantee you won't have a single plot of ground left by autumn, everything will be snapped up. In short, I congratulate you, you are saved. The site is splendid, the river is deep. Only, of course, the ground must be cleared . . . you must tear down all the old outbuildings, for instance, and this house, which is worthless, cut down the old cherry orchard—

LYUBOV ANDREYEVNA: Cut it down? Forgive me, my dear, but you don't know what you are talking about. If there is one thing in the whole province that is interesting, not to say remarkable, it's our cherry orchard.

LOPAHKIN: The only remarkable thing about this orchard is that it is very big. There's a crop of cherries every other year, and then you can't get rid of them, nobody buys them.

GAYEV: This orchard is even mentioned in the *Encyclopedia*.

LOPAHKHIN: (*glancing at his watch*) If we don't think of something and come to a decision, on the twenty-second of August the cherry orchard, and the entire estate, will be sold at auction. Make up your minds! There is no other way out, I swear to you. None whatsoever.

The audience knows everything it must to enjoy the main action and central question of the rest of the play before *The Cherry Orchard's* first ten minutes have passed.

Let's look at another example of character/conflict-driven exposition, this one from Sam Shepard's *True West*. It begins late at night in a kitchen. Austin, weary and tense, is trying to write at a typewriter. Lee, somewhat drunk, is at the sink, watching Austin.

LEE: So, Mom took off for Alaska, huh?

AUSTIN: Yeah.

LEE: Sorta' left you in charge.

AUSTIN: Well, she knew I was coming down here so she offered me the place.

LEE: You keepin' the plants watered?

AUSTIN: Yeah.

LEE: Keepin' the sink clean? She don't like even a single tea leaf in the sink ya' know.

AUSTIN: (*Trying to concentrate on writing*) Yeah, I know.

   (*Pause*)

LEE: She gonna' be up there a long time?

AUSTIN: I don't know.

LEE: Kinda' nice for you, huh? Whole place to yourself.

AUSTIN: Yeah, it's great.

LEE: Ya' got crickets anyway. Tons a' crickets out there. (*Looks around kitchen*) Ya' got groceries? Coffee?

AUSTIN: (*Looking up from writing*) What?

LEE: You got coffee?

AUSTIN: Yeah.

LEE: At's good. (*Short pause*) Real coffee? From the bean?

AUSTIN: Yeah. You want some?

LEE: Naw, I brought some uh—(*Motions to beer*)

AUSTIN: Help yourself to whatever's—(*Motions to refrigerator*)

LEE: I will. Don't worry about me. I'm not the one to worry about. I mean I can uh—(*Pause*) You always work by candlelight?

AUSTIN: No—uh—Not always.

LEE: Just sometimes?

AUSTIN: (*Puts pen down, rubs his eyes*) Yeah. Sometimes it's soothing.

LEE: Isn't that what the old guys did?

AUSTIN: What old guys?

LEE: The Forefathers. You know.

AUSTIN: Forefathers?

LEE: Isn't that what they did? Candlelight burning into the night? Cabins in the wilderness.

AUSTIN: (*Rubs hand through his hair*) I suppose.

LEE: I'm not botherin' you am I? I mean I don't wanna break into yer uh—concentration or nothin'.

In this scene, we see Austin and Lee's age-old sibling rivalry (conflict/ tension), the new situation (premise), the types of people involved (character), and the potential for the relationship to erupt later in the play (action). In the meantime, we also learn the vital exposition that Austin is a writer, Lee is his brother, their mother is in Alaska, and Austin is ostensibly in charge of the house. The opening lines of *True West* are a great example of active, character-driven, forward-moving exposition in representational theater.

Presentational exposition would appear, at first glance, to be an easier kind of exposition to write. If the play is aware of itself as a play—if there is a high level of self-consciousness—then the audience will accept the actors marching downstage at will and speaking to them whenever important information must be communicatated. But nondramatic exposition should be employed sparingly in drama. Gram Slaton, the playwright and teacher I learned a lot from early on, once said to me, "Monologues are the easiest kind of speeches to write. They're also the hardest to justify." He was right. And any actor saddled with expositional monologues will tell you that he becomes exhausted and the audience becomes restless if the exposition is communicated without a sense of urgency or dramatic need. No less so than in good dramatic dialogue, expositional monologues need character, conflict and action.

How can you achieve that sense of dramatic need in a monologue? The audience needs to know. And the character needs to tell. Only when this dynamic exchange exists is there a dramatic relationship between the audience and the actor delivering the exposition.

Let's look at two direct-address presentational monologues from Peter Shaffer's *Equus* and Shakespeare's *Richard III*.

Equus

Darkness. Silence. Dim light up on the square. In a spotlight stands ALAN STRANG, a lean boy of seventeen, in sweater and jeans. In front of him, the horse NUGGET. ALAN's pose represents a contour of great tenderness: his head is pressed against the shoulder of the horse, his hands stretching up to fondle its head. The horse in turn nuzzles his neck. The flame of a cigarette lighter jumps in the dark. Lights come up slowly on the circle. On the left bench, downstage, MARTIN DYSART, smoking. A man in his mid-forties.

DYSART: With one particular horse, called Nugget, he embraces. The animal digs its sweaty brow into his cheek, and they stand in the dark for an hour—like a necking couple. And of all nonsensical things—

I keep thinking about the *horse!* Not the boy: the horse, and what it may be trying to do. I keep seeing that huge head kissing him with its chained mouth. Nudging through the metal some desire absolutely irrelevant to filling its belly or propagating its own kind. What desire could that be? Not to stay a horse any longer? Not to remain reined up for ever in those particular genetic strings? Is it possible, at certain moments we cannot imagine, a horse can add its sufferings together—the nonstop jerks and jabs that are its daily life—and turn them into grief? What use is grief to a horse?

> ALAN *leads* NUGGET *out of the square and they disappear together up the tunnel, the horse's hooves scraping delicately on the wood.* DYSART *rises, and addresses the audience.*

You see, I'm lost. What use, I should be asking, are questions like these to an overworked psychiatrist in a provincial hospital? They're worse than useless: they are, in fact, subversive.

> HE *enters the square. The light grows brighter.*

The thing is, I'm desperate. You see, I'm wearing that horse's head myself. That's the feeling. All reined up in old language and old assumptions, straining to jump clean-hoofed on to a whole new track of being I only suspect is there. I can't see it, because my educated, average head is being held at the wrong angle. I can't jump because the bit forbids it, and my own basic force—my horsepower, if you like—is too little. The only thing I know for sure is this: a horse's head is finally unknowable to me. Yet I handle children's heads—which I must presume to be more complicated, at least in the area of my chief concern. . . . In a way, it has nothing to do with this boy. The doubts have been there for years, piling up steadily in this dreary place. It's only the extremity of this case that's made them active. I know that. The *extremity* is the point! All the same, whatever the reason, they are now, these doubts, not just vaguely worrying—but intolerable . . . I'm sorry. I'm not making much sense. Let me start properly: in order. It began one Monday last month, with Hesther's visit.

Richard III

> *Enter* RICHARD, DUKE OF GLOUCESTER, *solus.*

RICHARD: Now is the winter of our discontent
Made glorious summer by this son of York;
And all the clouds that lowered upon our house
In the deep bosom of the ocean buried.
Now are our brows bound with victorious wreaths,
Our bruised arms hung up for monuments,
Our stern alarums changed to merry meetings,
Our dreadful marches to delightful measures.
Grim-visaged war hath smoothed his wrinkled front,
And now, instead of mounting barbed steeds
To fright the souls of fearful adversaries,
He capers nimbly in a lady's chamber
To the lascivious pleasing of a lute.
But I, that am not shaped for sportive tricks
Nor made to court an amorous looking-glass;
I, that am rudely stamped, and want love's majesty
To strut before a wanton ambling nymph;
I, that am curtailed of this fair proportion,
Cheated of feature by dissembling Nature.
Deformed, unfinished, sent before my time
Into this breathing world, scarce half made up,
And that so lamely and unfashionable
That dogs bark at me as I halt by them—
Why I, in this weak piping time of peace,
Have no delight to pass away the time,
Unless to see my shadow in the sun
And descant on mine own deformity.
And therefore, since I cannot prove a lover
To entertain these fair well-spoken days,
I am determined to prove a villain
And hate the idle pleasures of these days.
Plots have I laid, inductions dangerous,
By drunken prophecies, libels and dreams,
To set my brother Clarence and the king
In deadly hate the one against the other;
And if King Edward be as true and just
As I am subtle, false, and treacherous,
This day should Clarence closely be mewed up
About a prophecy which says that G

Of Edward's heirs the murderer shall be.
Dive, thoughts, down to my soul—here Clarence comes!

In both presentational monologues, an intriguing, articulate and engaging character presents information to the audience. It's information we need to know before the play can progress. Where is the conflict? Where is the action? What is the need to tell?

In *Equus*, Dr. Dysart is engaged in solving a mystery. Why did Alan Strang blind six horses? He needs to find the solution to the mystery. And he needs to understand why his life of the mind feels so emotionally incomplete compared to that of the boy charged with the violent act he has been asked to investigate. Dr. Dysart needs to solve the mystery, but he also needs to make sense of his own life. He is a psychiatrist, and *he needs a listener.*

In *Richard III*, the Duke of Gloucester is about to set in motion the murderous plot that will bring him the crown. He must establish his background—the pains, the slights, the resentment. He must establish his ability—his chameleonlike nature, his strategic thinking, his wit. And, like many men of action, he must have a sounding board for his plans, his "brainstorming." Richard must commit crimes to gain the throne, and *he needs a confidant and coconspirator.*

In each case, the character is either in conflict or is about to enter conflict. In the midst of action, he needs someone to hear his story. The audience fills his need.

In review, then, representational exposition requires a subtle, sometimes coded, but dramatically active approach. Presentational exposition may be more overt in its delivery of information but must play by the same taut dramatic rules to be dramatically effective.

TWO WAYS TO START THE JOURNEY

A play is a journey, both for the characters in the play and for the audience attending it. Kira Obolensky, a talented playwright who's writing a stage adaptation of *Don Quixote* for Trinity Rep, said to me once, "You begin a play on a highway. Either you drop the audience right onto the fast lane, or you bring them down slowly off the entrance ramp." A play can start with a bang and we're off, or it can begin by slower increments. There are good arguments for both methods. Let's title each: We're off! and Slow Immersion.

We're Off!

We live in a caffeinated time. A late twentieth-century theater audience is much more apt to be attuned to the speed and rhythms of popular music, film and electronic entertainment (TV, video, the Internet) than to the slower tempos of the past. For the modern audience, slow and easy may be dull and deadly. The faster the play gets out of the starting gate, the better. There's an immediate rush, a sudden jolt to the senses a play can achieve by starting with a bang. But what can deliver the bang?

It could be an image. An onstage murder. A dance. A rapid entrance. A joke. Anything theatrical that arrests the eye and ear and connects the audience immediately to the action that is taking place and the story that is about to be told. It is always connected both to the back-story of the play (the inciting incident) and the major dramatic question and action of the play (the point of attack).

Look at the opening of *Six Degrees of Separation* by John Guare.

> *A painting revolves slowly high over the stage. The painting is by Kandinsky. He has painted on either side of the canvas in two different styles. One side is geometric and somber. The other side is wild and vivid. The painting stops its revolve and opts for the geometric side. A couple run on stage, in nightdress, very agitated. FLANDERS KITTREDGE is 44. LOUISA KITTREDGE is 43. They are very attractive. They speak to us.*

OUISA: Tell them!

FLAN: I am shaking.

OUISA: You have to do *something*!

FLAN: It's awful.

OUISA: Is anything gone?

FLAN: How can I look? I'm shaking.

OUISA: (*To us*) Did he take anything?

FLAN: Would you concentrate on yourself?

OUISA: I want to know if anything's gone.

FLAN: (*To us*) We came in the room.

OUISA: I went in first. You didn't see what I saw.

FLAN: Calm down.

OUISA: We could have been killed.

FLAN: The silver Victorian inkwell.

OUISA: How can you think of *things*? We could have been murdered.

An ACTOR appears for a moment holding up an ornate Victorian inkwell capped by a silver beaver.

FLAN: There's the inkwell. Silver beaver. Why?

OUISA: Slashed—our throats slashed.

Another ACTOR appears for a moment holding up a framed portrait of a dog, say, a pug.

FLAN: And there's the watercolor. Our dog.

OUISA: Go to bed at night happy and then murdered. Would we have woken up?

FLAN: Now I lay me down to sleep—the most terrifying words—just think of it—

OUISA: I pray the Lord my soul to keep—

FLAN: The nightmare part—if I should die before I wake—

OUISA: If I should die—I pray the Lord my soul to take—

FLAN AND OUISA: Oh.

OUISA: It's awful.

FLAN: We're alive.

FLAN stops, frightened suddenly, listening.

FLAN: Hello?

HE holds HER.

FLAN: Hello!

OUISA: (*Whispers*) You don't call out Hello unless—

FLAN: I think we'd tell if someone else were here.

OUISA: We didn't all night. Oh, it was awful awful awful awful.

THEY pull off their robes and are smartly dressed for dinner.

FLAN: (*To us*) We were having a wonderful evening last night.

OUISA: (*To us*) A friend we hadn't seen for many years came by for dinner.

FLAN: (*Portentously*) A friend from South Africa—

Now look at the opening of Shakespeare's *Hamlet*.

Enter BERNARDO and FRANCISCO, two sentinels.

BERNARDO: Who's there?

FRANCISCO: Nay, answer me. Stand and unfold yourself.

BERNARDO: Long live the king!

FRANCISCO: Bernardo?

BERNARDO: He.

FRANCISCO: You come most carefully upon your hour.

BERNARDO: 'Tis now struck twelve. Get thee to bed, Francisco.

FRANCISCO: For this relief much thanks. 'Tis bitter cold,
    And I am sick at heart.

BERNARDO: Have you had quiet guard?

FRANCISCO: Not a mouse stirring.

BERNARDO: Well, good night.
    If you do meet Horatio and Marcellus,
    The rivals of my watch, bid them make haste.

Enter HORATIO and MARCELLUS.

FRANCISCO: I think I hear them. Stand, ho! Who is there?

HORATIO: Friends to this ground.

MARCELLUS: And liegemen to the Dane.

FRANCISCO: Give you good night.

MARCELLUS: O, farewell, honest soldier.
    Who hath relieved you?

FRANCISCO: Bernardo hath my place.
    Give you good night.

Exit FRANCISCO.

MARCELLUS: Holla, Bernardo!

BERNARDO: Say—
    What, is Horatio there?

HORATIO: A piece of him.

BERNARDO: Welcome, Horatio. Welcome, good Marcellus.

HORATIO: What, has this thing appeared again to-night?

BERNARDO: I have seen nothing.

MARCELLUS: Horatio says 'tis but our fantasy,
    And will not let belief take hold of him
    Touching this dreaded sight twice seen of us.
    Therefore I have entreated him along
    With us to watch the minutes of this night,
    That, if again this apparition come,
    He may approve our eyes and speak to it.

HORATIO: Tush, tush, 'twill not appear.

BERNARDO: Sit down awhile,
  And let us once again assail your ears,
  That are so fortified against our story,
  What we two nights have seen.
HORATIO: Well, sit we down,
  And let us hear Bernardo speak of this.
BERNARDO: Last night of all,
  When yond same star that's westward from the pole
  Had made his course t'illume that part of heaven
  Where now it burns, Marcellus and myself,
  The bell then beating one—

  Enter GHOST.

MARCELLUS: Peace, break thee off. Look where it comes again.
BERNARDO: In the same figure like the king that's dead.
MARCELLUS: Thou art a scholar; speak to it, Horatio.
BERNARDO: Looks 'a not like the king? Mark it, Horatio.
HORATIO: Most like. It harrows me with fear and wonder.
BERNARDO: It would be spoke to.
MARCELLUS: Speak to it, Horatio.
HORATIO: What art thou that usurp'st this time of night
  Together with that fair and warlike form
  In which the majesty of buried Denmark
  Did sometimes march? By heaven I charge thee, speak.
MARCELLUS: It is offended.
BERNARDO: See, it stalks away.
HORATIO: Stay. Speak, speak. I charge thee, speak.

  Exit GHOST.

What is the similarity here? In both plays, we start with a mysterious opening depicted in dialogue of short, staccato sentences. The impression of urgency is communicated to the audience. Something is wrong. A balance has been or is just about to be disturbed. A balance in the kingdom, and a balance in a home.

In *Hamlet*, it is the balance between the known world and the "undiscovered country" of the dead. In *Six Degrees* it is the balance between privileged complacence and the dangers of intrusion. In each play, a world is established. And then there is a change. Something is wrong: a ghost is roaming the battlements of Elsinore castle; the Kittredges have just survived the shock of an intruder.

In the first moments of both plays, the playwright has provided a highly theatrical means of communicating the jumping-off point of his story. In *Hamlet*, we witness this through peripheral, supporting characters (none of the major players has made his first appearance). In *Six Degrees*, the couple at the center of the play begin their own story. And we're off. In these cases, the scenes pave the way for both the revelation of the inciting incident and the point of attack. *Six Degrees* is a perfect example. In this opening moment, we see the results of the evening the Kittredges spent with Paul, the young con man who pretended to be the son of Sidney Poitier (the inciting incident). Following this scene, the Kittredges will decide to find out who Paul really is and embark on their own investigation (point of attack). Guare has found a theatrical and dramatic way to start his plot at the fulcrum of his inciting incident and his point of attack.

But when using the "we're off" approach, the playwright must be mindful of the audience's level of observation and attention. It can be argued that the opening of a play provides ultimate attention for an audience, ultimate focus. But it can also be argued that at this early stage of the proceedings, the audience may not have yet found its bearings, may not yet have readied itself to focus its full attention on the performance. Perhaps an audience member has just sat down moments before the curtain has gone up. Perhaps he's thinking about a fight at home. Perhaps she's thinking about a problem at the office.

In the plays cited above, the playwrights employ a shrewd technique to energize the performance, begin the story, turn on the plot and introduce characters. But the playwrights also do something else. They return to the moment later on—just in case. In the opening of *Hamlet*, we encounter the ghost and are introduced to the mystery of its appearance. Why is it on the battlements? What is its purpose? A dramatic question has been posed, but Shakespeare will pose it again in Act One, Scene Two, and again in Act One, Scene Three, and again and again in Act One, Scene Five. No audience member could possibly miss it. In *Six Degrees*, Guare moves from his dazzling opening to a flashback as the Kittredges tell the story of what happened to them the night before. In twenty-five minutes of playing time, the action will come full circle. The Kittredges will discover the intruder with his "friend," and the opening dialogue will begin again, as if in a "loop." If the audience didn't quite catch the dialogue the first time in the opening, Guare has made sure to bring it back again. That's craft.

The "we're off!" method buys theatrical excitement, but it also requires dramatic insurance. The key point to remember is that the "we're off!" method is designed to provide the background for the major action of the play, the inciting incident, and to lead toward the character's major conflict and pursuit, the point of attack.

Slow Immersion

The alternative to the "we're off!" approach of starting a play on the high-speed lane is the "slow immersion" approach, a way of acclimating the audience to the plot. Imagine a person calmly and deliberately lowering himself into cold water inch by inch, step by step, until his body is fully inured to the new environment. Slow immersion.

This method is employed more often in representational theater and finds its greatest examples in plays written between the end of the nineteenth century and today. This method underlines the audience's need to believe in the world being represented to them. Slow immersion into a play or a scene requires time. But the best examples of this method are never slow moving. Look at Henrik Ibsen's *Hedda Gabler*.

Act One

A large, nicely furnished drawing room. In the rear wall is a wide doorway with curtains drawn back. The doorway leads to another smaller room which in turn communicates with other rooms in the house. A large framed mirror on the upstage wall dominates this smaller room.

In the stage right wall is a doorway leading to the entrance hall.

In the stage left wall is a large window. In the down left corner of the wall is a small door to the outside.

In the down right corner is a white tile, wood-burning stove. The chimney extends out of sight.

Also in the room, a high-backed chair, a cushioned footstool, an oval table, a two-seater sofa, several side chairs.

Up left is a baby grand piano, on which numerous bouquets of roses have been arranged.

It is early morning. Sunlight through the window.

MISS JULIANA TESMAN, about sixty-five, wearing a simple gray suit, wearing a hat and carrying a parasol, enters from the hall.

She is followed by BERTHE, *the Tesmans' maid.* BERTHE *carries yet another bouquet of roses.*

MISS TESMAN: (*Hushed*) I can't believe it. They're still in bed.

BERTHE: (*Also hushed*) I told you, Miss. With the boat getting in so late last night and then the young lady couldn't rest until I'd unpacked every one of the trunks.

MISS TESMAN: Yes, yes. Well, let them sleep in. But goodness knows they'll want some fresh morning air when they finally do emerge.

SHE throws windows wide open.

BERTHE: There's just nowhere left for these poor flowers. Maybe I could just put them here, Miss.

MISS TESMAN: So here you are, Berthe, with a new master now—and a new mistress. God knows it nearly finished me to let you go.

BERTHE: (*Near tears*) Think of *me*, Miss! What do you think it's like for me after all the blessed years I've been with you and Miss Rina?

MISS TESMAN: We must rise above, Berthe. We must rise above. There's nothing else we can do. George *must* have you here with him in this house. He simply *must*. You've looked after him since he was a tiny boy.

BERTHE: Oh, I know, Miss. But I can't help thinking about Miss Rina, lying there, helpless, poor thing. And the new girl! She doesn't know the first thing about looking after someone so sick.

MISS TESMAN: Oh, we'll manage. I suppose I'll have to take most of the burden on myself. But we'll manage, dear Berthe. Don't worry yourself over my poor sister.

BERTHE: There is something else, Miss. I'm frightened that the young lady won't find me to her liking.

MISS TESMAN: Oh, you're being foolish, Berthe. Certainly at the beginning there may be one or two little problems, but—

BERTHE: I have a feeling she'll be very demanding.

MISS TESMAN: Well, of course she will! She's General Gabler's daughter. Just think what her life was like when he was still alive! Remember her out riding with her father, galloping past us in the street? In that long, black dress with a feather in her hat?

BERTHE: Oh, yes, I remember. I couldn't have dreamt then that she'd wind up married to our little scholar.

MISS TESMAN: No, no, neither could I. But Berthe dear, our George is no longer a little scholar. You mustn't call him that. You have to say, "Doctor."

BERTHE: Yes, yes. So the mistress told me last night, as soon as they walked through the door.

What do we learn from this initial "slow immersion" into *Hedda Gabler*? Hedda has not even come onstage yet. Neither has her husband George Tesman, her former lover Eilert Lovborg, the sly Judge Brack, or the naive Mrs. Elvstead. Miss Tesman and Berthe are the smallest roles in the play. But Ibsen is patiently laying his groundwork. His set description tells us a lot: we're in an upper-middle class drawing room at the turn of the century. Lots of flowers suggest a woman's presence and a homecoming. All of the entrances and exits will be used to maximum effect later in the play, as will the furniture, especially that stove. We know that someone has just returned from a trip. We know that the maid used to work for Miss Tesman but now works for the young master of the house. We know that Miss Tesman's sister Rina is dying. We know that "General Gabler's daughter" is spectacular and difficult. From these opening moments we learn:

- the central characters (Hedda—"General Gabler's daughter"—and Dr. George Tesman, her husband)
- the foreshadowing of the central dramatic action (Will Hedda survive this setting?)
- the tone of the play (Serious)
- the style of the play (Naturalism)
- and the design—setting, sound, light, costume—of the play (A realistically depicted drawing room)

The "slow immersion" strategy is different from the "we're off!" method, but the key point to remember is that the "slow immersion" method is also designed to provide the background for the major action of the play, the inciting incident and to lead toward the character's major conflict and pursuit, the point of attack.

Two points of departure. One destination. Quoting Aristotle, "The case is made." And the play has started.

EXERCISES

1. Introduce two characters. In twenty lines of representational exposition, let your audience know that one is a construction worker, the

other a psychiatrist; that the setting is a church; that the two characters are waiting for the same person to enter; that the president of the United States is visiting the city in which the scene takes place. Use code words/ phrases/references to suggest professions, place, offstage characters in a natural manner.

2. Decide when the action of your story starts. Write down the first action of the play. Consider this first action. Is this the point of attack? Or is this action the inciting incident to the point of attack. Or is it a lesser action? The way to tell is this: The most dramatically exciting action is the one that comes at the point of attack.

3. What does your audience need to know in the first few minutes of your play? Write a presentational scene that delivers exposition at the beginning of the play. Put the key exposition in a monologue. Choose a character in your story who has a strong need to tell someone—either the audience or an unseen character—the exposition.

4. Now write the same exposition in representational dialogue. Use code, use conflict.

5. Now try to write the exposition without dialogue. Use stage action without words. Use the set. Use sound and music. Use slides above the stage if need be. Be as economical as possible.

6. Write the first scene of the play in the "we're off!" method. This may lead you toward a presentational mode. Find the dramatic, theatrical moment in the early part of your story that will grab the audience's attention in the first seconds of the play. Will it entice the audience? Will it confuse them? Will it make them lean forward and want to learn more? Will you have to go back and fill in some blanks, a la *Six Degrees of Separation*?

7. Write the first scene of the play in the "slow immersion" method. You'll probably find you employ a representational mode here. What small questions can you pose to hook the audience as you move toward revealing the inciting incident and then pushing toward the point of attack?

8. In *Six Degrees of Separation* John Guare *shows* us the inciting incident—the night Ouisa and Flan spent with Paul "Poitier"—that propels his play forward. For your play, write a scene where you depict the inciting incident onstage. If you were rewriting *Hamlet* you would write the scene of King Hamlet's murder by his brother Claudius.

9. In *Hamlet*, Shakespeare does *not* show us the inciting incident that propels the play forward. It is *told* to Hamlet and the audience by the

ghost. Now write a scene that *reports* on your inciting incident as an event that took place in the past, as Shakespeare does when the ghost tells Hamlet about his murder. If you were rewriting *Six Degrees*, you'd write a scene where Ouisa Kittredge tells someone about the night she and her husband spent with the intruder, Paul.

10. Decide which of the above two methods is more conducive to the story you wish to tell and the plot you wish to structure.

CHAPTER SEVEN

Great Middles

In every play, almost *everything* takes place in the middle. No writer has yet found a way to jump from beginning to end without crossing that pesky territory in between. A play that begins strongly with a terrific point of attack and then suddenly rushes to its climax is a play without a center. The middle takes up 50 to 75 percent of a play. For most full-length plays, that's seventy to one hundred pages. In running time, it's probably sixty to ninety minutes.

Many plays fail because they never get off to a strong beginning. Many plays fail because they have a weak, confusing or predictable ending. But *most* flawed plays fail because nothing much happens in the middle. The characters run out of goals too quickly. They run out of obstacles. They run out of ideas and strategies. Opportunities don't arise.

You might want to look at your play this way:

As a map, with a point of departure and a point of arrival.

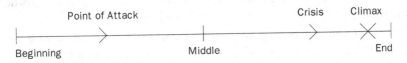

As a football field, with goals and lines along the way.

As an arc, with many arcs within arcs, as Martin Esslin suggests.

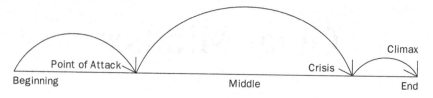

There may be other ways to draw your play, and frankly, you don't have to draw anything. I am convinced, however, that writers need to think in terms of shape and journey, and if there's a way for you to visualize that shape and journey, do it. Use whatever works for you. But you can see from my three diagrams that the middle of your play is the part that covers the largest number of miles; it has the most yardage; it contains the most arcs (and arcs within arcs).

You want to fill the great middle of your play with two primary ingredients: forward-moving action on the part of the main character(s); and complications.

Forward-moving action is fairly easy to grasp. It's any direct or indirect action performed by the main character(s) to achieve the major goal of the play. These actions include murders, robberies, seductions, searches, confessions, lies, kindnesses, cruelties and sacrifices. They are struggles toward the goal(s).

Complications can be found in many actions:

• A sudden entrance that interrupts a character's plan (the maid comes in while a murder is in progress).

• An exit that leaves a character alone and adrift (the wife deserts her husband just before his big client comes to dinner).

• A tempting diversion that pulls a character from her action (the jewel thief can't resist stealing a small ring en route to a much bigger heist).

• A roadblock (a man tries to secure a business deal, but he finds his prey has signed what appears to be an ironclad contract with someone else).

• An opportunity (the one person who knows that the "princess" is an impostor arrives at the party).

• A challenge (a duel is fought just before one of the duelists is to be married).

• A withheld secret (a little boy spies an illicit kiss but doesn't let on that he's seen it).

• A pursuit (a woman is trying to tell a man that she's in love with him, but other suitors keep running after her).

• A revelation (the woman the hero is about to marry is unmasked as his sister).

• A reversal of fortune (a witness the defense lawyer thought would give the accused an alibi incriminates him instead).

As you plan your middle section, think of all the potential complications that could arise. Are they strong enough? Are they believable? Could they really happen, given the rules you've established for your play? If it's a crime drama, think about criminal law and the rules of probability. If it's a children's fantasy, think about childhood beliefs and the rules of magic. Are there too few complications? Too many? Compare your work to the plays we listed earlier.

In *Hamlet*, the big questions are these: Did Claudius kill the king? Will Hamlet prove it? And will he kill Claudius when he does? Hamlet gets his proof at the performance of "The Mousetrap," the play he stages for the court. "The Mousetrap" is rewritten by Hamlet (the detective as playwright!) so that its plot mirrors Claudius' murder of the king. When the murder scene is performed, Claudius becomes upset and has the play stopped. Hamlet knows this incriminates Claudius. Hamlet has his evidence. All he has to do next is kill him. But when he does go to kill Claudius, Hamlet finds him praying; Hamlet fears that if he kills him in the middle of a prayer, Claudius will go to Heaven (roadblock/complication). Hamlet will have to wait a few moments until Claudius is finished. Just then Hamlet is summoned to his mother's bedroom (diversion/complication). He goes to the queen. Unbeknownst to Hamlet, Polonius is hiding behind an arras in order to spy on Hamlet (secret/complication). Hamlet and his mother argue. Polonius calls out from behind his hiding place (surprise/complication). Hamlet, thinking the voice is Claudius', stabs his rapier through the arras. (Remember: An action need not be intentional. Hamlet didn't *mean* to kill Polonius; he thought he was stabbing Claudius. Still his stabbing of Polonius is an action that causes further reactions.) Polonius falls forward, dead (mistake/complication). Claudius and his soldiers come after Hamlet (pursuit/complication).

Remember context. Your complications don't have to involve stabbings and murders. Your complications might involve a neighbor bringing over a bundt cake during an anniversary party. If the neighbor's timing is off (the husband and wife were about to embrace each other), or if the bundt cake shows that the neighbor is too familiar with the husband's taste in desserts (the neighbor and the husband were having an affair), it's a good complication.

You also have to remember where you're going. It's easy to get sidetracked when thinking up obstacles and complications. You may come up with a terrific scene that really puts your hero in the hot seat—so terrific he finds it impossible to get out of it. Or, if he does find a way out, it puts him in a place too far away from the main line of action. Test your ideas. Don't be too hasty. The entire point of your great middle is to reach your great ending. You must pace yourself. Your plot is like a car or a speedboat. Like these vehicles, your plot is always moving forward. But your plot is also the traffic on the highway, the choppy waves in the sea. Your plot is forward motion resisted by opposing forces. That's what makes the great middle full of exciting events and actions.

INTERMISSIONS

A key component in a contemporary full-length play is its intermission. As we noted in chapter five, there are many variations in acts and running times:

Hamlet has five acts in five hours
Hedda Gabler has four acts in three hours
Who's Afraid of Virginia Woolf? has three acts in three hours
Glengarry Glen Ross has a first act that is thirty minutes long, its
    second fifty-five minutes long
Six Degrees of Separation has one ninety-minute act

Some contemporary plays don't have intermissions. There are one-acts from ten to ninety minutes long. Some writers have written plays that require a continuous experience without interruption. Marsha Norman's *'Night, Mother* is written that way. Its power derives, in part, from its concentrated, unbroken action. The character of Jessie has told her mother that she plans to kill herself within the hour; the clock is ticking. But if you decide that your play needs one or more intermissions, plan the intermission for optimum effect. There is one rule to remember about the placement of your intermission: If you've written a play that demands an interval or rest stop for your audience, always place your intermission at a moment in the play when there is maximum expectation, and suspense—a surprise that generates a question, an action that creates a mystery, a cliffhanger. In the three-act plays of the early twentieth century, the first intermission usually came about thirty-five to forty minutes into the play. The second act was forty-five to sixty minutes in length, followed by a second intermission. The third and final act was twenty to thirty minutes long. In a contemporary two-act play, the intermission usually comes fifty to sixty-five minutes into the performance. The second act is usually slightly shorter in length. A good intermission is part of the playwright's strategy. You want the audience to get a little rest, but you also want them to be excited by what they've just seen and eager to find out what happens when the curtain goes up again.

The diagram of a contemporary, two-act, 130-minute play, including its fifteen-minute intermission, might look like this:

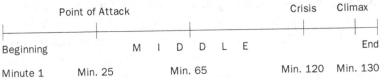

ACTIONS IN THE MIDDLE

Remember the goals and obstacles in the causality link of the story of *The Changeling*, the Jacobean revenge play we discussed in chapter three? Look at those goals and obstacles again.

Goal: Tomazo and Beatrice are in love with each other.

Obstacle: Beatrice is betrothed to Tomazo's brother, Alonzo.

Solution action: Beatrice and Tomazo plot to kill Alonzo.

Further obstacle: Neither can perform the murder without arousing suspicion.

Solution action: Hire DeFlores, Beatrice's servant, to kill brother.

Further obstacle: DeFlores will only commit murder if Beatrice allows him to sleep with her after the killing.

Solution action: Beatrice acquiesces to DeFlores' wish.

Action: DeFlores murders Alonzo.

Payoff: Beatrice allows DeFlores to make love to her.

Complication: After sex with DeFlores, Beatrice falls in love with DeFlores.

In looking at the above list of actions, problems, solutions and obstacles, where would you say the divisions of beginning and middle came? It came at the first solution action: Beatrice and Tomazo plot to kill Alonso. That's the action that starts the plot in motion. That's the point of attack. But there's still more play. In the rest of *The Changeling* there are murders heaped upon murders, more plans, more reversals, discoveries, revelations and surprises. A subplot involving a madhouse is brought into play. In the end Beatrice and DeFlores are both dead. The list above covers only about half of the play's middle actions. Where would you place an intermission in *The Changeling*? I know where I'd place one: after Beatrice sleeps with DeFlores.

THE END OF THE MIDDLE: CRISIS TIME

The *last* action of your middle is vitally important. It is where all the rising action comes to a head. It is the crisis of the play.

Ben Krielkamp—a playwright, actor and director—once talked to me about this crisis point in reference to Edward Albee's *Who's Afraid of Virginia Woolf?* The play is written in three acts with two intermissions. It is the story of George and Martha, a bitter, battling married couple at a small university. The play takes place late in the evening after a faculty party. Martha has invited a new couple, Nick and Honey, back to the house for drinks. As the doorbell rings, George hisses to Martha: "Just don't talk about the *bit*. The little bugger. Our *son*." (Threat/conflict/exposition/foreshadowing.)

As the evening progresses, George and Martha's "party" reveals their marriage, their history, and their deep animosity towards each other. And Martha does indeed talk about their son. George and Martha begin to *use* Nick and Honey as weapons to bludgeon each other. Late in the play, at the end of the second act, Martha takes Nick offstage to have sex with him while George and Honey are left in the living room. We have reached a crisis.

Ben and I were speaking about the end of this scene between George and Honey. Ben said: "There's a point in this scene—and it's the same with every great play—when something happens. And that something, that action, is the result of everything that has happened before it; and everything that happens after is the result of that same action." The crisis is a fulcrum, a point of action on which everything in the play turns. In this case, it's a decision—George's. Here's the scene:

From off-stage comes the sound of MARTHA's *laughter and the crashing of dishes.*

GEORGE: You know what's going on in there, little Miss?

HONEY: I don't want to know anything.

GEORGE: There are a couple of people in there . . . (MARTHA's *laughter again*) . . . they are in there, in the kitchen. . . . Right there, with the onion skins and the coffee grounds . . . sort of . . . sort of a . . . sort of a dry run for the wave of the future.

HONEY: (*Beside herself*) I . . . don't . . . understand . . . you . . .

GEORGE: (*A hideous elation*) It's very simple. . . . When people can't abide things as they are, when they can't abide the present, they do one of two things . . . either they . . . either they turn to a contemplation of the past, as I have done, or they set about to . . . alter the future. And when you want to change something . . . you *Bang! Bang! Bang! Bang!*

HONEY: Stop it! . . . (*Shivering*) I don't want to listen to you . . . I want to know who rang.

GEORGE: Your husband is . . . and you want to know who *rang*?

HONEY: Who rang? Someone rang!

GEORGE: (*His jaw drops open . . . he is whirling with an idea*) . . . Someone . . .

HONEY: *Bang!*

GEORGE: . . . someone . . . rang . . . yes . . . yessss . . .

HONEY: The . . . bells . . . rang . . .

GEORGE: (*His mind racing ahead*) The bells rang . . . and it was someone . . .

HONEY: Somebody . . .

GEORGE: (*He is home, now*) . . . somebody rang . . . it was somebody . . . with . . . *I've got it! I've got it, Martha . . . !* Somebody with a message . . . and the message was . . . our son . . . *our son!* (*Almost whispered*) It was a message . . . the bells rang and it was a message, and it was about . . . our son . . . and the message . . . was . . . and the message was . . . our . . . son . . . is . . . *dead!*

HONEY: (*Almost sick*) Oh . . . no.

GEORGE: I'll tell her myself . . . in good time. I'll tell her myself.

George has made a decision, a decision based on the events of the evening. Martha's use of "the bit, the little bugger, our son" has pushed them over the line. They have reached their crisis. George is determined to destroy Martha when she and Nick are finished having intercourse. Their final confrontation will take place at the ending—in this case in the third act. And in the above scene we see how he plans to do it.

In the end of *Who's Afraid of Virginia Woolf?* George tells Martha that their son is dead. Martha is horrified. But we also discover the truth of his "death." They couldn't have children, so they invented a son they could talk about together, as a kind of solace. But it was a private consolation—a secret fantasy shared between the two of them—and Martha broke the rules by mentioning him to their guests. Hence, George felt justified in ending the game. By announcing their son's death in front of Nick and Honey, George has effectively ended their solace forever. They will have to learn to live without it.

The point I want to stress is that good drama always has a crisis moment that leads to an action much like George's decision. It's an action that brings the middle of your play to a close and paves the way for the final confrontation. In *Hamlet*, it's Claudius' plot with Laertes to challenge Hamlet to a duel. In *The Odd Couple*, it's the fight between Felix and Oscar that sends Felix off into the night and, finally, to the Pigeon sisters. In *'Night, Mother*, it's the moment when Thelma confesses that she wishes Jessie had never told her she was going to commit suicide; she'd rather not have known in advance; after this Jessie shoots herself. Not all these actions are *exactly* alike, but they are similar in their general effect and provocation.

When you're planning your play and you've determined your middle and your ending, ask yourself: Do I have a crisis point, a fulcrum for the end of the middle and the beginning of the end? Can you look at the climax of your play and then find the crisis action late in the middle of the plot that moved the characters in the direction you had determined? Don't be blurry on this point. Audiences *love* crisis moments like these. Moments like George's decision make an audience say these things to themselves:

- What's going to happen when George puts his plan in action?
- How will Martha respond?
- What will we finally learn about "the little bugger" when George "kills" him?
- Who will win the final battle?

• What will the outcome of the conflict tell us about the characters, their world and our own?

Your great middle needs that moment of high expectation. You can feel the excitement in an audience build. You can hear an audience say to itself: "I can't *wait* for *this*!"

A play is a strip tease. The end of the middle is that moment when the stripper's hand hovers above one key piece of clothing. All it takes is a flip of a finger to reveal everything. The playwright's hand is poised and ready.

And then you reach the end.

EXERCISES

1. Pick a play idea you developed in one of the previous chapters. You've already chosen an ending, and you've chosen a beginning. You know your inciting incident. You know your point of attack. Between the point of attack and the climax is the middle of your play. Study the point of attack and the climax. What combination of (a) plausible forward pursuit by the protagonist of her goal, (b) obstacles thrown in the way by antagonists of every kind, (c) coincidences, and (d) opportunities can connect these two points in your play? Write down at least twenty actions performed by your character(s) that could link these two points.

2. Once you've determined this chain of actions, find the crisis point at the end of your middle, the moment at the end of the middle that propels your characters towards their final confrontations. Is it a decision on the part of a character? Is it a challenge? Is it an outside, offstage event? An opportunity? Is it a revelation, a surprise, a reversal? Write it down and add it to the twenty actions. Put yourself in the mind of the audience. You've been watching the play for a long time now. If it's a one-act, you've been watching it for many minutes. If it's full-length, it could be two hours or more. You want the audience to have a sense of expectation prior to the final conflict. What expectations does your crisis raise? If the expectations prompt questions like "What will happen next?" "What will one character do to another?" "How will one character respond?" and "What do these questions and their potential answers mean in terms of the play's themes?" you're on the right track. If not, can you find another crisis that can propel your play toward its conclusion?

3. If you find yourself stranded in the middle of your play, unsure about how to reach the climax you've already determined, try this first: reassess the climax you've chosen. Then look back over the play to earlier decisions you made about action, plot and character. Were there any earlier decisions that now seem to have less potential? Are there some scenes, characters and actions that have potential but seem to push your play in a direction you don't really wish to pursue? Or could those directions lead you to a more interesting and satisfying climax than the one you'd first planned? Revise.

4. Have you left clues for yourself in the earlier parts of the play? Details, lines of dialogue, physical actions—even ones that seem odd or extraneous at first glance—that you can go back to, focus on and use to push the play toward the most, effective, most dramatic and most interesting crisis and climax. If so, use them. Revise again.

CHAPTER EIGHT

Great Endings

The Russian actor, director and teacher Konstantin Stanislavsky once said that the most important part of any play comes in its last five minutes. Stanislavsky guided the four great plays of Anton Chekhov through their premieres at the Moscow Art Theater a hundred years ago. He knew from experience that a well-crafted play moves its audience forward in their seats in expectation of its conclusion, at its end.

Many times, after a successful play ends, you'll hear this uttered by an audience member: "It took a while to get going, but once it did, the show was great." But here's something you *never* hear after a successful play: "The play was great, but the ending was disappointing." Why will an audience forgive a disappointing beginning, but not a disappointing ending? The point, of course, is not to disappoint—*everything* in a play should be terrific. But audiences, even ones that are extraordinarily difficult to please, will often give a playwright time to establish the rules and set up the game. They'll give the show some leeway, but they want to *arrive somewhere* by the time they've reached the play's end. And an ending that does not provide that sense of arrival is not satisfying. That's why we call it a climax. Your job as a playwright is to provide satisfaction.

Don't frustrate your audience at your climax. Frustration is a useful sensation for an audience to experience at strategic points throughout the play, especially when you want to generate suspense. But a sense of frustration at the end of a play, by design or error, is worse than a wasted opportunity. The playwright who accidentally flubs the ending and frustrates the audience's expectations is incompetent. The playwright who *chooses* to frustrate the audience is immature, arrogant and hostile.

Certainly writers may play tricks on audiences and pull the rug out from under expectations (murder mysteries and comedies come to mind), but those tricks must be done with affection, on the level of a favorite uncle playing peek-a-boo and yelling "Fooled you!" to a roomful of delighted nieces and nephews. The trick about trick endings (O. Henry endings) is that the trick should be delightful.

HAPPY VS. SAD ENDINGS

A play can have a happy ending, a sad ending, or an ending that mixes the two. But when crafting your climax, a question I suggest you consider strongly is this: Was there hope for a happy ending? Novelist Erica Jong, in her preface to *Three Eighteenth-Century Novels* once wrote: "The best novelists of all periods . . . usually have in common their ability to suggest the redemptive possibilities of human life. They complete the action as the arc ascends. That it can also *descend*, we surely know. But we *need* (to be reminded) of the possibility of ascension." Jong was writing about novels, but I think her point is just as true for plays. Audiences believe in redemption. They believe in the possibility of goodness asserting itself over evil. They hope for a happy ending. If the playwright has provided no chance for her characters to achieve their goals, suspense is lost—as is the audience's sympathy and interest.

Tom Szentgyorgyi, a director and writer whose play *A Family Man* won the 1994 Jefferson Award for Best New Play, once told me about reading a script which had as its subject matter war, rape and genocide. On the last page of the script, two of the characters were savagely beaten by thugs. The last image Tom read on the page was: "They lie still." Tom put down the play. Pretty bleak stuff. What would an audience take home with it after such an ending? A few weeks later, Tom got a call from a colleague, eager to know Tom's reaction to the script. Tom said the ending had left him with a flat, cold feeling. The colleague was surprised. He had found the ending very moving.

"Moving?" Tom said. "With the two bodies lying 'still'?"

"That's not the ending!" exclaimed his friend.

It turned out Tom had read a copy of the play *with its last page missing*. On that last page were these simple stage directions:

(After a moment, they rise from the ground, helping each other to their feet. They begin to exit the stage, in each other's arms.)

An amazing difference. These few lines of stage directions don't change the fact of the beating. The characters are still badly hurt, but the action of helping each other to their feet and moving offstage together suggests a different world-view entirely, one in which characters make an effort to stand up rather than stay beaten. Ascension and grace.

Hamlet ends with carnage but Hamlet does achieve his goals before his death. In *The Cherry Orchard*, the estate is lost, the orchard is cut down, lovers break apart, and an old servant is inadvertently left alone to die; but love is not lost, the past is not forgotten, and the old man is still trying to serve his masters faithfully as he enters the stage for the last time. In *The Odd Couple*, Felix and Oscar will not live together anymore, but they will preserve their friendship and affection. When Jessie succeeds in killing herself at the end of *'Night, Mother*, her death is painful for the audience, but we have listened to her arguments, we have come to know her, we have come to respect her choice, and she has asserted control over her own life. These are endings that suggest the possibilities of the human spirit, the hope of love, the angels of our better natures. Within the darkness evident in these plays, the glimpse of light is both welcome and necessary.

A SUCCESSFUL ENDING

Glengarry Glen Ross by David Mamet is one of the best American plays of the 1980s. It is a taut, savage, vibrant, visceral, very funny, very frightening and very moving play about salesmen, money, and what it means to be a man in a brutal business world. The real estate salesmen—they're practically con men—of the play try to sell property to unwitting buyers ("suckers"). They also try to "sell" each other. Their motto is "Always Be Closing"—always be in the act of signing the deal. In his deft, efficient thirty-minute first act (three scenes in succession taking place in a Chinese restaurant) Mamet introduces us to four real estate salesmen, each of whom needs the "leads"—the information cards that provide tips to possible buyers. The man who controls the leads is Williamson, the ice-cold office manager. One of the salesmen, Ricky Roma, is on top, but the others—Shelly Levene, Moss and Aaronow—are desperate. Jobs, careers, families depend on their success or failure. They will bribe, cheat or steal to get those leads from the main office. As the act ends, we know that those leads are locked in Williamson's office.

As the second acts opens, we find ourselves in the real estate office. It has been ransacked. The leads have been stolen. Someone broke in the night before. Each of the salesmen is to be interrogated by the police. As the men file into the office, they react to the break-in. The audience suspects one of them to be the culprit. Is it the cocky Ricky Roma? The vicious Moss? The weak-willed Aaronow? The old warhorse Shelly Levene? The main plot of the second act focuses on the investigation, but the important subplot has to do with Ricky Roma's sale the night before of Florida property to a man known as James Lingk.

Into this scene comes Lingk, browbeaten by his wife. He has been told to retrieve the check he signed the night before and cancel the deal with Roma. Roma has to play for time. If he can put off Lingk for a few hours, the check will be cashed, the deal with go through and there's nothing Lingk will be able to do about it. Roma enlists Shelly Levene to help him by having Levene pretend to be a client. Levene's assignment: help get Roma out of the office. Roma and Levene do a marvelous vaudeville turn in this scene; they almost have Lingk bushwhacked when Williamson enters. Williamson misunderstands the situation, inadvertently revealing that Shelly is an employee. He also tells Lingk that he has nothing to worry about, that despite the break-in Lingk's check went to the bank to be cashed. This is the last thing Roma wanted Lingk to hear. Lingk leaves, horrified. Roma and Levene berate Williamson. Roma storms out. Levene continues to mock Williamson. He even tells Williamson that if "you're going to make something up, be sure it will help."

(*Williamson blinks.*) "How do you know I made it up?"

Crisis! Williamson smells blood. How did Levene know the check *hadn't* been cashed. It was on Williamson's desk the night before. The desk is in the office where the leads were. The only way Levene could have seen that uncashed check was if Levene was in the office the night before—when the leads were stolen.

The tables have been turned.

Conflict one: In the first act, Williamson had the upper hand, as Levene begged him in the Chinese restaurant to give him some leads.

Conflict two: In the second act, Levene had the upper hand, when, unbeknownst to Williamson, he had the leads and had just made a sale.

Conflict three: At the climax, following Shelly's foolish slip of the tongue, Williamson has information that will destroy Levene. Levene begs Williamson not to turn him in, but it's no use. Levene is sent into the inner office where the police wait. He is doomed.

There are a few lines after Shelly leaves the stage: Roma comes back and talks to Aaronow; Roma goes to lunch; Aaronow stares at the ruined office. A few lines. A few seconds. And the play is over.

Where was the climax of the play? What happened in this climax? Read the play. Focus on the last ten to fifteen pages. And look at everything Mamet is doing in this ending. You'll see that the climax came when two combatants waged one final war: one won, one lost. The climax came when Williamson destroyed Levene.

What's fascinating to note is that the climax is also identifiable by its activation of all six Aristotelian elements:

Character—We've seen what Shelly Levene wanted. We've witnessed what Moss, Aaronow, Roma, Lingk and Williamson wanted. We've seen them act throughout the play to get what they wanted. We've seen them threaten, bargain, negotiate. The characters define themselves constantly, by what they *speak* of doing and what they *actually* do. They are always "closing." In the end, they are revealed in their most pressurized state. The ending of any successful play shows its characters under the maximum challenge, in their greatest clash. In the last scene of *Glengarry Glen Ross*, we see Levene in his glory and in his depths, all within seconds. Character is displayed through actions.

Action—When Levene is full of himself he tells Williamson off. The speech he gives to Williamson is full of fire, anger, humor, scorn and triumph. It is hubris (remember the tragic flaws of classical heroes?). And in his hubris, Levene is incautious. He mentions the uncashed check. He has incriminated himself. His action prompts ideas.

Ideas—The play is about selling. Selling property, selling the image of yourself, selling your soul. It is also about business in America and what it means to be a man in this world. We see the self-assured sheen of success (Roma), the frustration and resentment that fuels hatred (Moss), the withering effects of failure (Aaronow), the coldness of the new corporate mentality (Williamson), and the desperation that drives a once proud and confident man to his own destruction (Levene). We also see a man far outside this world, Lingk, the quiet man who, in tears just before the climax, admits to Roma, "I can't negotiate"—which is the ultimate confession of failure in this world. Says Roma to

Williamson, in one of the play's funniest moments: "Whoever told you you could work with *men*?" At the climax, we are even introduced to one more character—Baylen, the detective who's come to investigate the case. Baylen's presence, his few lines, his tough persona, remind us of the grim authority that exists in this dog-eat-dog world. Baylen represents the ultimate penalty these men may pay. When the detective says to Levene, "Mr. Levene, I think we have to talk," we know Levene, whose very life has depended on "talk," won't be able to talk his way out of this one. The idea is in the action embodied by the language.

Language—Mamet is a genius at dramatic dialogue. At first glance, his words suggest a hyperrealistic depiction of the way people talk. But repeated exposure to Mamet plays reveals a consciously poetic quality to his linguistic stops and starts, his ellipses, his scatological epithets. The language of a Mamet play is as recognizable and identifiable as Shakespearean blank verse. At its best, at its most dramatic and most theatrical, Mamet's language is completely in tune with his characters, the actions they perform, and the ideas behind the actions. In Mamet, words are always actions. And so, in this climactic scene, we experience this kind of dialogue indicative of character, actions and ideas:

ROMA: "Whoever told you you could work with *men*?"
WILLIAMSON: "I want to tell you something, Shelly. You have a big mouth."
LINGK: "I can't negotiate." "I don't have the power." "Forgive me."
BAYLEN: "Get in the room!"
LEVENE: "John, my *daughter* . . ."

This last line is my favorite in the play. Out of context, it could mean anything. It is spoken by Levene twice, once in the first act when he's at the Chinese restaurant with Williamson trying to get him to give him leads. Levene begins to say: "My *daughter* . . .", and Williamson cuts him off. The line returns at the climax just as Levene has suffered his defeat at the hands of Williamson. Williamson opens the inner door to tell Baylen that Levene is the thief. Levene tries to stop him. He blurts out: "John . . . my *daughter* . . ." Williamson cuts him off, saying "Fuck you." Williamson goes into the office, shutting the door behind him.

In this context, "my *daughter* . . ." takes on many forms. Greatly important is the ellipsis, the three dots. The sentence could have continued but for Williamson's dismissal. How would that sentence have ended?

"My *daughter* needs a heart transplant."
"My *daughter* is pregnant."
"My *daughter* is in debt."
"My *daughter* is (fill in the blank)."

Whatever "my daughter" is, it isn't good. Something bad is connected to this "my daughter . . ." And Levene's willingness to use his daughter's dire straits shows his desperation. "My *daughter . . .*" is a plea and a weapon. It means "Don't hurt me. Help me. Other lives depend on what you are about to do to me." And it does not succeed. We don't need to know specifically what the dire straits are connected to Levene's daughter. It is a tantalizing mystery. All we need to know and all Mamet wisely needs to tell us can be found in those two words. It is one of the most efficient, effective uses of language in the contemporary theater.

The language at the climax of *Glengarry Glen Ross* is a complete and organic outgrowth of its characters, actions and ideas. And in its rhythms, its staccato outbursts, it is very much a kind of music.

Music—*Glengarry Glen Ross* is a very spare masterpiece. There isn't a wasted syllable in the text, and there isn't much room for adornment throughout the play. But in the realm of music, the dialogue sings. And at its climax, especially in the raging arias Roma and Levene direct at Williamson, the full throttle force of speech takes on an operatic flourish. Men's voices raised in bluster and rage and power have that kind of force and volume. There's another sound however that has a repeated impact in the play, a sound not connected to speech. Remember the real estate office's inner office? There's a door to that office, and when it shuts behind one of the men, there is a firm, recognizable clank as the interrogation begins. When it shuts for the last time behind Shelly Levene, we know that sound—a sound heard in countless offices every day—is the closing of Shelly's life.

The music of this moment is inexorably linked to the sixth part of Aristotle: spectacle.

Spectacle—This is a world of men. Men in expensive suits, men in shabby suits; men surrounded by the blood-red dragons of a Chinese restaurant; men surrounded by the dull gray of an office. And, at the end, as we hear the sound of a door shut, we see a man—suddenly old—enter a room from which, figuratively, he will never return. At the end of *Glengarry Glen Ross*, we see Shelly leave the room and leave the stage for the last time. It is as if we are watching a man going to the scaffolds to be hanged, a man walking the last mile. The door shuts, and Levene is no longer part of the world he has so fully inhabited all his life. He is gone. He is in the inner office. And he will never come back.

CRAFTING YOUR ENDING

I spend time on *Glengarry Glen Ross* because Mamet realizes that for maximum effect, the climax of the play should activate all six of Aristotle's elements. By doing so, the shrewd playwright captures all of the senses in one concentrated period of stage time, hence making the climax memorable and full of dramatic impact. Some playwrights weave the elements without planning them. If you're the kind of playwright for whom these instincts come naturally, bless yourself and pass some of it around. If you are not, I think it's good strategy to do the following:

Write the words character, action, ideas, language, music and spectacle on separate cards. Now plant the cards around your desk or wherever you do your writing. If you're inclined toward sculpture, maybe you can even construct a mobile with these cards, a constellation of Aristotelian theory floating around your work. It is vitally important to keep the elements in mind when crafting your climax.

Remember that the great ending of your play is an action you decided on long before you actually started writing. Your climax, the resolution of your play's conflict, was decided prior to your typing the first stage direction. As we've seen with the above-mentioned examples, your ending can be frightening, shocking, disturbing, ambiguous—and satisfying. It is here that we must remember one of Aristotle's primary rules: The ending must be both surprising and inevitable.

In *Hamlet*, it is inevitable that there is death, even for the hero, but the surprises (Gertrude drinks the poison, Laertes confesses and implicates Claudius, Hamlet stabs Claudius before his own death) are truly unexpected.

In *The Cherry Orchard*, the estate seemed doomed from the beginning, regardless of the attempts to save it. But the inability of Lopahkin to propose to Varya and the incredible sight of Firs the butler roaming about the empty house after it has been locked are heartbreaking surprises.

In *The Odd Couple*, it makes perfect sense that Felix and Oscar cannot live together. We could see their "divorce" coming. But when Felix was missing, who could have guessed he'd gone to live upstairs with the Pigeon sisters? And who could have guessed Oscar would start to become neat at the play's end?

Your ending must delight us by its very unexpectedness ("Surprise!"), but it must make sense ("Of *course!*").

Here's a tip. When you're devising your ending, think of what the actors get to do. A play that attracts actors because of the juicy roles they'll play and the kinds of actions they get to perform is probably a play that is functioning very well on a number of dramatic and theatrical levels. If an actor reads your script and says, "Well, there's not much for me to *do* here," you've got a problem. What many actors first look for in a play is how their characters end up. You can watch them skip through a text looking for their last lines and actions. They want to know what happens to them. What do they *do* at the end? The climax of the play should provide the opportunity every actor hungers for—a duel, a death scene, a great speech—a chance to shine, to shock, to be a marvelous hero or a splendid villain.

And while your ending is surprising and inevitable, it must also achieve other specific goals. It must:

- answer the central dramatic questions;
- answer any minor dramatic questions (but not at the expense of blurring the major ones);
- provide a major action for the central character(s) to perform;
- resolve the conflict;
- underline the ideas of the play.

Some minor dramatic questions may remain at the end of a play. There is room for ambiguity, but never confusion. An ambiguous ending is one that poses a minor question that has specific, possible and articulated answers, even though the writer doesn't provide the answer at the end.

Finally, the Great End of your play will be most successful if it grows organically from the Great Beginning and the Great Middle. If, however, you are stumped by your ending, go back again to the work you've done on the earlier parts of the play. The chances are the flaw lies there.

When planning your ending, track the actions from the beginning. Remember the importance of the verbs. Emphasize the notion of character. What *would* your characters do? What *could* your characters do? Brainstorm; there may be dozens of actions your characters could perform. Don't settle for the first climax that comes to mind. Choose the climax that best underlines the ideas of the play. Choose the climax that best exhibits your characters under pressure. Choose the climax that is both inevitable and contains elements of surprise. Make sure the climax activates all six of Aristotle's elements. And do not write a word of your play until you know how it ends.

EXERCISES

1. Either from real life or from your imagination, identify a dramatic premise. "A stable boy blinded six horses" from *Equus* is this sort of premise. Now determine two key characters in the story suggested by the premise. Determine the primary nature of their conflict. Now decide on the climax of this conflict and the resolution that follows it. Who wins? Who loses? What is the resolution? What is the world of the play following the climax?

2. What elements can you employ to depict this climax onstage? List them.

3. What is the meaning derived from this climax? Write it down.

4. What are the last ten lines of dialogue? Write them.

5. What is the last stage image? Write it down.

6. Ascension Endings. The ending of Martin Sherman's *Bent* is an example of a climax that ends sadly but with ascension. This 1978 British play established Ian McKellan as a major actor on the English stage. In it, he played a homosexual in Nazi Germany who is interred in a concentration camp with other "undesirables." At the play's end, a fellow prisoner is shot dead by guards inside the barbed wire. McKellan's character, against all odds, moves to the fence himself, where he too is killed. Another grim ending? No. Because McKellan's character found courage in the end and made his attempt at escape. He failed, but he made the gesture of ascension, and in that gesture there is grace. While we mourn the character's death, it is his grace that stays with us.

Write a climax that combines a positive final action on the part of your protagonist with a failure of the protagonist to achieve his goal.

CHAPTER NINE

Dialogue

The award-winning playwright August Wilson has often said that he doesn't so much *write* his characters as *listen* to them. The art of dialogue writing lies in the way dramatists listen both to the outside world and to our inner voices and the means by which our listening is transformed into character, action and meaning. We've already discussed dialogue as exposition and dialogue as action. Any playwright will tell you it's difficult to teach the *talent* of dialogue writing; you either have an "ear" for dialogue, or you don't. But even a talented dialogue writer can learn a few tricks that may enliven the words on the page.

PAYING ATTENTION TO REAL LIFE

When dramatists write dialogue, they often worry about "getting the diction right." Diction, in this case, means the manner in which a character speaks. It means making a realistic character sound the way she would in real life: cab drivers talking like cab drivers; state department officials talking like state department officials. Different people use different code words and turns of phrase. Diction has to do with education, class, region, age and other character variables. For example, a seventy-year-old Boston-born attorney who graduated from Harvard would probably not say "pants." He'd say "trousers." A Pittsburgh mobster wouldn't say, "Do you want me to hit you?" He'd say, "Ya' want hit?" A young lady in Victorian England would never say, "I've dated weirder guys than you"—unless the lady were in a wacky comedy. In writing specific diction for your characters, you should avoid linguistic anachronisms at all costs, the exception being when the anachronism intentionally calls attention to itself for the sake of comedy. Inconsistencies and anachronisms are sloppy errors that take the audience out of the play, making them wonder why the playwright goofed.

As an example of inconsistent diction, let's look at David Mamet's *Oleanna*. Some critics argue that the character of Carol, the inarticulate student depicted in the first act of the play could never speak in the smooth, articulate manner she does in the second act.

The First Act Carol: "I failed. Flunk me out of it. It's garbage. Everything I do. 'The ideas contained in this work express the author's feelings.' That's right. That's right. I know I'm stupid. I know what I am."

Now look at the Second Act Carol: "You call education 'hazing,' and from your protected, so-elitist seat you hold our confusion as a *joke*, and our hopes and efforts with it. Then you sit there and say, 'What have I done?' And ask me to understand that *you* have aspirations too . . . if you possess one ounce of that inner honesty you describe in your book, you can look in yourself and see those things that I see. And you can find revulsion equal to my own. Good day."

As for anachronisms, we can turn to Kathleen Winsor's popular romance *Forever Amber*, set in seventeenth-century England and containing—as *New Yorker* critic Anthony Lane has pointed out—such twentieth-century slang phrases as "Thanks a million" and "Hey, just a minute."

A writer has to choose the right dialogue. Try this exercise: Go to a party and tape some of the conversations. You'll pick up speech rhythms, colorful phrases, regional accents, and the stop-and-start pattern of real-life talk. You'll also realize that, for our purposes, a lot of that real-life talk is useless. Remember Hitchcock's definition of drama—life with the dull bits cut out? Good dialogue is talk with the dull bits cut out. Look at the transcripts of a trial, or—better—read the published transcripts of the Nixon White House tapes. The Nixon-Watergate transcripts are wonderful examples of real-life speech recorded while most of the participants were unaware of the taping system's existence. Here's a June 1972 exchange between President Richard Nixon, his chief of staff H.R. Haldeman, and White House attorney John Dean.

NIXON: Hi, how are you? You had quite a day today didn't you. You got Watergate on the way didn't you?
DEAN: We tried.

HALDEMAN: How did it all end up?

DEAN: Ah, I think we can say well at this point. The press is playing it just as we expect.

HALDEMAN: Whitewash?

DEAN: No, not yet—the story right now—

NIXON: It is a big story.

HALDEMAN: Five indicted plus the WH former guy and all that.

DEAN: Plus two White House fellows.

HALDEMAN: That is good that takes the edge off whitewash really that was the thing Mitchell kept saying that to people in the country Liddy and Hunt were big men. Maybe that is good.

Nixon was asking John Dean if he was keeping a lid on the Watergate break-in scandal without giving the press the appearance that the White House was trying to cover-up—or "whitewash"—its involvement. The "WH former guy" is E. Howard Hunt, who worked in the White House and for the CIA. The "two White House fellows" are Hunt and G. Gordon Liddy. Haldeman's last speech refers to his hope that the investigation will go no further than Liddy and Hunt. Nixon campaign chairman John Mitchell had told lots of people that Hunt and Liddy were key operatives in the campaign structure, so Haldeman thinks most observers will assume the buck stops with them.

What parts of this real-life dialogue would be valuable to a dramatist?

- The immediate action ("You got Watergate on the way, didn't you?")
- The exposition ("Five indicted plus the WH former guy and all that . . . that takes the edge off whitewash.")
- The peculiar and authentic-sounding code words ("the WH former guy.")
- The interruptions ("—the story right now—" "It is a big story.")
- The sense of rushed, real-life fractured grammar and syntax ("That is good that takes the edge off whitewash really that was the thing Mitchell kept saying that to people in the country Liddy and Hunt were big men.")

But not all of this raw material is dramatically useful. Some of it is fat. Some of it is confusing. What "dull bits" would you cut out to make the scene sharper? What would you add to make the scene clearer? I'll bold-face my deletions and italicize my additions to the scene:

NIXON: **Hi, how are you?** You had quite a day today didn't you. You got Watergate on the way **didn't you?**

DEAN: We tried.

HALDEMAN: How did it all end up?

DEAN: **Ah,** I think we can say *it went* well **at this point.** The press is playing it just as we expect*ed.*

HALDEMAN: *Does the press think we're trying* to Whitewash *it?*

DEAN: No, not yet—the story **right now—**

NIXON: It'**is** a big story.

HALDEMAN: Five indicted plus the WH former guy **and all that.**

DEAN: **Plus** *T*wo White House *guys.*

HALDEMAN:That'**is** good. *Admitting that two of them were connected to the White House* takes the edge off *any accusation of a* whitewash. **really that was the thing** Mitchell kept saying that **to people in the country** Liddy and Hunt were *the* big men. **Maybe** *the investigation will stop with them.*

Let's look at the final version of rewritten reality.

NIXON: You had quite a day today didn't you. You got Watergate on the way?

DEAN: We tried.

HALDEMAN: How did it all end up?

DEAN: I think we can say it went well. The press is playing it just as we expected.

HALDEMAN: Does the press think we're trying to Whitewash it?

DEAN: No, not yet—the story—

NIXON: It's a big story.

HALDEMAN: Five indicted plus the WH former guy.

DEAN: *T*wo White House guys.

HALDEMAN: That's good. Admitting that two of them were connected to the White House takes the edge off any accusation of a whitewash. Mitchell kept saying that Liddy and Hunt were the big men. Maybe the investigation will stop with them.

Selected reality. The truth is there. The clarity and shaping is imposed. It's the same with fictional dialogue. It's the old question of what to keep and what to throw away. Jon Jory, the artistic director of Actors Theatre of Louisville, once said in an article in *The New York Times* that he knew Marsha Norman would be a successful playwright because she "knew how to rewrite." Cutting, shaping and clarifying dialogue is the largest part of rewriting. As you rewrite, draft after draft, you'll be amazed how much you find to change in your play. There's always more to cut, always more lines to be improved. According to the late critic Kenneth Tynan in a *New Yorker* profile, Tom Stoppard once read to a group of students twenty-four different versions of an invective spat out by Tristan Tzara to James Joyce in his literary-political comedy *Travesties*. The first version was "You blarney-arsed bog-eating Irish pig." The last was "By God, you supercilious streak of Irish puke!" Commented Stoppard, deadpan: "All this takes *weeks*." Getting it right takes time. And, as many writers have said, plays are not so much written as rewritten.

STYLIZATION

Stylization in dialogue is hard to define, but a true, original, effective style is always recognizable. Look at the language found in the plays of Oscar Wilde, Harold Pinter and Sam Shepard. An epigram like this one spoken by Lady Bracknell in Wilde's high-comic masterpiece *The Importance of Being Earnest*: "To lose one parent may be regarded as a misfortune . . . to lose both seems like carelessness" is identified by its perfect balance, its symmetrical rhythm, its precise repetition of the words "to lose," and the solemn silliness of its surprising punch line "seems like carelessness."

Look at a speech like this one from Harold Pinter's *Old Times*:

DEELEY: You sat on a very low sofa, I sat opposite and looked up your skirt. Your black stockings were very black because your thighs were so white. . . . I simply sat sipping my light ale and gazed . . . gazed up your skirt. You didn't object, you found my gaze perfectly accept-able. . . . There was a great argument going on about China or something, or death, or China *and* death, I can't remember which, but nobody but I had a thigh-kissing view, nobody but you had the thighs which kissed. And here you are. Same woman. Same thighs.

It's pure Pinter. Suggestive. Spooky. Full of menace and sexuality. It's also reminiscent of three of Pinter's great influences—the witty English drawing-room dialogue of Noel Coward, the absurdist flourishes of Samuel Beckett, and the speech rhythms of London's Jewish East End, where Pinter grew up in the 1940s.

The roiling, southwestern tang of a Sam Shepard aria from *The Tooth of Crime*, a futuristic tale of two desperado rock stars, is redolent not only of the mythical, violence-prone loners he often depicts but also of the rock lyrics that permeated his experience of living with the song-writer and poet Patti Smith: "Beat it! I'm too old-fashioned. That's it. Gotta kick out the scruples. Go against the code. That's what they used to do. The big ones. Dylan, Jagger, Townsend. All them cats broke codes. Times can't change that. . . . They were killers in their day. . . . Cold killers."

You can't *choose* a dialogue style, like those of Wilde, Pinter, Shepard, Tennessee Williams, David Mamet or Christopher Durang. That comes with you, or it doesn't come at all. But you *can* refine it and mine it for all its dramatic and theatrical potential. The danger comes when a playwright imitates another writer's language. A writer *can* borrow a plotline or a story. The British playwright Alan Ayckbourn, in his play *The Revenger's Comedy*, which concerns a man and woman who meet on a bridge while attempting suicide but instead decide to murder their tormentors, combines the plot of Murray Schisgal's *Luv*, in which a man and woman meet on a bridge while attempting suicide, with Alfred Hitchcock's *Strangers on a Train*, in which two men plot to murder their tormentors by trading victims. A writer can borrow an idea, he can even develop a language that is a hybrid of other writers; but a writer who slavishly impersonates another author's style is always a pale thief. Just as dangerous: a writer who starts with a recognizable style and then turns that style into a crutch. Tennessee Williams wrote some of the greatest dramatic language in the American theater. He wrote great stage poetry, evoking the hothouse passions, shattered psyches and honeyed tones of a baroque, dreamscape South. But the plays he wrote in the last fifteen years of life—when he was plagued by doubts and addictions—were parodies of that style—overblown and unintentionally funny. It can happen to the best writers. An original style is often millimeters away from going over-the-top. The finest stylists— Pinter, Mamet, Shepard among them—have often had to reign themselves in after becoming a bit too indulgent in one play or another.

DIALOGUE AS TEXT

George Bernard Shaw and Tom Stoppard are masters of "writing on the line." Writing on the line means that the characters *say* what they *mean*. There are exceptions, of course (see *Pygmalion*), but by and large when Shaw's Henry Higgins speaks, we know he means what he says, nothing more, nothing less (and with Shaw, there's seldom any less). When Stoppard's characters, such as Henry in *The Real Thing* or George in *Jumpers* or Lenin in *Travesties*, speak, they are speaking their minds—clearly—without filters. Other writers who do this "on the line" writing might include the British writers David Hare, Howard Brenton and Caryl Churchill, as well as Tony Kushner, author of *Angels in America*. What kind of plays do they—and Shaw and Stoppard—often write? *Political* plays. Writing on the line is direct and clear, and political plays usually attempt to clarify complicated ideas and issues. That doesn't mean a writer can't approach politics or other complicated subjects like religion or philosophy from the avenue of metaphor. Tom Stoppard often writes very direct, elegant speeches about various subjects and ideas, but look at this example of metaphor from his Tony-winning play *The Real Thing*. Henry is talking to his wife about writing and the power of words. He holds a cricket bat in his hand.

HENRY: This thing here, which looks like a wooden club, is actually several pieces of particular wood cunningly put together in a certain way so that the whole thing is sprung, like a dance floor. It's for hitting cricket balls with. If you get it right, the cricket ball will travel two hundred yards in four seconds, and all you've done is give it a knock like knocking off the top of a bottle of stout, and it makes a noise like a trout taking fly . . . (*He clucks his tongue to make the noise*) What we're trying to do is write cricket bats, so that when we throw up an idea and give it a little knock, it might . . . *travel* . . .

It's a metaphor, but it's written on the line. You can deliver ideas and information in overt sentences ("One should write well"), or you can say it with metaphor ("We're trying to write cricket bats"), but writing on the line means that the language used is a *direct, conscious attempt* by the characters to communicate what they're thinking. Below is the term we use for *un*conscious or *in*direct communication.

DIALOGUE AS SUBTEXT

Actors know what the term "subtext" refers to in performing dramatic scenes. Its strict definition is this: (1) the complex of feelings and motives underlying the actual words and actions of the character being portrayed, (2) an underlying meaning or theme. Subtext means, for example, trying to find ways of saying "I love you" without having the words "I love you" at your disposal. The "I love you" is *under* the text—*below* the line.

Playwrights have to develop their subtext muscles. As we've discussed before, dramatic action is as much about what doesn't happen as what does. The trick to writing dialogue that underscores a romantic subtext has little to do with alternative words or codes for "I love you." You don't have to write "I adore you," or "Hey, babe: '*eight letters*,' know-what-I-mean?" ("I love you" has eight letters). The trick is being able to write, "Pass the salt, please" or "Nice dress" or "When do you want me to be there?" and still be certain that the audience knows it means "I love you." In Shaw's *Pygmalion*, to take a famous example, we know that Henry Higgins is in love with Eliza Doolittle when he says he has "grown accustomed to (her) face."

Again, it's a question of context. In a play about infidelity, the audience takes its knowledge of the information it has received and applies it to the action they are watching.

Here's an example from Harold Pinter's *Betrayal*. Emma, under duress, has confessed her affair with Jerry to her husband Robert. No one has yet told Jerry that Robert knows. Robert, a publisher, and Jerry, a literary agent, are best friends. Jerry doesn't suspect a thing. They meet for lunch.

ROBERT: Emma read that novel of that chum of yours—what's his name? . . . Spinks.

JERRY: Oh Spinks. Yes. The one you didn't like.

ROBERT: The one I wouldn't publish.

JERRY: . . . Did Emma like it?

ROBERT: She seemed to be madly in love with it.

JERRY: Good.

ROBERT: You like it yourself do you?

JERRY: I do.

ROBERT: And it's successful?

JERRY: It is.

ROBERT: Tell me, do you think that makes me a publisher of unique critical judgement or a foolish publisher?

JERRY: A foolish publisher.

ROBERT: I agree with you. I am a very foolish publisher.

JERRY: No you're not. What are you talking about? You're a good publisher. What are you talking about?

ROBERT: I'm a bad publisher because I hate books. Or to be more precise, prose. Or to be even more precise, modern prose, I mean modern novels, first novels and second novels, all that promise and sensibility it falls upon me to judge, to put the firm's money on, and then to push for the third novel, see it done, see the dust jacket done, see the dinner for the national literary editors done, see the signing in Hatchards done, see the lucky author cook himself to death, all in the name of literature. You know what you and Emma have in common? You love literature. I mean you love modern prose literature, I mean you love the new novel by the new Casey or Spinks. It gives you both a thrill.

JERRY: You must be pissed.

ROBERT: Really? You don't think it gives Emma a thrill?

JERRY: How do I know? She's your wife. (*Pause*)

ROBERT: Yes. Yes. You're quite right. I shouldn't have to consult you. I shouldn't have to consult anyone.

The genius of this dialogue lies not in the speeches themselves, but in what Pinter has dramatized *before* the scene takes place. If we didn't know before this scene that Robert was aware of Jerry and Emma's affair, this exchange would appear to be a business-and-art discussion, a sad rumination on the state of publishing and fiction in 1970s Britain. But knowing what we know, the scene becomes electric with subtext, that subtext being: "You have betrayed me, best friend. You have broken my heart. I could kill you."

In other words, subtext in dialogue is transmitted to an audience more by the arrangement of actions than it is by code words and euphemisms.

Subtext is often found in two areas: understatedness and inarticulateness. The British are masters of the former (see that *Betrayal* scene), Americans of the latter.

Look at this example from *Private Lives* by the great British playwright Noel Coward. Elyot and Amanda have been married and divorced. In the first, famous scene of the play they meet on the joined terrace of a hotel in France. They have just remarried other people that very day. They are shocked to find each other so near. They try to act like nothing much has happened and they are not affected.

AMANDA: What have you been doing lately? During these last years?

ELYOT: Travelling about. I went round the world you know after—

AMANDA: (*Hurriedly*) Yes, yes, I know. How was it?

ELYOT: The world?

AMANDA: Yes.

ELYOT: Oh, highly enjoyable.

AMANDA: China must be very interesting.

ELYOT: Very big, China.

AMANDA: And Japan—

ELYOT: Very small.

AMANDA: Do they eat sharks' fins, and take your shoes off, and use chopsticks and everything?

ELYOT: Practically everything.

AMANDA: And India, the burning Ghars, or Ghats, or whatever they are, and the Taj Mahal. How was the Taj Mahal?

ELYOT: (*Looking at her*) Unbelievable, a sort of dream.

AMANDA: That was the moonlight, I expect; you must have seen it in the moonlight.

ELYOT: (*Never taking his eyes off her face*) Yes, moonlight is cruelly deceptive.

AMANDA: And it didn't look like a biscuit box did it? I've always felt that it might.

ELYOT: (*Quietly*) Darling, darling, I love you so.

The last line puts the subtext right back on top again. Coward's characters are wildly articulate people. They have no trouble saying what they mean and saying it beautifully with style, wit and grace. But knowing what we know—that Elyot and Amanda have been married, that they are together again on this terrace, and, *important*, that they do not leave to retrieve their new spouses immediately—we understand the subtext of this wonderful exchange fully and completely: "I love you and you love me and we are still wildly attracted to each other despite this pathetic attempt to behave as if we were actually interested in discussing world travel."

Let's look at an inarticulate American couple. Doc and Lola are the central characters of William Inge's dark drama *Come Back, Little Sheba*. But this time I'm not going to tell you what came before this exchange, the last scene of the play.

> LOLA *puts away the supplies in the icebox. Then* DOC *comes in the front door, carrying the little suitcase she previously packed for him. His quiet manner and his serious demeanor are the same as*

before. LOLA is shocked by his sudden appearance. She jumps and can't help showing her fright.

LOLA: Docky!

Without thinking, she assumes an attitude of fear. DOC observes this and it obviously pains him.

DOC: Good morning, honey.

Pause.

LOLA: (*On platform*) Are . . . are you all right, Doc?

DOC: Yes, I'm all right. (*An awkward pause. Then DOC tries to reassure her*) Honest, I'm all right, honey. Please don't stand there like that . . . like I was gonna . . . gonna . . .

LOLA: (*Tries to relax*) I'm sorry, Doc.

DOC: How you been?

LOLA: Oh, I been all right, Doc. Fine.

DOC: Any news?

LOLA: I told you about Marie—over the phone.

DOC: Yah.

LOLA: He was a very nice boy, Doc. Very nice.

DOC: That's good. I hope they'll be happy.

LOLA: (*Trying to sound bright*) She said . . . maybe she'd come back and visit us some time. That's what she *said.*

DOC: (*Pause*) It . . . it's good to be home.

LOLA: Is it, Daddy?

DOC: Yah. (*Beginning to choke up, just a little*)

LOLA: Did everything go all right . . . I mean . . . did they treat you well and . . .

DOC: (*Now loses control of his feelings. Tears in his eyes, he all but lunges at her, gripping her arms, drilling his head into her bosom*) Honey, don't ever leave me. *Please* don't ever leave me. If you do, they'd have to keep me down at that place all the time. I don't know what I said to you or what I did, I can't remember hardly anything. But please forgive me . . . please . . . please . . . And I'll try to make everything up.

LOLA: (*There is surprise on her face and new contentment. She becomes almost angelic in demeanor. Tenderly she places a soft hand on his head*) Daddy! Why, of course I'll never leave you. (*A smile of satisfaction*) You're all I've got. You're all I ever had.

It's a reconciliation scene to be sure. A homecoming. But if you know the play you know that Doc is an alcoholic. You also know that he married Lola twenty years before when he got her pregnant. She lost the baby and couldn't have other children. Their hasty marriage crippled their early promise. There is no passion or romance in their lives. The "Marie" referred to is a boarder they took in to earn money. Marie was young and sexually attractive, and Doc lusted after her. When he saw that Marie had slept with a young man, Doc fell off the wagon, got drunk, came home and threatened to kill Lola, raging at her about "sluts" and "whores" and letting her know just how much he despised their marriage, how disgusted he was by her. At one point he grabbed a knife and screamed that he wanted to "hack all that fat off" Lola. Finally, Lola called for help, and Doc was carted away to the hospital.

Knowing what you know now, what do you make of the subtext behind these lines:

- "Are . . . are you all right, Docky?" (Have you come back to tell me our marriage is over? Are you sober again? Have you come to kill me?)
- "It's . . . it's good to be home." (I have no place else to go.)
- "You're all I've got. You're all I've ever had." (Our lives may still be in shambles. You probably don't love me. But what else is there for us?)

Again it's context and placement. Your own play's action will tell you how to employ subtext. Once you know what is essential to the plot and story you're telling, you'll know what words the characters must say as well. If it isn't necessary to say, "I love you," don't say it.

PLEASE TAKE MY WIFE

Humor is essential to almost every play. There is a comedy in *King Lear*, in *Hamlet*, in *Death of a Salesman*, and in hundreds of other plays we think of as *serious*. An audience needs to laugh—for relief, for release or for pure joy. As for "official" comedies, the great scripts of Georges Feydeau, Kaufmann and Hart, Neil Simon, Wendy Wasserstein, Noel Coward and Christopher Durang cover every style from farce, drawing room comedy and satire to the borscht belt and surrealism.

There is comic action (pratfalls, chases, hiding under beds and slamming doors), and there is comic dialogue.

You can't learn to be funny.

You have to have a sense of the ridiculous. But the ridiculous has to have its own weird logic. From Durang's hysterically funny and very moving *The Marriage of Bette and Boo*, a conversation between a grown son and his mother:

MATT: Why do you call me Skippy? Why don't you call me Matt?

BETTE: *Skippy*'s my favorite movie.

MATT: My favorite movie is *Citizen Kane*. I don't call you *Citizen Kane*.

You have to understand irony. Irony is an awareness of the ridiculous coupled with perfect, deadpan, dry understatement, as in the following excerpt from Tom Stoppard's masterpiece about positivism, murder and morality, *Jumpers*, in which a philosopher attempts to explain logic and assassination:

GEORGE: Cantor's proof that there is no greatest number ensures that there is no smallest fraction. There is no beginning. But it was precisely this notion of infinite series which in the sixth century BC led the Greek philosopher Zeno to conclude that since an arrow shot towards a target first had to cover half the distance, and then half the remainder, and then half the remainder of that, and so on, ad infinitum, the result was ... that though an arrow is always approaching its target, it never quite gets there, and Saint Sebastian died of fright.

You have to mine the comic power of bottled anger when it's finally released, such as in this statement from *The Odd Couple*, in which Oscar is telling Felix he hates getting little notes on his pillow:

OSCAR: "We are all out of cornflakes. F.U." It took me three hours to figure out that F.U. was Felix Unger!

You have to be tough enough not to shrink from nastiness. Invective is essential to comedy, especially when it has the right setup and the correct number of syllables in the punch line. In Kaufmann and Hart's *The Man Who Came to Dinner*, the critic Sheridan Whiteside attacks his annoying nurse, Miss Preen:

MISS PREEN: Oh my! You mustn't eat candy, Mr Whiteside. It's very bad for you.

WHITESIDE: (*Turning*) My great aunt Jennifer ate a whole box of candy every day of her life. She lived to be a hundred and two, and when she had been dead three days she looked better than you do now.

You have to sense where to put the punch line. Imagine famous punch lines if they were mangled like this:

- "My watch has been stolen and it was taken from me by Hildy Johnson, who is a son of a bitch." (Apologies to Hecht and MacArthur, the authors of *The Front Page*.)
- "Last night I shot an elephant in my pajamas. Somehow he got into my pajamas, but I don't know how he did it." (Apologies to *Animal Crackers*' George Kaufmann and Groucho Marx.)
- "Please take my wife." (Apologies to Henny Youngman.)
- "Why did the chicken cross the road? The reason: the other side. He, the chicken that is, wanted to get over there." (Apologies to the ages.)

They sound like bad translations from Latvia. The rule? The key words should come at the end of the line. That's where the *punch* is. A "periodic sentence" is a line in which the meaning and intent of the sentence is only revealed by its last word or words. An example would be Dorothy Parker's famous cocktail party joke: "If you laid every woman at this party from end to end *I wouldn't be a bit surprised.*" Or Richard Greenberg's rueful observation from his one-act comedy about love, *Life Under Water*: "If I didn't trust you so much *I'd be a lot wiser.*" The audience expects the logic of the sentence to go in one direction, but the writer spins it in another. The crisp logic shift and the jolt of the surprise makes us laugh.

You have to know the difference between "witty" and "funny." Sometimes witty *is* funny. In Tony Kushner's *Angels in America*, two men discuss the loss of a pet:

LOUIS: Cat still missing?

PRIOR: Not a furball in sight . . . I warned you, Louis. Names are important. Call an animal "Little Sheba" and you can't expect it to stick around.

But sometimes witty is clever without being funny. From Noel Coward's famous *Private Lives*, Elyot is complaining about Amanda:

ELYOT: Women should be struck regularly, like gongs.

Clever, but not very funny, especially nowadays. What *is* funny in *Private Lives*—along with most of this great comedy—is this exchange between the adulterous Elyot and Amanda, who, as we saw in the exchange quoted earlier, used to be married to each other but are now married to new spouses.

AMANDA: Do you realize that we're living in sin?
ELYOT: Not according to the Catholics; Catholics don't recognize divorce. We're married as much as ever we were.
AMANDA: Yes, dear, but we're not Catholics.
ELYOT: Never mind, it's nice to think they'd sort of back us up.

Now *that's* funny.

And you have to be able to write comic lines that are funny, not only by themselves ("To lose one parent may be regarded as a misfortune . . . to lose both seems like carelessness") but funny in their dramatic context. Noel Coward, one of the funniest writers in the English language, said that the biggest laugh he ever got in the theater came after this line from *Hay Fever*: "Well, go on . . ." It's not funny by itself. But in context, it's a killer. The setup is that Judith Bliss is a charming and wildly egotistical actress. When a young man named Sandy comes to visit the Bliss family one weekend, Judith sits down with him for a chat. The subject of her acting comes up:

JUDITH: Have you ever seen me on the stage?
SANDY: Rather!
JUDITH: What in?
SANDY: That thing where you pretended to cheat at cards to save your husband's good name.
JUDITH: . . . "The Bold Deceiver" . . .
SANDY: You were absolutely wonderful. That's when I fell in love with you.
JUDITH: (*Delighted*) Was it really?
SANDY: Yes, you were so frightfully pathetic and brave.
JUDITH: (*Basking*) Was I?
SANDY: Rather!

(*There is a pause*)

JUDITH: Well, go on . . .

It's her grandiose desire for even more praise that brings the house down. The laugh is based on our knowledge of her character and our expectations of what she'll do. This is *active, character-based, situation-based* comedy. It's the most rewarding kind of comedy to write because it's the most dramatic way to write.

MONOLOGUES

Remember the playwright Gram Slaton's quote? "Monologues are the easiest speeches to write and the hardest to justify"—particularly when there's another character onstage listening to the speaker. One question you should ask yourself when you're experimenting with monologues is this: If there's someone else onstage, why isn't she interrupting the speaker? There has to be either (a) a specific dramatic situation that keeps the listener silent (mute, bound-and-gagged, unconscious), or (b) the monologue is so moving/thrilling/suspenseful/portentous that the listener would never *dream* of interrupting.

I faced this challenge when I was writing *Scotland Road*, a contemporary mystery about a woman found on an iceberg in the North Atlantic, who claims she is a survivor of the Titanic. I knew the mysterious woman was going to have a big monologue at the end of the play when she finally remembered what happened the night of the Titanic's sinking. I avoided writing that speech until I was in the right frame of mind, until I knew I had the woman's rhythm and syntax ingrained in my thinking. I knew I wanted to achieve a poetic effect as well as a dramatic one. The woman's speech was designed to unlock certain mysteries posed earlier in the story. It was also supposed to provoke her nemesis, an interrogator named John Astor, to make a decision and perform the final act of the play. The monologue would have to tell a story from the past—tell it in dramatic terms—and effect another action.

I waited a long time to write that speech. When I was ready I turned on my tape recorder and spoke for about three minutes. As background, you need to know that the woman claims to be a survivor of a disaster that took place almost a century before. John Astor has been interrogating her for six days, trying to get her to confess that she is a fake. The interrogations have taken place in a sterile, white room. But she has not broken down. The only clues John has are (a) that the woman has screamed the first time she heard the name "Astor," (b) that during her sleep she has been heard to mutter "Take me up, take me up, take me all the way to the Hebrides," and (c) that she has reacted strangely when she was shown an old ship's photograph of a man standing at the top of a flight of steps. Finally, John breaks down instead, confessing that *he* is in fact an imposter—not an Astor at all, but simply a lonely man obsessed with the romance and mystery of the great ship. When he confesses to her, the woman speaks:

WOMAN: The first time I saw him was at the Third Class Staircase. Sunday morning worship. Feeling the eyes across the room during the hymn and the admonition. And then the eyes meeting. A hat tipped. An offer of a walk along the deck on a Sunday afternoon. And then a spot of tea. And then supper. And more.

And the questions.

"What do you do before bed, darlin'?"

"I read the bible. And then—sometimes—my 'Strand.' But on Sunday, just the bible."

And you know how they keep us in third class. Men on one end, women on the other. Like we were children, and they who run the ship know better. But you can come from one end to the other. You can come down from high *above* as well.

And it's dark out. And the sea and the sky and the stars have gone by. And indeed there is the bible. Laid out on the blanket. Across my breast. Unopened. And the "Strand" even farther away.

And the rap on the door then comes. And, yes, a talk would be lovely, although it's not really proper in the room.

"Oh, I am going to work in the household of Mrs. George Haverland Coe of Pittsburgh, Pennsylvania. In-service just like yourself, but I could never claim a position as fancy as you. To be in service to such a fine family, I am very impressed indeed to be sure."

And then more talk. And laughter, very hushed and silent.

And then the question. And the question again. And again. And then an answer.

And the bible is placed aside near the "Strand."

And then, in the dark, in the silence, in the murmur of the machines in the heart of the ship, a finger draws along the side . . . and wakes.

"It's the ghost of your aunt, Mrs. James, wagging a finger at her naughty niece."

And I laugh. And we go on.

And then there is another knock on the door. And voices in the passageway.

"We should go up and see . . ."

"No, darlin', not yet."

"We should go up and see what it is . . ."

"No, not yet. A little longer, darlin'. A little longer."

But I want to see what it is, and I look out the porthole.

And it is a sea of ice, mountains of ice going by, so beautiful in such a calm, black sea. We've stopped, and we can look out at this beautiful field of ice.

"Let's go up," I say. "Let's go up and see."

But we don't.

"Listen to me, darlin'. I must go up to the master, or there'll be hell to pay. But I'll come back. You wait under the covers, and when I come back I'll take you up to see the ice. I know a way to get up to the First Class Promenade Deck where we can see, and no one will know. I know a way up through a central passageway, a passageway that runs all the way through the length of the ship, from bow to stern.

"The officers call it 'Park Lane.'

"The crew calls it 'Scotland Road.'

"We'll go up, we'll go up all the way on 'Scotland Road.'

"And I'll show you the ice, I'll show you the mountains of ice. I'll take you up 'Scotland Road.' "

"Take me up. Take me up. Take me all the way to the Hebrides."

He was so beautiful. My handsome valet to the Astors.

He never came back.

The monologue answers a lot of the play's mysteries and dramatic questions:

- How the woman came to be on the ship.
- Who the man in the photograph was.
- What the connection is with the Astors.
- Why the woman didn't get off the ship.
- How she died.
- And what the title of the play, "Scotland Road," refers to (it was never mentioned earlier in the play).

John is silent during this speech. He would never dream of interrupting her. Nor would the audience.

TECHNICAL TIPS

There are many different ways of "writing" dialogue, some of which have nothing to do with pens, pencils or keyboards. The playwright August Wilson has said that he doesn't so much "write" his characters as "listen" to them. If the author of *Fences* and *The Piano Lesson* is right—that dramatic characters speak to their creators—it's important for us to get their quotes right. Sometimes your fingers can keep up with the speed of their dictation—at the keyboard, at the legal pad—and sometimes they can't. In those cases, you can just *talk*.

I don't think one word of *Neddy* came from my brain straight to the typewriter. The legal pad was always an intermediary. But so was a tape recorder, a pocket-sized one I carried with me. Like a lot of writers I used to carry a notebook to jot down overheard dialogue, scraps of the world around me. But I can never find my pens, so I bought the tape recorder and started mumbling into it. I found that dictation was useful to me and still is, even in the computer age. For *Neddy*, I often dictated whole speeches, sometimes a whole scene into the tape recorder. That often facilitated the flow I needed, the stream of consciousness. This isn't to say I didn't rewrite these speeches or scenes later; I did. But sometimes your own voice can take you into the character or the scene in a completely unfiltered way. And so I used the tape recorder to help engender that flow. Much of the dialogue and all of the monologues I dictated stayed in the play. I can't recommend this for everyone, but it has its uses, especially for monologues.

ONSTAGE EXPERIENCE AS AN ACTOR

Every playwright should try her hand at acting, even if it's just in a sit-down reading of a script. Act in old plays (Shaw, Shakespeare, Chekhov, Williams), act in contemporary plays (Guare, Norman, Churchill, Albee, Mamet, Wasserstein, Durang), and act in brand-new plays that aren't finished yet (fill in your own names here). You'll learn a lot. You'll learn what it's like to get through an overwritten speech or a badly shaped joke. What it's like to read dialogue that doesn't move action. What it's like to say words that don't seem to come from the character who's speaking them. And if you're fortunate, you'll occasionally get to read dialogue that *works*.

EXERCISES

1. No dialogue please, we're dramatists.

Some of the most famous dramatic scenes have little or no dialogue: Nora's exit in *A Doll's House*; the final duels in many of Shakespeare's tragedies; the "blinding" of the horses in *Equus*; the ritual hari-kari suicide of Gallimard in *M. Butterfly*; the nursing of the dying man at the end of *The Grapes of Wrath*.

In one to two pages, write a scene with one, two or more characters involving tension, conflict, character-based action and suspense in which no dialogue is spoken.

2. What you don't say.

Subtext concerns the meaning and relationships that lie under dia-logue or action. In one to three pages, write a scene in which two charac-ters express love for each other. They will never say the words "I love you." They will never refer to their own feelings for each other. But it is vital that the audience understand that these feelings exist. Choose an action the characters have just performed, are performing, or are about to perform. *Note:* You may add a third character if you would like.

3. Do the same exercise. But this time change the word "love" to "hate."

4. Subtext and juxtaposition.

Many scenes only begin to make dramatic sense in context, when their actions are juxtaposed against the other scenes and actions. Harold Pinter is a master of juxtaposition; see "Betrayal."

Take this example:

Scene One: A man and a woman meet over a breakfast table. The man says, "I'll see you at seven tonight."

Scene Two: The woman with another man. She says to him, "He'll be home at seven."

What is happening? What's going to happen? What's the subtext?

Scene Three: The woman and the second man wait in a darkened dining room. The first man enters. Lights go on. A crowd of people emerge from the kitchen with a cake. They shout "Surprise!" It's a birthday party.

But what if Scene Three ended differently? A darkened room. The first man enters. A gun goes off. The lights are turned on. The first man lies dead. The second man holds a gun. Now it's a murder plot.

In each case, the meaning of the second scene subtext has been changed by what is learned in the following scene, juxtaposed against it.

In three scenes of no more than one page each, show how the dramatic, subtextual meaning of the second scene is altered by the information/action revealed in the third scene. Then write an alternative third scene, so that meaning is changed again.

CHAPTER TEN

Hedda Gabler:
A Script Analysis

A s you might have guessed by now, I believe in learning from the plays that have come before us. There's immeasurable value in analyzing great plays to learn how they work. In this chapter, we'll focus on one play from start to finish: *Hedda Gabler* by Henrik Ibsen. By analyzing the play's sources (where Ibsen got the idea for his drama), its structure, its characters, and its various dramatic devices, you'll gain a clearer understanding of how plays work, enabling you to apply these lessons to your own writing.

Written in 1891, *Hedda Gabler* is the story of a woman of passionate desires. These desires might have led her to a life of intellectual creativity, or one of bohemian nonconformity. But because of her bourgeois social upbringing, she has a great fear of scandal. Her fear is almost pathological, and it has caused her to make safe choices as opposed to adventurous ones. The play depicts a thirty-six-hour period in her life during which her desires and her fears clash, bringing her to a crisis and leading to the destruction of the man she loved and her own suicide.

By taking apart the components of the play, we can learn a lot about how it was conceived and built. A great play can't be *reduced* to its components, of course. A great play is enlarged by original thinking, exuberant spirit, gut instincts, and the beat of the human heart. But if a play can't be described in its component parts as well as its whole, then it isn't a successfully constructed play.

Hedda Gabler exists in one commonly accepted Norwegian text, and although its many English-language translations vary in tone and texture, there is no serious difference in what is most important—its dramatic structure, characters and actions.

The biographical material and many of the quotes in this chapter are taken from Michael L. Meyer's excellent 1971 biography *Ibsen*.

HENRIK IBSEN AND THE ORIGINS OF HEDDA GABLER

Henrik Ibsen began writing plays in his native Norway early in life. The son of a merchant whose financial failures disrupted the family's security and well-being, Ibsen's earliest position was as an apothecary's assistant in a provincial town, the setting for his first personal drama: the fathering of an illegitimate son. The mother was the apothecary's housekeeper, ten years Ibsen's senior. While he took a certain measure of responsibility for the child's welfare and upbringing, Ibsen never met his son until late in life, almost fifty years later.

Following his university studies, Ibsen married Suzannah Thoresen, the daughter of a well-known university dean, and began writing epic dramatic "poems" and nationalistic plays focusing on Norwegian themes and stories. Although these oversized plays were produced, they were not successful. It wasn't until 1867 with the publication and production of his great verse play *Peer Gynt* that Ibsen achieved fame and notoriety. *Peer Gynt* solidified Ibsen's reputation. He abandoned verse drama in 1873 and worked in prose dialogue form for the rest of his life. This radical departure from the traditional formality of verse was matched by Ibsen's embrace of radical social thinking and his adherence to a psychological approach to character and play structure that seemed shockingly new at the time.

Ibsen took the idea of psychological realism and poured it into the "machinery" of what was then referred to as the "well-made play"— melodramatic nineteenth-century comedies and romances, thrillers and tearjerkers stuffed with secrets, revelations, suspense and violence. Ibsen disdained the "well-made" play—its fakery and shallow theatrics— but we can still see its mechanism at work in his plays. He took this melodramatic form and used it as the vehicle for his own brand of realism. Ibsen was combining the psychological insights and social concerns found in the literary works of Emile Zola, Gustave Flaubert, Leo Tolstoy and others with his own, and focusing them inside the precise lens of the stage. In *Hedda Gabler* we find the finest observable example of his dramatic structure, a dramatic structure beholden as much to

Aristotelian theory as it was to the construction of nineteenth-century "well-made" melodramas and comedies. *Hedda Gabler*'s influence on the dramatic writing that followed—on George Bernard Shaw, on August Strindberg, on Anton Chekhov and countless dramatists working to this very day—is demonstrable and acknowledged.

By 1889, Ibsen had written a number of plays that dealt with crimes against society, the independence of women, the hypocrisy of religion and public morals, syphilis, and the dangers of social "do-gooding." Ibsen was often vilified by critics, artists, politicians, religious leaders, academics and other public figures. He was considered a socialist in England, a revolutionary radical, thanks to George Bernard Shaw's Fabian Society pamphlet *The Quintessence of Ibsenism*, a work that interpreted his plays in a Marxist light.

The first hint that Ibsen was contemplating the play that would later become *Hedda Gabler* comes in a letter he wrote to an admirer, Helene Raft, in October 1889. "A new poem begins to dawn in me." ("Poem" was another term for play.) What contributed to the "poem" that would become *Hedda Gabler*? Ibsen was a dramatist who explored numerous landscapes and shadows for his play subjects, both public and interior:

- Social concerns
- Contemporaries
- His own psyche

Hedda Gabler is a perfect amalgam of all three. The story of a passionate woman whose obsessive longing for excitement combines with her dread of humiliation to destroy her life and the lives of others, *Hedda Gabler* springs from Ibsen's:

Social Concerns. Ibsen's previous plays had championed new notions of the roles of the sexes. When the submissive Nora left her husband at the conclusion of *A Doll's House*, Ibsen ushered in a new understanding of the positions of men, women, marriage and sex in personal and societal interaction. It was an understanding that explored the complex connections between passion and money, between children and independence, between love and order, between law and the soul. Developing his artistic concerns along these lines, he was bound, at some point, to turn his eye to the frustration a talented, passionate soul finds in a stifling, bourgeois marriage. A frustration that leads not to "quiet desperation," but to rage, action and malevolence.

Hedda Gabler comes from an observation of the world.

Contemporaries. Ibsen's circle of friends, colleagues, enemies and acquaintances provided him with rich material. In 1885, Ibsen heard the story of Sophie Magelssen, a notorious beauty who, for some unknown reason, had married Peter Groth, a decent but uninteresting academic who had just received a major university posting following a "competition" with Hjalmer Falk, a writer and philosopher commonly held to be the more gifted of the two. Why had Sophie married Groth? Where would a marriage between these two lead? What events awaited this coupling?

Around the same time, Ibsen met Julius Elias, another academic, whose greatest ambition, as he often explained, was to burrow into other people's letters. (Ironically enough, Elias would later burrow into Ibsen's own letters, following the playwright's death in 1901.) In addition, Ibsen had long known the popular and dashing Danish writer Julius Hoffory and recalled the famous anecdote that concerned Hoffory's loss of his only copy of a much-awaited manuscript during a particularly infamous nocturnal orgy.

Others came into Ibsen's view at this time: a well-respected couple whose marriage shattered when the husband became obsessed with another woman; a famous composer whose newest score was burned by his wife when she found a note from her husband's lover; a man who had freed himself of alcohol only to be drawn back into drinking when his disturbed wife, in an attempt to display her power over him, tempted him one night to join her for an anniversary toast.

In Ibsen's personal life, we also find two women who influenced his thinking, his work and his heart. Emilie Bardach, whom Ibsen called the "May sun of a September life," was a young woman he met in the mid-1880s. They began a passionate friendship that, for all its suggestions of illicit romance, never blossomed into a sexual affair. Emilie's desire for independence and romance was matched by that of another woman who seemed to share a similar place in Ibsen's life: Helene Raft, who combined Emilie's passionate desires with a cool, hard-headedness that served to further attract Ibsen's interest. Neither were artists, but both seemed to have an artistic temperament that Ibsen recognized and from which he derived ideas and energy.

Helene Raft would write him at one point: "Women's will . . . tends to remain undeveloped. We dream and wait for something unknown that will give our lives meaning. As a result of this, women's emotional lives are unhealthy, and they fall victims to disappointment."

Neither Helene nor Emilie would ever consummate her relationship with Ibsen (biographers suggest this was because of Ibsen's inhibitions), and in the end, Ibsen severed ties with the two women who had seemed to bring so much joy, excitement and intellectual stimulation to his late middle age.

Hedda Gabler comes from an observation of other people.

The Author's Psyche. Just as French novelist Gustave Flaubert, when asked to identify the model for the title character of *Madame Bovary*, proclaimed proudly "Emma Bovary *c'est moi!*", one might as easily suspect Ibsen of a private acknowledgment that, as much as Hedda might be based on Sophie Magelssen, on Emilie Bardach, on Helene Raft, his platonic mistresses, in fact Hedda Gabler was Ibsen. Ibsen regretted the passing of his more fiery youth. He saw himself as a man who had turned his back on desire and settled for a life of respectability and comfort. Perhaps this was the price he had paid for his early romance with the apothecary's housekeeper—the birth and secret shame of his illegitimate son. Perhaps it was his early marriage, close on the heels of his affair, to a daughter of academia—a marriage that gave him love, support and sustenance, but less excitement than his nature craved. Perhaps it was a deeper and more complex fear of the sexual act; Ibsen and his wife had only one offspring, born early in their marriage, and he never allowed even his most trusted doctors to examine his sexual organs during a physical examination.

Whatever the reason, Ibsen regretted his loss of fire. He wrote in 1887: "The great tragedy of life is that so many people have nothing to do but yearn for happiness without ever being able to find it." Later, he would note: "It is a great delusion that one only loves one person." And still later: "Whatever a man turns his back on gets him in the end."

Hedda Gabler comes from an observation of the artist's own psyche—whether conscious or not.

HEDDA GABLER: COMPOSITION

How did these disparate elements—these shards of social concerns, salon gossip, diary entries, letters and midnight obsessions—combine to create *Hedda Gabler*? Can *any* playwright listen to these voices and come up with a well-made work? There isn't a formula. Ibsen was an artist, and an artist listens to his world, his friends, his inner voice. An artist has antennae and collects stimuli from every part of his experience—as much from an overheard lament in a cafe as from the stories of wars and upheaval found in the pages of newspapers, books and journals. A play comes as much from a small perception as it does from the big idea. In a great play a small perception can *become* the big idea.

There isn't a recipe, but a play that does not, in some way, combine an observation of ideas, an observation of living people, and an observation of the artist's own soul will probably never fuel a dramatic vehicle, no matter how well built. Another reminder that the essence of art, the meaning of a created work, cannot be taught, even while the methods and techniques of delivery can.

The writing of *Hedda Gabler* (originally titled *Hedda*) came slowly. Ibsen apparently thought about the subject for a long time. Actually, changing the title may have helped. *Hedda* is fine, but *Hedda Gabler* is more to the point, more firmly identifies the character. As a matter of fact, one of the wonderful details of the play is the fact that Hedda is almost always referred to by others—her in-laws, her former "lover," even her *husband*—as "Hedda Gabler," her maiden name, as opposed to her married name. It's as if the world recognizes Hedda's unwillingness to fully enter the dull domesticity her marriage to George Tesman brings. Few call her "Mrs. Tesman." When used by the sardonic Judge Brack, "Mrs. Tesman" becomes a kind of taunt. When used by Eilert Lovborg, it is with accusation and longing.

Planning for the play came in increments. Ibsen was a writer who approached plays first via theme. Anecdotes may have fueled the initial story idea of *Hedda Gabler*, but it's fair to say that Ibsen did not like to pursue a plot until he knew clearly what he thought about the issues and the characters. He was searching for the actions that would tell the story, the actions that would engender the themes he wanted to convey. Notes like "women lean towards sensuality, but are afraid of scandal"; and "the play is about the longing and striving to defy convention." Ibsen was putting together his three observations to create a set of ideas that would, in turn, create characters and actions.

He outlined the entire plot in longhand (the outline would change, but he had one, and that's the point). Then he began the play itself. He spent a month writing Act One. Then he stopped for many weeks. Then more ideas and actions came together. Acts Two, Three and Four evolved quickly, in just four weeks. In the next two months he revised.

When it opened, the play premiered to horrible reviews.

Moral? Sometimes a writer's work is beyond the comprehension of his time.

HEDDA GABLER: CHARACTER

Hedda was an original character. She is a female egotist (the first of her kind onstage) who seeks passion, romance, sensation, experiment, vicarious danger and adventure. But she is also pathetically afraid to act on her desires until the very end, until it is too late.

Hedda does terrible things, but she is always witty, always vital, always planning, plotting, full of energy. She wants things. That's the key. And even when we criticize her pettiness, her cruelty, her demonstrable *monstrosity*, she's always worthy of pity, understanding and, most important, awe. As a character, she is a giant.

Characters must fascinate, enthrall, surprise. Characters must want. We must care about them—and those they affect—to see the outcome of their goals, desires, obsessions and obstacles. *Hedda Gabler* achieves all this.

• • • • •

HEDDA GABLER: ANALYSIS

Hedda Gabler was written to be performed in four acts, four separate sections in four separate times of day in a single thirty-six hour period, a very close approximation of the Aristotelian notion of the "unity of time." Although there are four official acts, *Hedda Gabler*, as we shall see, still adheres to the three-movement model. Each act takes place in the same sitting room, displaying Ibsen's strict use of the Aristotelian "unity of space."

For this analysis of the play, I am using Long Wharf Theatre Artistic Director Doug Hughes' 1992 English language adaption. It has been staged at both Seattle Rep and at the Denver Center Theater Company. Numerous other translations are readily available. It is essential that you read a copy of the play as we analyze it. I suggest reading one act at a time, then referring to the analysis of that act. As we go over the text, keep in mind everything you've read so far:

- the definitions of drama and theater
- the six elements of Aristotle (character, action, ideas, language, music and spectacle)
- space/time/causality

- character/conflict/action/idea
- the three movements of a play
- inciting incidents, points of attack, goals, obstacles, wants, needs, desires, complications, crises, climax and resolution
- mysteries
- protagonists and antagonists
- concrete goals and abstract ideas
- suspense
- secrets
- sex
- love
- money
- power
- crime
- death
- ideas
- theatricality

ACT ONE

On the morning that starts the action of the play, the pedantic academic George Tesman and his wife of five months, Hedda, have just returned to their new home in the city. Their ship has docked the night before. The home is that of the late cabinet minister, Secretary Falk, purchased by George with loans from his family and assistance from his friend, the older Judge Brack. In the opening scene, George's loving but cloying Aunt Julie is discussing the young couple's arrival with the maid, Berthe, a domestic who is stoking the fire grate. Berthe worked in Aunt Julie's home but has now joined George and Hedda at Julie's insistence. Julie's sister Rina is ill, dying, and Julie will have to return home soon to care for her, but she is eager to see George and his wife, "the beautiful Hedda." Julie has even bought a new hat for their return. She places it on a sofa.

George joins them. He is excited and anxious. Hedda Gabler is a woman with expensive tastes. His new home and servants require a larger income, one that may come with the professorship he hopes to get. His friend Judge Brack has told him that the appointment at the university is assuredly his.

Julie quizzes George about his honeymoon. She alludes to the possibility that Hedda Gabler is pregnant. George will neither confirm nor deny the possibility. (Both refer to Hedda as "Hedda Gabler," not "Hedda Tesman.")

Julie is very proud of George, noting that his academic achievements outshine so many of his contemporaries'. Then she makes a reference to one of his friendly adversaries, a man known as "Eilert," whom Julie informs George has just published a book of some importance. George absorbs this information.

Hedda Gabler enters, as beautiful as she has been described. She refers to Julie as "Miss Tesman," to George as "Tesman." Hedda notes the hat on the sofa. She says it must be the maid's, because it's so "dreadful. People don't do such things."

Embarrassed, Aunt Julie retrieves her hat. She leaves.

Once alone, Hedda and George discover a card from a visitor who has apparently come earlier that morning, a "Mrs. Elvstead." Tesman remembers her as a woman he and Hedda knew some years ago, a woman who has married an older magistrate in a northern province. Hedda comments that it is the same province where Eilert Lovborg had moved to some time before.

At this point, "Mrs. Elvstead" is announced. She enters, nervous. It turns out she went to school with Hedda many years before, but Hedda was a much more popular figure. Thea Elvstead knows very few people in the city, and she has come to town to meet someone—a friend, the tutor of her stepchildren.

THEA: "Eilert Lovborg is back in town."

Lovborg's book has become a sensation. It was written at Thea's home, with her help. George is shaken by Lovborg's success, and Hedda seems to enjoy his discomfort. Thea must find Lovborg. Will the Tesmans help? Of course, says George. Hedda suggests he write a letter to Lovborg at the local address Thea has discovered. Hedda makes George leave the room to write the letter.

Once George is gone, Hedda interrogates Thea. Thea's marriage to the magistrate is a union of convenience (she used to be governess to the magistrate's children). She has left the much older magistrate to come to the city, so that she can be with Lovborg.

Hedda is taken aback by this "little woman's" courage. Thea seems not to care "what people will say," as Hedda puts it. Under questioning, Thea reveals that she has not only helped Eilert write his successful book ("like his partner"), she has also made him stop his "old habits," his drinking and carousing. Hedda is not pleased by this. Hedda brightens, however, when Thea says that even though she has left her husband, something stands between her and Eilert: "another woman," someone Eilert loved years before.

THEA: "When he left her, she threatened to shoot him with a pistol."
HEDDA: "Such melodrama."

Thea believes the woman is a famous singer (read: prostitute) whom Eilert once mentioned. The singer, Diana, is in the city, too, and her presence is driving Thea "mad."

George reenters. He has sent the note to Lovborg, inviting him to the house that evening.

The maid announces Judge Brack.

Thea exits.

The smooth, avuncular judge enters. Judge Brack and Hedda banter. It is obvious they enjoy an innuendo-filled relationship. George hints about a possible pregnancy. Hedda quiets him.

The three talk about the honeymoon, the costly home, and George's university appointment. There's a problem though.

BRACK: "Eilert Lovborg's back in town." (That *sentence* again.)

They know.

And his new book has caused such a sensation that the university is considering him for the same post George thought was his. There will be "a competition."

George is distraught. His own book—years in the making with still more years to go—is about the "the textile industry in the 14th century." Lovborg's best-seller is about the history of civilization.

Brack is sanguine. Does George remember the party at the Judge's scheduled for later in the evening? No, George has forgotten. And George has just invited Lovborg to visit. Brack doubts Lovborg will respond. Brack leaves, saying he'll be back to pick up George.

Alone again, Hedda berates George. Without a university post and its attendant salary, her dreams of servants and horses and a social whirl may be lost. George says that perhaps visits by his Aunt Julie will fill Hedda's time instead. Hedda doesn't respond to this. But she makes a pronouncement as she exits the sitting room.

HEDDA: "At least I still have one thing to kill time with."

TESMAN: "What's that?"

HEDDA: "My pistols, George. General Gabler's pistols."

And she exits.

End of Act One

Summary: Ibsen uses the "slow immersion" approach to begin his play. The opening dialogue between Aunt Julie and Berthe is classic nineteenth-century exposition. Hedda doesn't even make her first entrance for a good few minutes. Where was the point of attack? At the curtain line? Maybe. That's where we realize Hedda may be the woman from Eilert's past. Why does the curtain line tell us that? It's the revelation of the pistols. Was the point of attack at the Judge's mention of a "competition"? Maybe. Competitions are dramatic. Earlier?

Think of westerns. The first act turning point, the end of the beginning, comes when Thea enters the Tesman's home and says, "Eilert Lovborg is back in town," after which Hedda *acts* to make George invite him to the house. Nothing will ever be the same after this entrance (Thea's), this information ("Eilert Lovborg is back in town"), and this action ("George, send him a letter. *Now.*").

If you looked for the inciting incident, you saw the tip of its iceberg in the news that Lovborg has written a new book. Once Lovborg arrives onstage, we'll find out more about how that book came to be written.

Details and props in Act One are important. Think of them as seeds that will grow later in importance: the hat, dying Aunt Rina, the suggestions of pregnancy, the two books, Thea's declaration of love, the story of "the other woman," the Judge's sly grasp of information, the "competition," the pistols. Also, certain key thematic concerns have been layered in: "people don't do such things" (this about leaving the hat on the sofa), "burning," scandal ("Aren't you afraid what people will say, Thea?"), "partners" and "courage." Ibsen finds ways to plant these seeds in dramatic and memorable ways. They'll come back later. But the point of attack catalyst is a human one. A man from the past has returned. A central dramatic question has been posed (What will Hedda do now that Lovborg's back?). His presence will change their lives. And they know it.

ACT TWO

That evening. A fire flickers in the grate. Judge Brack has returned to pick up George. Hedda, beautifully dressed, greets him. (Why is Hedda beautifully dressed?) Hedda asks the judge why he has come back to bring George to the judge's own home. It becomes obvious: Judge Brack and Hedda have a flirtatious relationship, one made up of double entendres. Hedda even teases the judge by aiming her father's pistol at him in the garden.

They discuss her honeymoon—a bore.

They discuss Tesman—a bore. Brack asks her why she married George. She replies: He's solid. And there weren't any other "available escorts in the city."

The judge hints at his willingness to be the third side of a "casual triangle." Hedda laughs. She "accepts," in the veiled terms they are used to.

George enters, laden with more books for his research and dressed to leave. George also has Lovborg's book. He's read it that very afternoon. It's impressive. He also reveals that his Aunt Rina has taken a turn for the worse (A small detail? Or will it be important later?). George exits a moment, and Hedda reveals that she knew all the time that the infamous "hat" was Aunt Julie's. She was just torturing Aunt Julie for the fun of it. She also admits that her love for the home George has bought, the famed "Secretary Falk's villa" is not real at all. She and George had been walking home from a party the summer before (she chides the judge for "going in another direction"; otherwise he might have been the one walking her home); George was tongue-tied. They passed the villa. To break the silence, Hedda said she would love to live in the villa. So, in effect, the judge's "other directions" created a chain of events that lead to the Hedda/George courtship, to the myth of the adored villa, and the marriage itself.

Brack wonders about Hedda's goals. Doesn't she have any? She's bored, she replies. But she needs . . . *something*.

Brack alludes to a child. This upsets Hedda.

George returns. And a visitor is announced.

Eilert Lovborg enters.

Polite reintroductions. They're all old acquaintances. George praises Lovborg's book. Lovborg disparages it. It is pablum, he says, designed to flatter the readership. It is merely preparation for his next work, the one he wrote with Thea in the provinces. This next book, he says, will be a *real* masterpiece. He carries the manuscript with him.

And he's willing to read it to George.

George tries to appear thrilled (inside, he's dying—subtext) but explains he's on his way to Brack's party. Brack slyly suggests Lovborg join them at the party. He can read the book to George there. Brack will even set up a room. Brack is enjoying all this. Hedda is not.

George asks if Lovborg will indeed be giving a series of lectures in the fall, as he had heard at the bookstore.

Lovborg says he will. But only *after* George gets his university appointment.

Surprise. We thought there was to be a "competition."

Lovborg doesn't want the university job. He'll "let" George have it. He just wants everybody to know he could have beaten George if he wanted to. "I'll settle for the moral victory," he says.

George is ecstatic. But Hedda, Lovborg and Brack—and the audience—know George has been humiliated.

George and Brack exit for a moment.

Hedda asks Lovborg if he would like to see photos from her honeymoon. Once they're alone, we realize Hedda and Lovborg have been extremely close—soul mates, almost lovers. Lovborg keeps murmuring her name ("Hedda Gabler, Hedda Gabler") as she turns the pictures in the album (note the juxtaposition: a discussion of Hedda and Lovborg's passion while they peruse the photographic evidence of Hedda's connubial boredom).

LOVBORG: (Re: George) "How could you throw yourself away."

They refer to their earlier "partnership" (remember the word when Thea used it?) and their secret "understanding" that no one suspected.

HEDDA: "Did I have *power*, Eilert?"

Lovborg has a goal in this scene. He wants to know if Hedda had ever loved him, might *still* love him.

Hedda says she will not have an affair. She doesn't love George—that's obvious—but there will be no affair.

But did she *love* Eilert? Eilert is begging her to say "yes."

Hedda say he was "dangerous," "forbidden." They had a common "hunger for life." (Hedda's tragic flaw #1.)

The "fire" was the attraction (read: sex). But Hedda also feared Lovborg's passion and fire. His danger. Lovborg asks her why she didn't shoot him when she threatened him with her pistols (confirmation of our suspicions).

HEDDA: "Because I'm too terrified of scandal!" (Hedda's tragic flaw #2.)

This is Hedda's inner conflict (self as antagonist):
(1) Hedda wants passion, but (2) she's afraid of the scandal that may come with it.

Hedda's inner conflict is firmly depicted for the audience. It is still early in the play (not quite the 40 percent point), and this vital exposition is revealed in a scene of great conflict, tension and suspense.

As their scene ends, Hedda admits the heat of her feelings for Lovborg. We know the attraction is still there. The fire is crackling again. But Hedda must reject Lovborg.

Thea Elvstead enters.

Thea melts at the sight of Lovborg. Lovborg, hurt and angered by Hedda's rejection, needles Hedda by referring to Thea's "partnership," her "courage," her "willingness to *act*." By using all these phrases—phrases Ibsen has earlier linked to the relationship between Lovborg and Hedda—and applying them instead to Thea, Lovborg is forcing Hedda into a corner.

Suspense/tension: What will Hedda do?

It looks like Lovborg has put Hedda—the woman he loves, the woman he has been hurt by, the woman he both hates and desires—in her place.

And then Hedda mentions "the punch."

The characters—and the audience—know Lovborg is a former drinker. Thea has helped reform him. It is one of her points of pride.

Then Hedda suggests Lovborg have a glass of punch. Lovborg and Thea are shocked. Of course, he wouldn't dream of drinking anything with alcohol. But Hedda uses Lovborg's weakness, his fear of not being thought of as courageous, to make him drink. She says Brack and George were mocking him earlier when he twice refused a drink. Didn't he notice? Surely someone who doesn't *need* liquor can show his independence by having *one* drink?

Conflict/Tension/Suspense

Against his better judgment and against Thea's protestations, Lovborg takes one drink (acts)—to prove himself in front of Hedda. He has shown Hedda that he has both courage and self-control. (But has one drink been one too many?) Lovborg decides to join George and Brack at the

THE ART & CRAFT OF PLAYWRITING

party. Thea will stay with Hedda, and Lovborg will return at ten to take Thea back to her rooms. The men leave, Lovborg carrying his manuscript. Hedda comments to Thea that they will sit together until Lovborg's return.

HEDDA: "He shall return with vine leaves in his hair." (A phrase that sounds like an old shared reference.) "On *fire* with life."

Hedda also says she'd like, for once in her life, to have power over another human being.

Hedda and Thea go into the dining room.

End of Act Two

Summary: The development of the plot is furthered in this act, the first half of the Great Middle. So is character. So are themes. What has Ibsen used in the first act that he now uses in the second act? Phrases, memories, lines, images, actions and ideas. And what has he inserted into the second act that he may use in Act Three and Act Four? What details seem minor but may have importance later? Remember: A good play uses its details as it moves along. They come back. They transform. They are used again. It is in this act that the full story of the inciting incident—Hedda and Lovborg's past affair and the subsequent writing of his manuscript—is explained to the audience. The second act is firmly part of the middle of the play. Hedda has been moving toward her goal—exercising power over Lovborg. She has met with opposition: Lovborg's abstinence and his unwillingness to compete with George, Thea's presence, the presence of Brack and George, her own fears. She has acted: The challenge to Lovborg is a key action; so is keeping Thea with her. And Act Two ends on a note of rising action and suspense: What will Lovborg, George and Brack do at their party? When will they return? What will Hedda do? It is after Act Two that most directors place their "official" intermission.

ACT THREE

Dawn. Seven hours past ten. Hedda and Thea sleep on the settee. Lovborg has not returned. Neither has George.

Suspense—what is keeping them? What has happened?

The maid has stirred the fire again. She delivers a letter for George in Aunt Julie's handwriting (remember the importance of Aunt Rina's physical condition?). It is left unopened. (A mystery.) Thea leaves the room to sleep in Hedda's bedroom. Then George returns, dishevelled. He tells Hedda:

- that Lovborg read him the book. It's incredible.
- that Lovborg got drunk and out of control. It's believable.
- that Lovborg led them into the street, toasting "the woman" who inspired the great work. It must be Thea, says George. (We doubt that.)
- and . . . that Lovborg dropped the manuscript in the street, and George found it. (Surprise/complication.)

George carries the manuscript with him. No one knows he has it. George says it must be returned to Lovborg soon. Hedda argues that they should keep it in the house.

George finds the letter. Aunt Rina is indeed dying (not *dead*, this is a key distinction). If he hurries, he may see her one last time. (If she's dead, no hurry, right? Sly Ibsen.)

George leaves. Hedda will take care of the manuscript. She hides it.

Brack arrives. He has news about Lovborg. It seems his late night travels took him to "Mademoiselle Diana"—the "singer." All was well until Lovborg started accusing Diana of stealing something. (What could it be?) The police took Lovborg away.

HEDDA: "Were there vine leaves in his hair?" (That phrase again!)

How does Brack know all this? A man in his position has powerful friends and good contacts, he says. Brack tells Hedda that Lovborg has now so embarrassed himself "that every respectable door must now be closed to him." (Scandal.)

Hedda understands what the judge is implying: He wants *Hedda's* door to be closed to Lovborg. Brack wants Hedda for himself. Hedda and Brack discuss his advances toward her. She knows what he wants. But she's ahead of him. The judge may have power, she says, but he has no power over her.

Brack accepts this uneasy draw. He leaves.

Lovborg arrives. (Ibsen is always the efficient traffic cop, even though the rapidity and felicity of his characters' arrivals and departures remind us of the melodramatic roots of this beautifully constructed play.) He bursts in. He's a mess.

And Thea enters. She wants Lovborg, cares for him, needs him. (Hedda is watchful.)

Lovborg has come to break it off with Thea. He has news for her:

He has destroyed their "child"—the manuscript. He says he has torn it into a thousand pieces the night before (lie/complication). Hedda is baffled by this lie, but she's smart, and she keeps her mouth shut.

Thea is distraught. She leaves, in tears.

Lovborg tells Hedda the truth. He got drunk and lost the manuscript. He looked for it everywhere. It's gone. He couldn't admit "carelessness" to Thea about "their child." That seems to Lovborg worse than intentionally destroying it. That's why he lied. Far better to say he had *acted*, than to admit to such pathetic, inadvertent failure. He doesn't have the willpower he thought he had. Thea had helped him, but now he's a lost man.

HEDDA: "Thea had such power over a human life?" (Hedda seems obsessed by this notion of power.)

Lovborg starts to leave. Without Thea, without his great work—and, by implication, without Hedda—his life is over. Lovborg will kill himself.

Hedda doesn't try to stop him. Hedda doesn't reveal her possession of his lost manuscript.

Instead Hedda gives Lovborg General Gabler's pistol. (Remember how Ibsen has used this gun?) Hedda has finally achieved her goal: to have power over another human being.

HEDDA: "Do it beautifully."

LOVBORG: (*Smiling ruefully*) With "vine leaves in my hair"?

We realize we were right. That line *is* a shared reference between the two of them.

Lovborg exits with the gun.

And then, in one of the great curtain moments in all drama, Hedda retrieves Lovborg's manuscript and burns it in the fire grate (the fire that has been going all during the play), saying: "I'm burning your child, Thea."

Burning, fire, children, power.

It all comes together.

The curtain falls as the firelight plays over Hedda's smiling face.

End of Act Three

Summary: Act Three is the second half of the Great Middle. It depicts the rising action (or acceleration of actions) of the play. If we compare the actions of the first two acts with those of this third act, it's easy to see that the rapidity of the actions, as well as their number, has tripled. The first two acts paved the way for conflict. Act Three has conflict and action in full flower: George and Hedda battle over the discovered manuscript; Brack propositions Hedda; Hedda rejects Brack; Lovborg lies to Thea and rejects her; Hedda rejects Lovborg again; Hedda provokes Lovborg to suicide; and Hedda destroys the manuscript. Where was the second turning point of the play? The Crisis? The end of the middle?

Was it George's revelation about his finding the manuscript? Brack's pass at Hedda? Lovborg's rejection of Thea?

No. As we saw in the chapter on Great Middles, the crisis/turning point comes late in the play, two-thirds or three-fourths of the way through. It is the moment to which all other previous actions and events have been pointed. It is the moment that leads inevitably, irrevocably, toward the end. It is when Hedda hands Lovborg the pistol and then burns the manuscript. Nothing can be the same after these actions. In *Hedda Gabler*, the crisis/turning point comes at the close of the act, sixty seconds from the curtain coming down. Masterful. The climax and conclusion, full of incident, will come when the curtain rises again.

ACT FOUR

That evening. Darkness. Hedda, dressed in black (mourning?), paces. Julie enters to tell Hedda that Rina is dead. George enters after a day of making funeral arrangements. George suggests that perhaps Aunt Julie should now come to live with them. Hedda reacts negatively, but keeps quiet.

Aunt Julie leaves.

George is worried about Lovborg. Hedda tells George she has burned the manuscript. George is horrified. Hedda says she did it for George's sake, to help him, to erase any future competition from Lovborg. George thinks Hedda loves him and has done this to make him happy. Hedda also reveals, in veiled terms, that she is pregnant. Now George is delighted. Hedda's "crime" will be kept hidden. No one must know the truth, says Hedda—especially Judge Brack.

Thea enters with a large suitcase. She has heard rumors about Lovborg, something about "the hospital." (Suspense—what has happened?)

Brack enters. Always the man with powerful friends and powerful information, Brack tells the others that Lovborg has shot himself, that he's dying. It was a shot to the heart. (Hedda had hoped for a bullet in the head, but the heart will do.) As is his wont, Brack reveals this information bit by bit, piece by piece, never the whole story in one gulp.

George bemoans the loss of Lovborg, and he mourns the loss of the manuscript which, as Thea says, was "torn into a thousand pieces." George and Hedda can feel safe. (But they are now co-conspirators. They have a secret.) Lovborg's masterpiece won't be able to hurt them.

But just then Thea holds up the suitcase. Thea has Lovborg's original notes. The book could be pieced back together. (surprise/reversal/complication). And since that's what George does best—research other people's work—he can help Thea rebuild the text. George decides to dedicate his life to re-creating Lovborg's book. He'll work with Thea. They'll start that very evening (reversal).

They exit to the study.

Hedda is shocked. Still, Lovborg has killed himself, performed a "courageous" act, done it "beautifully." Hedda has exhibited her power over a human life. So she must have achieved her primary goal. Right? The central dramatic question must have been answered. Right? Is this the end of the play?

No. Judge Brack is still in the room.

Alone, Brack tells Hedda that the *real* story is not quite the one he told a few moments before.

Lovborg is already dead. Lovborg didn't return to his rooms and commit suicide. Lovborg went back to Diana's, caused a ruckus again, went into Diana's bedroom . . . (Hedda looks sick) . . . said he wanted his "lost child" . . . (Hedda sinks into a chair) . . . and shot himself *by accident*. A gun was in his pocket, it went off, it hit him—not in the head, not in the heart, but in the groin.

Hedda's goal has been frustrated, by accident, fate and human nature.

There's something else, says Brack: "The gun."

Just then—for the sake of suspense—George reenters to get something from his desk.

The tension is killing us.

George exits.

"The gun." Brack has recognized it. After all, it was pointed at him playfully just the evening before. It's Hedda's.

BRACK: "Lovborg must have stolen it."

Hedda, desperate, plays along. Yes. Stolen. When she wasn't looking. Who has the gun? The police. Will they try to trace it? Of course.

HEDDA: "Do you think they will succeed?"

BRACK: "No, Hedda Gabler. Not as long as I keep quiet. If they do trace it, though, you can always *say* the pistol was stolen." (Implication: No one will believe that, Hedda.)

HEDDA: "I would rather die."

BRACK: (*Smiles*) "People *say* such things. They never do them." (We've heard a variation of that line before.)

If the pistol is traced to Hedda, and the police show it wasn't stolen, says Brack, ". . . well, then, Hedda, there would be scandal." A trial. Hedda on the witness stand. The same witness stand as the "singer," Diana.

Scandal! What Hedda fears most. Her Achilles' heel. The second part of her tragic flaw. She exhibited the first part of it when she gave Lovborg the gun (her desire for passion and danger). Now the other half (fear of scandal) has returned to finish her off.

But Brack assures her. He'll keep quiet.

HEDDA: (*Looking up at him*) "So I'm in your power, Judge." (The line about power comes back to haunt her.)

The judge has achieved his goal. Hedda seems to have failed at hers. The protagonist destroyed by herself (self-antagonism), actions she cannot control (Lovborg's botched escapade—fate), and another character (Brack as adversary-antagonist). In some plays, this would be the end. But Ibsen is moving toward something larger, something greater. Ibsen is moving toward the classic conception of tragedy. The hero must fall even further. What follows the judge's revelations is a fairly long (two minutes) scene that seems to suggest the future Hedda sees for herself:

"A Domestic Setting"

* George and Thea (a "partnership") at work on Lovborg's posthumous masterpiece (the "child" Hedda thought she had "burned")
* the prospect of living with Aunt Julie (that "dull, dull boredom")
* Brack seated next to Hedda ("power over another human being")

It is Hedda's nightmare come true.

Hedda plays an annoying ditty on the piano for a moment. George enters and remonstrates her. He and Thea need quiet. Hedda looks around at all of them. This is her future?

Hedda will act.

She walks into the other room and closes the curtain.

A shot rings out.

Hedda has shot herself in the head with her father's second pistol. She has "done it beautifully."

George and Brack rush in and discover the body. Hedda has eluded Brack's power—at the cost of her life.

BRACK: "People don't do such things."

Curtain. End of Play.

Summary: This Great Ending, with its resounding climax and resolution, is one of the most famous, shocking conclusions in theater history. The entire act is a marvel. In a sense, Ibsen heaps crisis upon crisis, reversal upon reversal, but never so many as to make the play's action appear ridiculous. What's most important is that the character asserts her power at the play's end. In one sense, she is defeated. In another, she has exerted a victorious and violent control over her own life.

Does *Hedda Gabler* fulfill the expectations of a well-constructed play? Read the play again. Look at the sources of Ibsen's ideas for the script and how he combined and energized them in the text. Look at his use of drama and theater. Look at his use of the six elements. Look at space, time and causality. Look at the three-part structure. Look at his use of dialogue. Look at character, conflict, action and ideas. Look at goals and obstacles. Look at tension and suspense. Look at secrets. Look at sex. Look at money. Look at power. Look at crime. Look at theatricality, the world of gunshots, onstage fires, and the compressed excitement of two secret lovers talking about passion while looking at honeymoon pictures.

Then see the play. Stage the play.

CHAPTER ELEVEN

Three Interviews

Lee Blessing
Marsha Norman
José Rivera

For this section of the book, I talked to three well-known playwrights who have a great deal of experience in the contemporary theater: Lee Blessing, Marsha Norman and José Rivera. Each has had many plays produced by hundreds of theaters in the United States and abroad. Lee is the author of *A Walk in the Woods*, among other plays, screenplays and television scripts. Marsha wrote the Pulitzer-Prize winning *'Night, Mother* and won a Tony for her book and lyrics for the musical *The Secret Garden*. And José is a playwright whose work moves easily from the world of television and film to the theater of magic realism, including his FDG/CBS award-winning play *The House of Ramon Iglesia*, which was later filmed for PBS.

In these interviews, we discuss craft issues; inspiration; theatricality; personal passions; what is learned from adaptation; what is learned from other writers, directors, actors and designers; rules and rule-breaking; getting ideas; structuring and outlining; first drafts; rewriting; play development; production; rehearsal; and the joys and frustrations of collaboration. I tried to ask each writer the kinds of questions I thought you, the reader, might ask.

Lee Blessing

Lee Blessing was born in Minnesota and started writing plays in the late 1970s. He studied poetry and drama at the University of Iowa, and his earliest works were performed at such theaters as Actors Theatre of Louisville, Brass Tacks and the Cricket Theater. He is best known for his two-character play about U.S. and Soviet arms negotiators, *A Walk in the Woods*. *A Walk in the Woods* was produced by Yale Rep and La Jolla Playhouse prior to its Broadway premiere in 1988. It was nominated for both a Tony Award and the Pulitzer Prize. Since then the play has been produced dozens of times, including stagings in London (with Alec Guiness in the lead) and Moscow. It was filmed for American Playhouse with the New York cast, Robert Prosky and Sam Waterston. His other plays include *Two Rooms*, about a U.S. hostage held in Beirut; *Cobb*, about the controversial baseball star; *Riches*, about a battling couple; *Fortinbras*, a comic "sequel" to Shakespeare's *Hamlet*; and *Patient A*, based on the story of Kimberly Bergalis, the woman who died of AIDS after contracting the disease from her dentist. Blessing has won numerous grants, fellowships and awards, including an NEA, a Bush Fellowship and a McKnight Fellowship. He has been a member of both New Dramatists in New York City and The Playwrights' Center in Minneapolis. He has written the screenplay for the film *Steal Little, Steal Big* and teleplays for such series as *Picket Fences*. Blessing and his wife, the director Jeanne Blake, live in Los Angeles.

Jeffrey Hatcher: You grew up in Minnesota, in a suburb outside Minneapolis. Did you see a lot of plays when you were young?

Lee Blessing: The first experiences I had with drama were at high school. I was at school when the Guthrie Theater started. My family was not a theatergoing family, and I don't think I saw any shows there until the second season. The first production I ever saw was *Saint Joan*. So by the time I was beginning to experience any theater at all, I'd already written a play—done in a "barn," so to speak.

Hatcher: Do you think there's a difference between writers who are able to experience plays at an early age and writers who, for whatever reason—education, the city he or she grew up in—aren't able to see plays until later in life?

Blessing: I think it might affect how quickly you develop. A kid who grows up in New York with parents who are avid theatergoers, and who's been going to see plays since he was ten, well, his *abilities* as a playwright might develop more quickly, and he might be writing plays in his twenties that maybe I wasn't writing until I was in my thirties. I think that's possible.

Hatcher: What's the difference between the plays you wrote in graduate school at the University of Iowa in your twenties and the ones you wrote six or seven years later?

Blessing: For me, it's been a very gradual and even progression in terms of my abilities as a writer, as I matured as a person—assuming that's occurred. So I don't think there have been big moments of change. When I was starting out writing plays, the big pitfall was that the dominant playwrights in the world, whose influences were felt in America, were mostly Europeans, like Samuel Beckett, Eugene Ionesco, Jean Genet, Harold Pinter, theater-of-the-absurd playwrights. Playwrights who had nothing to do with the American tradition of playwriting. And yet those were the writers I read first, and quite avidly. Of course, at the same time I was reading Shakespeare and Shaw and Sophocles. These things didn't tend to go terribly well together, and, again, none of them was in the rich American tradition of the previous one hundred years. So I was rather lost, I think, when I first started writing plays. I didn't quite understand how you did it. I'd read Eugene O'Neill, but again he's a rather unusual playwright. So the first thing I had to do was unlearn how to write like a theater-of-the-absurd writer because I slowly came to realize that wasn't what I had to say. It was a style that wasn't getting me anywhere.

Hatcher: Do you think a lot of writers imitate a style they're drawn toward? Even if it isn't their own?

Blessing: Constantly. I noticed it in writing poetry. The writers I enjoyed the most were those who, when I tried to imitate their style, eluded me. I ended up with terrible poetry. I'd read a Theodore Roethke poem or a James Wright poem, and try to write that way, and it didn't get me anywhere. The same thing can happen in drama. They're wonderful writers, but they're just not me.

Hatcher: At what point in your development as a writer did you become aware of the audience? Some playwrights say they never think about the audience while composing a play.

Blessing: That's really an individual concern. If they think too much about the audience, they'll become self-conscious. When I'm writing the play, I don't spend a lot of time consciously thinking about the audience. But every time I think about writing a new play, one of the questions I know I have to ask myself is does an audience care about this? Do they care about it in the same way *I* do? If they *don't*, can I *get* them to? Do they have a strong investment in this issue anyway? Because if they don't, it's a big climb to get them to.

Hatcher: When you get an idea for a play, do you think it tends to come from one source, or do they come from all sorts of things: an overheard line of dialogue, a place, a concern . . .?

Blessing: Sadly, from a lot of different sources. Otherwise I'd just go back to the same old one.

Hatcher: Is it hard to pick and choose?

Blessing: It can be. If I'm fortunate, I find something I'm excited by, and I get an idea and it stays with me. I don't ever write a play I haven't thought about for a couple of months—and often for years. This is to make sure that at least *I* continue to be interested. It's a lot of work to write a play, and why would you do that unless you continued to be fascinated by it?

Hatcher: When you're thinking about a play, be it a year or so, or a couple of months, is there a particular process you've come to depend on?

Blessing: It's changed. A lot of this has to do with the opportunities that have been presented to me combined with the work patterns one has. Before *A Walk In the Woods*, I would be writing a play, and no one would be much concerned with that fact. And I would get the play read at The Playwrights' Center, and if it went well I would rewrite the play, and if it went badly, I guess I'd rewrite the play more, and then I'd have a second reading there or at New Dramatists in New York, or something like that. And ultimately I'd try to interest theaters. From first draft to premiere, this might take a couple of years. After *A Walk in the Woods* got done in 1988 there was a period of years in which I got a lot of commissions to write plays for theaters. There was a commission every year. And when someone says, "We'd like you to write a play, and we're going to do it next year," you really only have about a year to put a play together from conception to a producible form, and that's not a great deal of time, as you know. It's enough, but barely enough. In the case of some of those plays, I'd missed that early process of getting a play read in a sit-down reading, and felt I had to go back and do a *second* production of the play, considerably rewritten, to feel as if I was really finished with what I wanted to do with it.

Hatcher: Is there a particular period of gestation, from conception to production?

Blessing: I'd hate to characterize it. Some plays get written very quickly. The first draft of *A Walk in the Woods* got written very quickly. The first draft of *Patient A* got written very quickly. But with *Patient A*, that draft came after two years of planning and research, whereas some plays have stuck with me and taken quite a while. The play I'm writing now is one I've been thinking about for a year and a half. And things get in the way as well. As my wife, the director Jeanne Blake, and I have done more television and film writing, suddenly playwriting, which doesn't pay as well and as dependably, has to find its own niche in the amount of time you can spend on it. It's always a complex sort of calculation, so in a sense I couldn't say it takes two years to write and complete a play. But generally for me it does.

Hatcher: When you get an idea for a play, what comes first: the big idea? The setting? Situation? Or do you always see a person?

Blessing: It's usually more related to people than concepts. Sometimes I'll give myself an assignment. If I've been writing certain sorts of things or emphasizing certain sorts of ideas in plays, I do the opposite. So after the first few plays, which were all about men, I assigned myself some plays with women. But beyond that, there was no specific assignment. They didn't have to be any particular women in any particular place with any particular dramatic problem to solve. I wrote *Independence* and then *Eleemosynary* and the assignment was: no men. Just don't write men in these plays. Later, after completing *Riches*, which was a husband/wife play, I decided I wanted to write something that was really more off page one, the news, a headline kind of play, a public issues kind of play since I'd never done that. I didn't know which public issue I wanted to write about, but eventually it occurred to me that it would be interesting to write about arms control. *A Walk in the Woods* got started that way. After that, I gave myself another assignment. From my first play through *A Walk in the Woods*, all of the plays I'd written had a great deal of humor in them, and used humor a lot to entertain, even in my most serious plays. So—for some odd reason—I decided to banish humor from some plays for a while and write about things I really couldn't joke about.

Hatcher: Were you conscious in choosing those subjects that by banishing humor it would be good for your writing, a good challenge? That in the challenge you would develop some different muscles?

Blessing: That was the point. The point of not writing men is to write women better. The point of not using humor is to make sure I'm not using humor as a crutch. To feel as though I can encounter a serious theme and treat it in a serious, *sober* manner and still make that entertaining, still make people want to watch that.

Hatcher: When you get an idea for a play, do you know where your characters are going to go? Do you start writing the play before you know the end?

Blessing: All my training taught me that you have to know the climax before you write the play, otherwise you don't know what it's going to do to the audience, and therefore you don't know why it exists. By far, the most efficient way to write a play is to know where it's going. And I still think that's true. But it's hard to do that all the time because one also has to maintain a sense of interest and wonder and excitement about the journey as one is writing. And writing takes a long time. If one is still trying to write exactly the same moment that one conceived three months earlier or six months earlier, it may feel a little stale by the time you get there. So I'm always alive to a play growing and changing as I write it. I do tend to have a plot plan when I start. It's not always the strongest feature in my mind when I think about the play. The characters will be stronger. The way they say things will be stronger. The relationships, the premise, are all more vivid to me than perhaps where it's going to go. But if I don't have a very strong clue as to an action, a climax that's going to compel me as well as an audience, then I'm not terribly confident that the play is going to work out as a good piece of writing.

Hatcher: Have you ever mapped out a play—decided where it was going to go, identified its climax—and then somewhere along the way moved away from that route and found a more interesting way to go?

Blessing: Sure. That happens. I've heard that was true of *A Streetcar Named Desire*. Tennessee Williams had fully intended to take it one way and about half way through the writing he saw a different route that was far more interesting and took that. That certainly can happen, and so it's important to stay alive to possibilities. There are times when you realize, suddenly in the middle of writing it, that you can take the play much further, that it could be about much more than you thought it could be about. Sometimes the fruit of writing characters well is that you suddenly discover they're far more interesting people than you'd ever expected them to be.

Hatcher: Isn't there a difference, though, between a playwright who chooses a route, chooses a climax and then discovers a different route or climax, and one who starts off without a route?

Blessing: A considerable difference.

Hatcher: Is it because a decision on a climax means your writing is being pulled *toward* something, even though you may abandon the climax you've chosen?

Blessing: Sure. The conscious mind and the subconscious mind are both working on anything you're writing. You may have all these conscious intentions, this conscious road map for where a play's going to go, and subconsciously something else is going on.

Hatcher: Is there a way, when you're working on a script, to *lean in* to that subconscious? You've planned the plot, you've structured it, but now you want to look for the clues in the woods.

Blessing: For me, it goes back to my background as a poet. When I'm writing a scene, I try to stay alive to things that develop or dialogue that comes along which has a resonance with everything that has gone on, with the characters as they are developing, with the ways they've been speaking, with the linguistic possibilities they have and are still developing as the play goes on. So, in a sense, it's almost a matter of one's "ear" picking up things. And it's an "inner ear" that tells you when you come across something valuable, something that you should pick up and carry with you on your journey. And it may lead you down a different path. That's when it can become an exciting process.

Hatcher: Do you make these discoveries in character, action, dialogue, images . . . ?

Blessing: In all those areas. And the different path I'm speaking of may be a path that ultimately gets you near the same goal you anticipated getting to in any case, but the route you may get there by could be different and richer and more surprising. Sometimes it can take you somewhere totally different too, and that may be a virtue for the work and it may not. That's when you have to go back to your fundamental reasons for writing the play and check your work against that. Have you ultimately created something that people can get a genuine emotion out of, one that they not only feel but know what to do with? And really I like that tension between what you planned to do and what you did at the moment. It's very valuable.

Hatcher: You've worked in the theater for over fifteen years, with various directors, actors, designers. What have you learned about the theater, and about your own writing, by working with collaborators?

Blessing: You learn a tremendous amount. Certainly you learn a great deal about how what you write needs to be a useful tool for somebody to take on to stage and speak in a three-dimensional medium and make real in front of other people. You can't write a line or a moment that you yourself would be embarrassed to perform, assuming you had all the talents of a good actor. So over time, by working with any set of actors or directors, you learn a certain level of respect for the medium.

Hatcher: Sometimes you hear playwrights talks about actors who've taught them about the length of a line of dialogue—this is a question, say, of breath control and how playwrights often don't realize the stamina it will take to get through an overwritten speech. You'll also hear playwrights talk about how some parts of plays are more difficult for actors to memorize than others because there's something missing in the emotional or psychological through-line, scenes that don't have a clear intent or a clear objective.

Blessing: I'm leery of things that are as technical as worrying about the length of a line and an actor's breath. When I used to act, I remember doing Shaw, and I remember what a challenge it was to me, a relatively untrained American actor, to be able to mouth those words, to speak those long sentences and speeches one after another. Yet, it can be done. Technically it can be achieved. And when it is, it's an extraordinary effect. But actors, having to go through the experience of putting something on a stage, have to make the event convincing. That there's a level of credibility that the writer has to have emotionally—on whatever level. The writing has to have that, or the actor can't really perform it convincingly.

Hatcher: Is that the "emotional build" actors talk about? I've heard actors say, "Well, I can *get* to where you want me to go in a script, but I'll have to make quite a jump. It might help if you give me dialogue that gets me between A and Z."

Blessing: That can often be a very helpful exchange with actors. I've had actors say to me, "This is nice, I love where it's getting to, but what if something like *this* happened between A and Z." And I've often worked to rewrite scripts or scenes on that basis. I've also had the direct opposite experience, of an actor being so unhelpful as to tell a director in my presence, "Well, I can only do the scene one of two ways" in order to get a change they want but which I think is wrong or unnecessary. Or they'll do the opposite, as a defense mechanism, to stop me from changing *anything* in the script.

Hatcher: Let's talk about theatricality. You'll hear someone talk about theatricality and you think they mean actors dressed as puppets running around on stage saying, "Look at this blanket, it's really a cloud." But some of your plays take place in rooms that look like rooms and feel like rooms—and others take on a different kind of reality. *Two Rooms* is an example. *Fortinbras* is an example too. Could you talk a little bit about how you move from one kind of theatrical depiction to another?

Blessing: I love sets. I'm always fascinated by what set is ultimately chosen for a play or suggested to people by a script. I try not to spend a great deal of time thinking about the set when I'm writing it other than to get the most fundamental ground rules set up. In *Two Rooms* I wanted one room, one space. I wanted it to be empty. There were still lots of choices to be made by the set designers. Marjorie Kellogg designed the first production at the La Jolla Playhouse and did a magnificent job with minimals, you know. The choices she made were texture and color and some other choices which were just wonderful and did a tremendous amount for the play.

Hatcher: And the idea in the play, just so everybody knows, is that you're primarily in two rooms, one in the United States and one in Lebanon.

Blessing: It's his office in his Washington home which is stripped of all furniture. And the other one is the empty room where he's being held in Beirut.

Hatcher: But at any given time the characters are in the same space onstage, but we understand that they are in totally different places.

Blessing: They are in one place or the other, and then of course imaginatively the characters bleed from one place to the other.

Hatcher: Now that kind of theatrical idea is one that comes up when you're writing the play. Do you remember the first time you came up with an idea that was that theatrical—or was your very first play like that?

Blessing: Yes, it's interesting—because *Two Rooms* was not a play that I could have started to write without knowing that about the set. So that was a set decision that came very, very early, whereas *Fortinbras*—I said to myself, "I know it's in Elsinore. That much I know, but where in Elsinore, what the sets are . . ."—that slowly developed as I started the scenes and decided where, and then the play was sort of telling me where it wanted to go next. Some of my earlier plays were set in more realistic situations that were very specific. In *Independence* it started out as a play about three sisters, and it happened in one small town in Iowa, in an apartment one of them had. And then in later drafts their mother kept calling, and finally she became so important on the phone that I introduced her into the play—and, before I knew it, they were all at her house in a different Iowa town so the set shifted as the story shifted and settled in Independence, Iowa.

Hatcher: Change of topic. This is the "seductive lollipop" question. Some plays find more success than other plays, either commercially or artistically. You've spoken to me about the ingredients a playwright often puts into a play to entertain, hook, bring in an audience— seductive lollipops you called them. Then there are those plays that don't have that same kind of hook, but still attention must be paid.

Blessing: I think any actor knows that he's going to play a whole spectrum of roles in his career, and some of those are going to have an absolute magnetism for an audience. Zero Mostel played a lot of roles, but they weren't all Tevye in *Fiddler on the Roof.* He played even more wonderful roles in other important plays. But there are some that just click, like Tevye. It's what every actor hopes for—that's the one they'll be remembered for, that's the one that will enhance their career. It's similar when you write plays. They all have value as projects. Almost all of them are intensely enjoyable to create and produce. Not all of them have whatever that magical thing is, and you can't always tell what it's going to be either. It's not always in the realm of what's humorous or appealing or sentimental or massaging or easy or melodramatic. Or seductive. Sometimes it can simply have to do with a question the society is asking itself subliminally and intensely at the time. A good play can hit for that reason. *'Night, Mother* was like that. It said something to people that was important to them about life and death, about the value of living life as a woman in America today, in a country that didn't value a certain class of women or women as a class in a way it probably ought to.

Hatcher: What do you find most troubling about a play? Let's say a friend or colleague has written a play or you've written a play and you think it's dealing with a subject matter that should be dealt with— maybe it's addressing issues that other people aren't addressing, you think it's a good play. And yet it's not cooking in all the right ways. The audiences aren't flocking to see it. Do you think that some dramatists "write out of their time" and that it will take twenty years for their plays to win favor?

Blessing: I don't think a playwright can spend his or her time worrying about that. One simply has to write and do as well as one can with each project—be as ambitious as one can be as a writer with each project and try to work with the best people one can work with. I honestly think, especially from a writer's point of view, there is no way to predict or try to manipulate how a play will do with audiences in general. You can try to learn from how your earlier plays have done, but I think it only can diminish you as a writer to start making that your top priority. As for people writing for their own time or people writing ahead of their time, I'm sure it happens. We write plays because it's a challenging genre, we have a talent for it and there is on some level pleasure in producing good plays, good scripts. If audiences happen to like it as well, that's wonderful.

Hatcher: Now you're working on something new, but you don't want to talk about it because . . .

Blessing: Because it would be bad for me to talk about it.

Hatcher: Why do you think it's bad?

Blesssing: It tends to diminish one's energy for actually writing the piece. Every writer wants to get out of writing to begin with. That goes without saying. When you're a writer your highest priority is how to keep from writing. And so you have to guard against too many things that make it too easy not to write. One of the things that I think makes it easy not to write is to be able to go down to the coffeehouse and sit with your friends and tell them all about this great new idea you have. Once you've expressed it, you sort of have the entire pleasure of getting the feedback from the original conception, and it's very hard to bank up sufficient energy then to go to all the trouble of writing it. Writing takes a long time. It's slow going, and you need to keep the carrot out in front of you a little bit. I want to keep that carrot.

Marsha Norman

Marsha Norman won the 1983 Pulitzer Prize for her play *'Night, Mother.* The play also won four Tony nominations, the Dramatists Guild's prestigious Hull-Warriner Award and the Susan Smith Blackburn Prize. A feature film, starring Anne Bancroft and Sissy Spacek, with a screenplay by Norman, was released in August 1986. *'Night, Mother* has been translated into twenty-three languages and has been performed around the world.

Her first play, *Getting Out*, received the John Gassner Playwrighting Medallion, the Newsday Oppenheimer Award and a special citation from the American Theatre Critics Association. Her two one-act plays, *Third and Oak: The Laundromat* and *The Pool Hall* premiered at Actors

Theatre of Louisville. Her play *The Hold-Up* was workshopped at ATL as well. *Traveler in the Dark* premiered at American Repertory Theatre and was later staged at the Mark Taper Forum under the direction of Gordon Davidson. *Sarah and Abraham* premiered at Actors Theatre of Louisville in 1987 and was produced at the George Street Playhouse in the fall of 1991.

Norman received a Tony Award and Drama Desk Award for her Broadway musical *The Secret Garden.* Her play *Loving Daniel Boone* had its premiere at the 1992 Actors Theatre of Louisville Humana Festival, and her latest play, *Trudy Blue*, premiered in the 1995 Humana Festival. She wrote the book and lyrics for *The Red Shoes*, with music by Jule Styne.

Marsha Norman, Four Plays was published by Theatre Communications Group in 1988. Her first novel, *The Fortune Teller*, was published in 1987. Norman has worked in television and film, including most recently *Face of a Stranger*, starring Gena Rowlands and Tyne Daly.

Norman has received grants and awards from the National Endowment for the Arts, the Rockefeller Foundation, and the American Academy and Institute of Letters. She has been playwright-in-residence at the Actors Theatre of Louisville and the Mark Taper Forum in Los Angeles, and she has been elected to membership in the American Academy of Achievement. She serves on the Council of the Dramatists Guild, and on the boards of the New York Foundation for the Arts and the Independent Committee for Arts Policy. She is the recipient of the Literature Award from the American Academy and Institute of Arts and Letters.

Jeffrey Hatcher: How do you recognize a play idea that lends itself to drama and theater? Is there a rule of thumb you use when you're thinking up plays and receiving ideas from the world?

Marsha Norman: I think that the pieces for the theater clearly have to be events that must be witnessed. You have to see it to believe it. This is the rule about a theatrical piece—"You Were There." You would never believe that this thing could happen. That is, I think, a quality of a good piece for the theater. Somehow your presence as an audience is required. Pieces that have to do with great geographic scale—obviously those things are better done in films. Quite frankly, pieces that are about sort of domestic interiors that require close but not deep attention are better for television. We're in a curious place in the development of the theater where we need to think a lot about what can only be done in the theater and just do that. My new play, for example, takes place entirely in the leading character's mind. You don't know that because you are flipping around from scene to scene seeing all kinds of events and hearing people who were never in the same room together and all that kind of life of the mind on the stage. That's what I think we need to be looking for more overtly, to find the theatrical event.

Hatcher: If you were to see something in the newspaper or overhear a conversation and you started to apply certain tests to it and you thought to yourself, "Well, I'd like to write it as a play; but I can see it just as readily as a novel or a screenplay," would you avoid it entirely as a theater piece or would you search for something theatrical about it?

Norman: When I have ideas for plays I try to dismiss them immediately so that I only end up writing the plays I *have* to write.

Hatcher: The ideas that insist themselves?

Norman: There are lots of unnecessary plays written. Those are the ones that cause you lots of pain. The good ones are pieces that have to be, as I say, witnessed by a group. They are communal from the beginning, and those are the things that work best in the theater. Look at a play like Brian Friel's *Faith Healer*, for example. The telling of it has to be in the theater. That's the way that it best moves people. *Our Town* would be the dopiest novel in the world, and it would make a really silly movie. Whenever there are elements of the paranormal, the extranormal, the nondomestic, those are the things that belong best in the theater.

Hatcher: In his book *The Empty Space* the director Peter Brook says that when he was shooting the film of *King Lear*, the problem was that he actually had to film the real beach where Gloucester dies, but the wonderful thing about the stage is that the blind Gloucester *thinks* that he is on a cliff, his son *knows* they're on a beach, and as far as the audience is concerned they're on a set of stage planks—you can be in three different spaces at the same time; but you can never do that in film. You've got to be specific.

Norman: Right. We actually experience our lives closer to the way that they are presented in the theater than the way they are presented in film and TV. I think people get disenchanted when their lives don't work out the way they do in film and TV, and they don't have all the correct costumes and they don't have people who say the right things, and they don't look the right way. Television has created a world full of spectators.

Theater always creates a world of participants.

Hatcher: This is a quote of yours: "In the theater you're in jail for two hours, and if you don't make the audience happy they're going to be really pissed off."

Norman: That's true. That's why I think that criticism for the theater is often so brutal, because the critics actually get mad. You kept them there for that time, and they didn't like it. They had other ideas about what to do with their evening.

Hatcher: When you're looking at an idea for a play and it's demanding to be written, how quickly does it turn into a question of character?

Norman: It's almost always a question of character. I know that other people write from different motivations, but I almost always write with a desire to understand the action of one person. Why did *this* person do *that*? In other words, I become aware of an act. If we could use *'Night, Mother* for a moment, I became aware of the act of this woman who killed herself, who lived with her mother for her whole life, who suddenly said, "'Night, Mother," went in the bedroom and killed herself. And you think, "Why did she do that? How did she do that? And why do I think it was an act of courage?" I tend to only write about acts of courage, so it's easy to answer questions about this. I see somebody doing something that I think is a really powerful move, and I know that it's not generally recognized as a powerful move. I know that it's my task as playwright to get it into the right category. I know people who would say, "Oh, well, Jessie, that's just a selfish thing to do" or "That's just a defeatist weak thing," and I think that, no, actually in *this* case for *this* woman committing suicide was the realization of her own power over her life; and that's what she wanted to do with it. She could have at the moment made any number of decisions. At that place of power she could have decided to go to beauty school, for example; but I don't think they would have given me the Pulitzer Prize for it.

Hatcher: You've talked a lot about the need for characters to take control of their lives, just as people need to take control of their lives. Is that the primary action of a two-hour play?

Norman: It's very important to select the two hours from that person's life or the collected moments that add up to two hours from which the whole life is visible. You want to be able to see how they got into this predicament, you want to see what the predicament is, and you want to have a sense of what they're going to do and where the life will take them. Lots of time people choose the two hours too soon or two hours too late. You can easily imagine a *'Night, Mother* play that's written from the viewpoint of the funeral. Jessie's in her casket and Momma and all her friends are gathered around and the play begins then and the whole thing is done in flashbacks. This would be just silly, hopelessly boring. In *'Night, Mother* the way it's structured you know that she is going to kill herself, but you don't believe it. And it's your lack of belief, it's your struggle against this inevitability that somehow creates the drama—because this is the drama that everybody lives with all the time: Am I gonna make it to the end of this?

Hatcher: How much do you think about the audience before you write a play and while you're writing it?

Norman: I don't think about them too much, but I know a lot about them instinctively. I know that they have to laugh every now and then or they'll get fidgety. I know that they have to be rooting for something for that character and they have to know what it is that character wants and be able to see that that character is trying very hard to get it. The audience loses patience so fast with characters who aren't really active in their own behalf.

Hatcher: Do you think a character has to be likeable?

Norman: I don't think they have to be likeable, but I think they have to be understandable. The audience has to be able to say, "If I were that person, I would do that. If I had that history, that experience, those disabilities, that anger, that whatever-it-is, then I would do that." It has to be comprehensible. It's like the writing of villains—you know, the better reasons they have to be villains the better villains they are.

Hatcher: Your connection to an audience is instinctive?

Norman: Yes. People who are storytellers have grown up telling stories and watching the audience, whether it was their parents or their friends in school or people on the telephone or whatever, and you know about the timing of individual lines, you know the things that make people interested. You know how to drop little hints so that the audience begins to unravel the story for itself.

Hatcher: Were you a storyteller when you were a kid?

Norman: I was, but I also grew up at the knees of a great one. My grandfather was one of the most gifted storytellers in the world. He grew up in New Mexico where there were all these great stories to be told, things about ranching and wheat-threshing crews and tangles with snakes.

Hatcher: So did you find that storytelling came naturally to you?

Norman: Absolutely. It's an instinct. I think that somehow there is this ancient occupation of the storyteller, the tribal storyteller; and these occupations—just like the other ones of shoemakers and cobblers and canners and beer-makers—are all passed down. There is a need in the community for someone to tell the stories of the tribe and tell what has gone before and preserve a sense of what it has felt like to be alive in this time. It's oral history on the hoof, as it were, and there's basic survival information in the plays that we keep around. *Oedipus* has been around not just because it's a great piece of writing; it's because there's something in it that everybody has to know. We write them and present them and then the culture decides whether to retain them. Obviously when a society forgets an important story, we can get into trouble.

Hatcher: When you started to attend the theater, did you observe and absorb lessons about theater craft or did you study it later?

Norman: I was a thirsty child who spotted water. I think that I knew that this was somehow the world that I belonged in. I didn't act on that for a long time because I didn't really believe it was possible. I was under the impression I was going to have to be a missionary or something; but I watched, I listened, I absorbed lots of this. I don't think there's a better way to learn about the theater than just go *a lot* because what you want to do for an audience as a writer is create a theatrical experience. In other words, you don't want to create a reading experience, it's not an intellectual experience, it's an experience of being in the theater and responding as a body, as a human physical body to what's going on on the stage. Your mind, your body are all one. You can't get a play just from reading it. You have to be there. So, when the idea is to create an experience for people, what you can do to learn about it and learn how to do it is to have the experience as much as possible. If you were designing roller coasters, you would go and ride all the great ones. You would listen and watch for when people screamed. You wouldn't *read* about them.

Hatcher: Let me jump over to the subject of rules. You like to experiment with the rules of playwriting. Which are the unbreakable ones and which are the breakable?

Norman: The unbreakable ones are no passive central character and no more than one central character. The central character has to want something that is within his or her means. I used to think that the Aristotelian notion of time was an unbreakable rule, but I no longer believe that. I do think that the action has to be circling around one issue and be driven by the needs of one character. The reason audiences respond better to *one* protagonist is because this is how we experience our own lives. We have a collection of issues, and we deal with them one at a time. We all feel that we are the center of our own story.

Hatcher: Aside from the question of breaking time frames, what other rules do you like to play with onstage? You've experimented with time travel and multiple story frames in *Loving Daniel Boone* and *Sarah and Abraham*, for example.

Norman: What I like best to play with is the notion that the visible and the invisible are quite close and in fact they are both sensible and active realms in which we play. That the invisible is woven around and through the visible in our daily lives. By the invisible I mean there are people from the past, people who are dead, people who never existed, people we dreamed of, ideas that we had, dreams, hopes, fears, those things all might as well be characters that are walking around on a stage. My own fear of heights, for example, in certain circumstances could very well be dressed up with me and screeching at me the whole time. Our minds operate in a world where fears become personified. On the other hand, people transform into other shapes. I'm sure that my mother in my mind is actually seventy to eighty feet tall and very loud and very powerful, in spite of the fact that she is a sixty-four-year-old woman who died five years ago. In the theater we can present things as they seem, not as they are. In *Trudy Blue*, for example, when I have people who are fantasy figures walking around in between conversations that are actually happening, this is how it is. This is actually what happens. Our world is populated by the people that we dream about and that we fear and not just the ones that we could actually go pinch.

Hatcher: In the battle between those theater artists who say theater should be linear and those who say, "Well, life is nonlinear and hence why should theater be linear?"—is it fair to say that you play with *some* nonlinear ideas while holding onto Aristotelian structure?

Norman: So far I do, but I may be breaking out of that. I think that our ability to perceive story is all changing rapidly with the amount of television that we watch and the effects of the computer world. Those things really do change the way people think. For a very long time people pretty much thought in the same ways. They remembered stories in the same ways and they presented them in the same way—the Charles Dickens version. This is how stories were presented more or less from the beginning of time. There's not a lot of difference between *Tale of Two Cities* and Sodom and Gomorrah. It's kind of the same story.

Hatcher: Jon Jory, the artistic director of Actors Theatre of Louisville, said that one of the attributes that told him you were going to be a terrific writer was your ability to rewrite. When you go into a first draft, how conscious are you of how you're going to be progressing as each draft comes? Do you say to yourself, "Well, I know I can't do such-and-such in this draft because I'll be able to get back to this problem in about two months"?

Norman: All that I know in terms of a first draft is that it's more important to get it down than it is to get it right, you know? You have to get the hundred pages filled up first. This is *the* thing that most people never do. Most plays never get finished. That does not mean you just force yourself to fill a hundred pages. My view of it is you wait until you can fill the hundred pages before you start to write. You feel this gathering force within you. When it reaches this critical point and you know that you've got enough to fill the hundred pages, then you start and you write it. You just get it down, and you don't let yourself labor over individual sentences, individual scenes. You get things good *enough* so that you can go forward. The trick about that first draft is to get your excitement onto the page, this sort of need, this urgency, this "Listen, I have to tell you this. You are not gonna believe this."

Hatcher: We're all supposed to learn from our mistakes. Were there any plays that you have written and said of later "Well, I guess that wasn't that necessary" or "Maybe I shouldn't have been writing that scene that day"?

Norman: I feel like I've made almost all the mistakes. I haven't made the mistake of quitting entirely, and this is what saved me. I've continued to do this. I think that obviously there are plays I made mistakes with. *Circus Valentine* was a play about too many people. *The Hold-Up* was a play that had characters that didn't belong together naturally. Those are characters that *I* put together, and the audience somehow knew that these are not people who would naturally appear in the same scene. There have been lots of times when the content of something has been at war with the form of it. In fact, this is one of the things I believe most strongly about the theater—that you have a chance for a great piece of work when the form and the content meet and lock instantly. You can't just put content in any kind of form. If you have marbles you can't put them in a black felt bag.

Hatcher: As an example of form meeting content, *'Night, Mother* could never have been written with an intermission. You could never have written that play out of its natural sequence because you would have lost the compression of time and the compression of ideas and the urgency and ferocity of the debate.

Norman: Right. In *'Night, Mother,* I got away with writing an argument; by that I mean a philosophical argument. To live or not—to be or not to be. This is the question of *'Night, Mother.* It's great that by shutting down everything else and creating the sense of urgency in the debate I allow people to listen to what's being said and follow it as though it were action. It's not physical action, but it feels like it is because there's threatened action at every moment.

Hatcher: What's exciting about the younger writers you work with today?

Norman: I do think that writing plays is primarily a thing for young people to do. There is a kind of inherent struggle in the form that is echoed by the struggle in the lives of young people to say, "Here's who I am, here's what I'm gonna do, and watch out. Here are the things that scare me, here are the things that seem unfair." It's almost a kind of petulance of form. "I *insist* on telling you this. I'm gonna interrupt your life to tell you this." Later on in people's lives they become less demanding or they realize, "Well, hey, you know, if you want to look at this in a couple of days, fine." What thrills me about working with young writers is the fact that youth is exactly when those real thematic, dramatic issues of a career are being established. As for writing about old age, Shakespeare was the only guy that could actually write plays about the sunset years. Nobody since then has really been able to do that. Older playwrights *try,* and obviously some writers have written some nice things, but that striving of youth is very exciting, and somehow it seems to be central to our survival as a species.

Hatcher: Imagine you're working with a young writer who seems to be a very theatrical writer yet is more attuned to computer-age, MTV kind of thinking—very fast, very nonlinear. You think the writing is really sizzling, but there's something about the plays that doesn't work. Maybe it's the structure. Maybe the drama isn't as conflict-oriented as it could be. Would you suggest to that playwright that she should try to write something in strict tried-and-true Aristotelian structure, or would you let that writer just keep going and discover the right way for herself?

Norman: I think writing exercises are great. You need to have as much flexibility and power and skill and craft as you can gather up because you never know what's going to be needed by any one project. There are people who belong in film and TV and don't have that kind of sense of urgency and presence that you need to work in the theater. There's a great sentence that Lillian Hellman has in this introduction to Chekhov's letters, and she says playwrights all have this killer instinct. I think this is true. There is something about the end of *Hamlet*—everybody ends up dead. Movies aren't like this. Nor is television. But there are some times when you lose really big in life, and this is part of what the theater is willing to show. There are just some situations that end up killing everybody. I think that there's something about that kind of boldness, that sort of risk-taking that is natural to theatrical writers. The real people that belong in the theater know that, just *know* it. I'm sure that it's the same with great trapeze artists; there is probably some great thing that you have to know in your blood if you're gonna be a great trapeze star. Playwriting is a physical craft, and it's a thing that requires muscle, intellectual and emotional. People who are afraid of that, people who are afraid of doing damage—those are the people who'll never make it. You have to be willing to be a killer.

José Rivera

José Rivera was born in San Juan, Puerto Rico. His play *The House of Ramon Iglesia*, winner of the 1983 FDG/CBS New Play Contest, aired on the public television series *American Playhouse*. *The Promise* premiered at the Los Angeles Theatre Center and was recently seen at the Orange Tree Theatre, London. *Each Day Dies With Sleep* premiered at Circle Repertory Theatre, was seen at the national theater of Norway, and at the Orange Tree Theatre. The Los Angeles production of *Each Day Dies With Sleep* received six Drama-Logue Awards, including Best Play. *Marisol* premiered at the Humana Festival at the Actors Theatre of Louisville. The La Jolla production of *Marisol* received six Drama-Logue Awards, and the Joseph Papp Public Theatre production received a 1993 Obie Award for Outstanding Play. *Giants Have Us in Their Books: Six Naive Plays* premiered at the Magic Theatre in San Francisco. *Cloud Tectonics* was part of the 1995 Humana Festival at the Actors Theatre of Louisville and is scheduled at the La Jolla Playhouse and the Goodman Theatre, Chicago. Honors include grants from the NEA, the Rockefeller Foundation, and the New York Foundation for the Arts. In 1989 Rivera studied screenwriting with Nobel Prize-winner Gabriel García Márquez at the Sundance Institute. In 1990 he was writer-in-residence at the Royal Court Theatre, London, while on a Fulbright Arts Fellowship in Playwriting. In 1992 he received the prestigious Whiting

Foundation Writing Award. Film and television credits include the critically acclaimed NBC series *Eerie, Indiana* (co-creator and producer), *P.O.W.E.R.: The Eddie Matos Story* (ACE Award nomination) for HBO, and the screenplay *Lucky* for Interscope Films. Rivera is married to writer Heather Dundas; they have two children, Adena Maritza and Teo Douglas.

Jeffrey Hatcher: You're a playwright who also does a lot of work in television and film—you've written screenplays, produced a television show (*Eerie, Indiana*), but you keep coming back to the theater. Why?

José Rivera: It's hard to leave a first love behind. Here is something I fell in love with early, very early in life, and even before I knew I wanted to be a writer I knew there was something about the theater that I loved. It's hard to let that go. I like the idea of dedicating my life to something like this. I think in more practical terms I find the opportunities for personal self-expression are far greater in the theater than in movies and television. I feel theater is the most personal of the media, *then* film, and *then* television. I also find that I need to tell stories in imagery. I consider myself an imagist, and I find that when I write through images, theater is the natural form for that type of expression, much more so than film.

Hatcher: When you talk about imagery, do you mean in terms of imagery within language or stage visual imagery?

Rivera: Somewhat visually, mostly within language, mostly in terms of how we express the inexpressible, how we can take the English language—its vernacular—and mold it in such a way that it expresses the things that we normally leave unexpressed. To me that is what the theater can do that the other art forms can't do and that I find missing in those other art forms when I do practice them. I find that certain stories need to be told in pictures, and when those stories urge themselves on me I write them as film. Certain stories are told through *language*, and those are the stories that I devote to the theater. In discussing *Cloud Tectonics* for a second, I knew that in discussing the nature of time and the definition of "relationships" and what "love" is that I needed all the verbal dexterity I could possibly muster—and I didn't think I could do that in pictures. Also, the theater allows a playwright a level of artistic control unheard of in the other two forms. A writer in television, once he's risen through the ranks and becomes a writer-producer, exercises an enormous amount of creative and financial control over the work; but that's rare. Most TV shows have a show runner and a staff, between six and fifteen writers; but only one person gets to run the show and call the shots—and of course, as we know, film is the director's art form. But in the theater the playwright still has enormous power to shape the outcome from casting to design; and I have tended to work with directors who are extremely comfortable with my power and do not feel, in terms of ego or territoriality, that I am a threat. You know, working for instance with Tina Landau, the director of the Actors Theatre of Louisville premiere of *Cloud Tectonics*, is that kind of experience. So those are the things that keep me coming back to the theater. What's kept the force going the *other* direction has never really been TV and film as a seduction. The disappointments that happen in a playwriting career are the things that actually have threatened me and have pushed me away. The times when I have thought to myself, "I am never going to do this again; this is just crazy," it's because the theater *itself* has disappointed me, not because TV and film has been so attractive and seductive, as I said. The times when I have sweated blood for a production that has fallen short or has been mauled by the critics or for some reason the actors didn't connect with the material—when the theater itself has hurt me, that's when I've wanted to leave this. But those things have been rare and not enough to push me away permanently.

Hatcher: Let me ask you specifically about *Cloud Tectonics*. You said the play is about time and love, and certainly in theatrical language you can focus on the imagery of time—the play is filled with time references—but the discussion of time is also in the very nature of the theatrical performance. In fact, the conventions of the theater will often admit that time is compressed or time elongates onstage. Audiences are quite used to the idea that something that should take many weeks takes two hours on stage or something that should take ten seconds has been elongated to four minutes. I think we have an inner appreciation of that even if we don't think about it while we're watching a play. *Cloud Tectonics* is very much about this idea. So when you have an idea for a play like this one, (a) where does it come from, and (b) how do you then develop it into a play?

Rivera: Everything that I write comes from some kind of image, either something that I see or something I've heard or even just imagined or dreamed. *Cloud Tectonics* came from an airplane flight that I took. Plate tectonics is the study of the continental plates under the earth and their movements. When you study earthquakes, for instance, you study plate tectonics. So I was on a plane and I was looking out the window. I was trying to imagine if you had to define what "love" was or "sexuality"— how would you do it? I was really stuck. I couldn't figure out a good definition, and I realized that trying to do that is very similar to trying to understand the structure of clouds. As I was looking at the clouds going by, I kept trying to ask myself: How do you describe that structure, how do you describe that shape and those myriad shapes and those ever-changing shapes? And I realized you couldn't do it, but if you tried to and created a science to do that you would call it "cloud tectonics," which is essentially a nonsense phrase because the clouds don't move like the plates. But I like the idea that even the title itself is somewhat meaningless, because grasping the idea of cloud tectonics makes as much sense as trying to grasp a definition for "love."

Hatcher: "Cloud" sounds amorphous and billowy and "tectonics" sounds like something scientific and mechanical.

Rivera: It is the juxtaposition of two contradictory images which is the definition of surrealism. Like Magritte. Just about every one of my plays begins with that kind of imagery or that type of imagery tied to some deep emotional experience. The imagery of homeless people in New York, for instance, became critically personal once I found out that an uncle of mine had died homeless in San Diego. And that was enough to make a play out of. I get images from things I overhear, things my children say to me. There are many, many sources. And what I tend to do is gather these images. I collect them, even to the point of keeping them in a diary, and these things stay with me and I let them simmer, I let them stew for years at a time. Certain images in certain plays took many years to cook after the initial image came to me. And I tend not to be an impulsive writer. If I get an idea I don't go rushing off to write it. I had an image not too long ago of a dinner between two people who had multiple personalities. One character had three and the other character had thirteen, and if those two people had dinner what would happen? What personalities would come out and on what cues and what relationships would they have? That image came to me about a year and a half, two years ago; it stayed with me and I keep thinking about it constantly. I obsess about it, and it's that kind of thing that will stay in me until eventually the obsession grows to such a point that it demands to be written. It demands my time and I will then sit down and write the play. Once I've done the writing it goes quickly. It may take me three or four months to write a reasonable first draft—and then from that point on, as you know from your work, it becomes a process of refining and getting feedback, and that kind of thing. But the initial impulses are always images.

Hatcher: In *Cloud Tectonics*, although the *subject*, the *themes* and *ideas* may be time and love, the *story* and the *action* involve a man, a baggage handler at the Los Angeles airport who picks up a pregnant woman during a torrential rainstorm, the storm of the century, and takes her home ostensibly for one evening. During the course of the play, during the course of their relationship, we realize indeed two years have passed in one evening. Your idea for a play about time and love could have gone in a thousand different directions. What made you choose this particular story to discuss these images and ideas? What brings the idea and the story together?

Rivera: That's a very good question. When I was going about my work of gathering imagery, one of the other images that stuck with me came the day I was driving through Los Angeles, and I passed a pregnant hitchhiker on the road who was soaking wet. She was there with her thumb out, and there was fast traffic. I didn't stop, I just kept on going, and I kept wondering what happened to her, what got her to that point. I kept asking myself the dramatic question, What would have happened if I had stopped? So what happens to me is that I will—just in the course of living and having experiences—gather fragments of unrelated images. And at any one time I could be thinking of a dozen, two dozen things or subliminally carrying them around or having them in my dreams or whatever—or my notebook. And they will form a pattern. Sometimes images find each other and they form a pattern. They belong together. Compatible images are like magnets, and when enough of those images come together and the pattern becomes vivid enough, then the play takes shape. Once I was able to put together the image of my uncle dying on the street, a conversation I overheard about a woman who'd seen an angel, my experiences living in the Bronx when I was attacked by a man with a golf club, the news stories about homeless people being set on fire in New York—once all these things came together, by some natural, mental, creative process found each other and *agreed*, then I had the play, *Marisol*. And there might have been fifty other images I had floating around that didn't agree, so they just disappeared. So these things created a pattern, and that pattern becomes the play. It's a very subconscious process. Later, it becomes a more conscious process, a more writerly process of putting pen to paper and crafting the imagery in such a way that it does agree on the stage, that they're compatible and they build on each other and that an image described in the first five minutes of the play pays off in the last five minutes. That process becomes more conscious and active.

Hatcher: In *Cloud Tectonics* one of the major scenes is when the woman asks the man to massage her toes, her feet, and the audience senses—and you can feel this in the house—that this may lead to other things, as well it does. At the very end of the play after many years have passed and the man is now very old and on his deathbed, the woman returns, but the woman hasn't aged a day. She returns to him and she asks him if there is anything she can do before she leaves, and he says, "Well, you could massage my feet." You can feel the excitement and the titter and the giggle go through the audience again. That is, I would think, one of those conscious arrangements of actions on the part of the playwright.

Rivera: Yes, that was very conscious on my part. I think the art of playwriting isn't some kind of mystical connection with a muse; the nuts and bolts of playwriting demand strict attention to craft. Good writers or lucky writers have access to imagery and to ideas and to voices, but the active part of the brain has to be engaged in a craftsman-like alignment of imagery and ideas and actions in order to make the play work, because it wouldn't work if things dangled. People talk about my plays in terms of magic realism. The fact is that the architecture of these plays is very, very strict—very, very thought out and preplanned. Those massage scenes illustrate a perfect example. Sometimes things take me by surprise. I will get to a certain point and something will happen and something prior in the writing will come back, simply insist itself and it'll be right. And the good writer takes advantage of that, listens to those happy accidents. Neil Simon talks about that in one of his books, about the "lucky accidents" that have happened in his work, and he is smart enough to leave those things in the play.

Hatcher: There's the old story of the screenwriters of *Casablanca* driving around Hollywood trying to figure out the ending to the movie, and suddenly one of them looks at the other and says a line spoken earlier in the film, "Round up the usual suspects." And they've got their ending.

Rivera: You have to be awake to those possibilities.

Hatcher: Do you think writers leave clues for themselves in plays, especially in a first draft or second draft?

Rivera: I think writers leave *opportunities*. Good writers leave enough open-ended, unresolved, unfinished material in first drafts that can be somehow tied up later on or paid off in some way. There is a danger of doing that *too* far and then the play seems contrived, but it's like a biofeedback mechanism where ideas create new ideas which create new ideas which create new ideas. I think that good writers are always in tune with that.

Hatcher: Do you always know how a play is going to end before you start it?

Rivera: Yes, I have a good idea where I want it to go. Before I write the first draft I have the structure more or less decided. It's very important for me to find closure, to find where the parentheses end. I don't begin a project until I know where it ends. Until I know, I'm not going to commit myself to the act of writing because I can't write in an open-ended way. It just won't work for me.

Hatcher: When you get into trouble in a draft of a play, even one that eventually turns out to be very successful, do you know what things pulled you toward the trouble spots? And do you know how to get yourself out of them?

Rivera: I know from long experience that I have certain bad habits. I have a tendency toward long-windedness and repetition. So when I do get into trouble, it's usually because I've fallen into one of my own bad habits, one of my own traps. I'm now a fairly good editor of my work. I have a theory about writer's block. This will answer your question in an oblique way. I think writer's block is the best thing that ever happened to writers. I think it's nature's way of insuring that fewer bad books are written and fewer bad plays are written—because I find that when I'm blocked, I'm blocked not because I have a lack of ideas. It's because I have told a *lie* somewhere in the process. I have laid out a premise, I have set something in motion, I have created a character motion or something that is basically not true—either not true to the work or not true to real life—and that when I have a block I know that I'm lying about something, that I must go back and sniff it out. And once I've destroyed that premise, then the block disappears and the writing continues.

Hatcher: Can it destroy an entire play?

Rivera: I think it could. If I had gotten to some point in writing *Cloud Tectonics* that reached a logical impossibility—because when you deal with time you're so vulnerable to that—if I had reached that point I would have said, "I don't have a play here. I have something that is just not true. No matter how clever or interesting it is, somehow it's just not going to ring true." I took a workshop with Gabriel García Márquez, and he said to us seven writers, "You know, when you create a work of fiction that is fantastical, you get to lie once. That's your premise, and you're granted that."

Hatcher: The lie is the premise?

Rivera: Yes, whatever it is—like in this case that there is a woman who lives outside the field of time. That's obviously not true. It's never happened, never will happen; but that is the premise of this play. So you're granted that premise by the willing suspension of disbelief.

Hatcher: But it would be unfair, for example, if she also turned out to be a witch.

Rivera: Exactly—or a mermaid. García Márquez would say, "Okay, this premise is the fundamental lie that you are allowed to tell in order to get at the truth or a deeper truth elsewhere." But from that point on everything must be consistent with that particular change in the physics of life. I have changed the basic physics of these particular people's lives, so everything must conform to those new rules. And part of the fun and difficulty of writing is, What are those rules? What is the world that you're making up? Because to me what's most exciting about playwriting as opposed to writing a novel is that you get to create the entire world. You get to create the color of the furniture and the smell in the room and the clothing they wear, and then you get to *see* it! But all those elements must be true to your original premise: What *is* that world, how do you define that world. In *Marisol* the premise is that a guardian angel leaves the person she's guarding, and that's a big leap of faith; but it's something that a good smart theatergoer would accept. Everything must follow from that. So when I get stuck, when I'm in trouble, I know it's because I violated that initial rule.

Hatcher: I wanted to ask you about some of the playwriting rules you do adhere to and the rules you like to break. I suppose one rule might be: Always keep the characters moving forward. Always keep track of what they want. Are there times when you say, "All right, I know the play's got to have the basic A-B-C's, but I certainly want to subvert D this time"?

Rivera: It's hard to answer that question because I know the playwriting rules by instinct, but I don't know if I'd even be able to express what they are. I know that somehow the action must move forward and I know that the language must not obscure the ideas of the play but underline them. The rules I tend to break deal with how we experience reality, what the logic of reality is. I tend to be very free with that logic. Like in my play *The Promise*, the dead can come back to life. It's not unheard of that corn can bleed, for instance, which is the end of that play. I tend to break rules that way by adding elements to what we normally call reality and experience that are completely unreal, completely works of the imagination. But I don't care. They're going to be part of the reality that I represent. Those are the rules I tend to break. I don't write like a documentarian, writing life as it is, but really life as it can be imagined. Not even life as it ought to be. Because in many of the works that I've done which are works of the imagination, the worlds are pretty bleak and difficult and dire. So it's not like I'm writing an idealized world. But I am writing worlds that can be imagined—as if there were a blurring between what happens in dreams and what happens in life. Worlds in which juxtapositions are slightly more daring than they would be in a conventional play. So those are the rules that I tend to deal with. In some ways I think actually I'm a very conventional writer because my plays have a beginning, a middle and an end most of the time. And I believe in the integrity of characters. I don't write like Sam Shepard, for instance, who creates fragments of characters or has a character basically decompose into two or three different parts. I've never done anything like that. What I do is break the rules of reality and then put that "broken" reality in the theater in a conventional form. I don't break those conventions. And even when I play with conventions, like breaking the fourth wall, I break them in a conventional way. I do it the way it's been done many times. Other kinds of rule-breaking—no plot, for example—I've never really attempted. It seems very postmodern to me. What I tend to do is to leave the larger architecture of theater more or less accessible to people and then *within* that to challenge their perceptions. For instance, in my play *Each Day Dies With Sleep* there is a young couple, just married. They're very hot for each other, they're very in love, and that is symbolized by an orange tree which they have in the house. And the orange juice itself is an aphrodisiac, and every time they want to sleep together they cut open an orange and smear orange juice on each other. Which is unconventional. I mean, it's just not something that happens in real life. The audience goes with it and says, "Oh, this is very strange." And then what I tend to do is take that thing which is already slightly beyond the rules of the game of life and the next step. For instance, in this case the next step is that when the marriage becomes difficult and bad, those oranges turn black and the juice inside the oranges turns to gasoline, and the main character uses that gasoline to burn his house down. So it's taking something slightly unconventional and pushing it to its complete logical extreme—that the orange juice turns to gas—and, then, taking it even a step further, using that in the plot and saying that's how he burns his house down.

Hatcher: But even that is organic.

Rivera: Absolutely. That's completely organic.

Hatcher: But if the orange turns into a banana which then becomes a revolver or something? That's *not* organic.

Rivera: Exactly, and that kind of organic changing of the rules to me is the realism of magic realism. In *Cloud Tectonics* "magic" (this woman who's outside of time) and "realism" (the guy who is the baggage handler) are equal, they're *married*. They're a pair, and it's the juxtaposition of those two things that makes the play.

Hatcher: I'm going to leap to another subject. Many beginning playwrights struggle with dialogue. Can good dialogue writing be taught? I think structure can be taught, if it's not instinctual, and I think you can learn about character and action and how to move a play forward. But can you learn how to write good dialogue?

Rivera: The bad news is I would have to weigh in on the side of those who say no. When you read a lot of new plays, you can recognize the author who clearly knows how to write dialogue. That's the play that jumps out at you. And it may be a horrible play in lots of other ways, but you know instinctively this person has "it." They have that gift. I think there is this intangible thing called talent and this intangible thing called inspiration. You can develop certain habits. You can develop skills. You can make a mediocre writer into a good writer that way and a good writer into a better writer. But I don't think you can teach the art of dialogue. The art of *listening*, which I think is absolutely the most important aspect of playwriting, the art of an open ear, an *active* ear is something I don't believe you can teach. You can teach eavesdropping, and I think you can teach people to go into the street, listen to what people are saying and write everything they've heard. But that's not theater. Theater is not a tape recorder; theater is a poetic reinterpretation of the tape recorder.

Afterword

When I started to write this book, two thoughts zoomed to my mind:

1. There are lessons I've learned about playwriting over the years— truths, constants, tricks of the trade—that every writer, including me, should recall from time to time, lessons I think can be useful to other playwrights, lessons I'd like to share.

And

2. I'm a fraud; what could I possibly have to teach anyone?

Writing successful plays for the theater depends on a lot of factors. In this book I've emphasized how much it depends on study and craft. But more than anything else good dramatic writing depends on a writer's heart, soul, wit, imagination, sensibility, history, travails, luck and whatever gifts she's acquired since the day she was born. It's wrong to approach a form of writing that has so much to do with personal intangibles as if it were a technical exercise that could be imitated by learning five easy steps. I didn't want this book to be a cookie-cutter manual. I wanted this book to be a reminder of the qualities and techniques all good plays possess, qualities and techniques that come either by nature or through trial and error. Every play teaches its playwright something new about his work and skills. Sometimes it's a hard lesson, sometimes it's a joyful discovery. We go two steps forward and more steps back. But we do go on.

Sometimes the lessons have surprised me. In 1992 I wrote a four-character, one-set play called *Scotland Road*. *Scotland Road* was a mystery with a strange twist. It took place in a locked room and focused on a man obsessed by the Titanic. In this locked room he interrogates a woman who has been found floating on an iceberg in the North Atlantic. When she's rescued she says one word: "Titanic." Apparently the woman claims to be a survivor of a disaster that took place eighty years before. The man's goal: crack her story and get her to confess she's an impostor. He has six days. In the end, the tables are turned. The woman proves she is who she says she is. The man is unmasked, and his surprising identity is revealed.

Before I wrote the play—based on my fascination with the sinking of the Titanic and prompted by a tabloid headline I glimpsed one day in a 7-11 store ("Titanic Survivor Found on Iceberg: She Thinks It's 1912, and Her Dress Is Still Wet!")—I knew the Titanic had an emotional pull on a lot of people, but I never knew it had its grasp on so many imaginations. I never knew that the sinking of that ship held such resonance for so many—and on the same metaphorical level as it did for me. And it was a deep satisfaction to discover that my treatment of the subject and the ideas of identity and heroism and completion struck such a chord with so many audience members.

What, then, were the lessons I learned from *Scotland Road*? There were many:

• that there was an exciting tautness my writing took on when I wrote a play with one "locked room" setting and a "ticking clock" to keep the characters moving forward;

• that my play had a special kind of drive when the lead character's dramatic need was the strongest motivator in his life;

• that audiences love a classic mystery, but more important, they love a mystery with a difference, a special twist and perception—call it a "gimmick";

• that there is a palpable sense of delight the audience feels when power shifts from one character to another;

• that there is an emotional and intellectual lift a play can benefit from when the audience roots for its characters, no matter how bizarre or otherworldly their goals;

• that a playwright shouldn't ignore the "big subject"; if something like the Titanic has stayed in the minds of people for almost one hundred years, there's a reason;

• that a playwright shouldn't ignore the fact that people *want* to believe in the unbelievable;

• that a playwright should never ignore his own deepest desires. I was afraid *Scotland Road* would be too quirky, too odd a fascination, too personal for audiences to identify with. But it turned out to be a shared obsession, and the play has been produced dozens of times. Writers can make mistakes by imagining that their own childhoods and experiences are more fascinating to the average audience member than they are, but finding the universality in something as specific as the Titanic makes these *personal* experiences a *shared* experience for the audience.

So what did I do for my next play? Look at more tabloids? Try to find another big disaster subject? The Lusitania? The Challenger explosion? Did I fix on every little obsession I'd ever had? No. Lightning tends not to strike twice. And many playwrights will tell you that going back to the same well more than once almost always means going back once too often. A playwright learns from success and from failure. But I think the wise playwright learns not from narrow specifics (Always write four-character plays set in locked rooms with a ticking clock) but rather from wide generalities (Find subjects an audience can care about in the same way you do; and if they *don't*, try to find a means of getting them to).

Here's what I'm doing. I'm keeping my eyes open. I'm listening to the universe. I'm preparing myself to come up with the next idea.

The best I can recommend for myself and other playwrights is this:

Work with actors, directors, dramaturgs and designers as much as you can—at whatever level. Get involved with groups or organizations that read plays and support the work of emerging playwrights, like The Playwrights' Center in Minneapolis, New Dramatists in New York, and the O'Neill Theater Center in Connecticut. Apply to every contest. Send your plays to every theater you can think of. Give yourself time. Write. And learn.

Learn from the plays that have come before you.

Learn from the writing you've already done.

Listen to the world around you.

Listen to yourself.

Compel us.

About the Author

Jeffrey Hatcher is the author of numerous plays, including *Three Viewings, Scotland Road, Neddy, Sockdology, Fellow Travelers, SMASH, Comfort and Joy, Vandals,* and *The Turn of the Screw.* His plays have won many awards and have been produced in the United States, Great Britain, Germany, Chile and elsewhere. He taught for six years at the Playwrights' Center in Minneapolis, and has been a guest lecturer and playwright-in-residence at a number of colleges and theater centers.

Index

Printed in the United States
by Baker & Taylor Publisher Services